# Critical Literacy as Resistance

# COVNTERPOINTS

## Studies in the
## Postmodern Theory of Education

Joe L. Kincheloe and Shirley R. Steinberg
*General Editors*

Vol. 326

PETER LANG
New York • Washington, D.C./Baltimore • Bern
Frankfurt am Main • Berlin • Brussels • Vienna • Oxford

# Critical Literacy as Resistance

## Teaching for Social Justice Across the Secondary Curriculum

Edited by Laraine Wallowitz

PETER LANG
New York • Washington, D.C./Baltimore • Bern
Frankfurt am Main • Berlin • Brussels • Vienna • Oxford

Library of Congress Cataloging-in-Publication Data

Critical literacy as resistance: teaching for social justice across the secondary curriculum /
Edited by Laraine Wallowitz.
p. cm. — (Counterpoints: studies in the postmodern theory of education; vol. 326)
Includes bibliographical references.
1. Critical pedagogy—United States. 2. Literacy—Social aspects—United States.
3. Educational sociology. 4. High school teachers—In-service training—United States.
I. Title.
LC196.5.U6W35   370.11'5—dc22   2008036178
ISBN 978-1-4331-0063-5
ISSN 1058-1634

Bibliographic information published by **Die Deutsche Bibliothek.**
**Die Deutsche Bibliothek** lists this publication in the "Deutsche
Nationalbibliografie"; detailed bibliographic data is available
on the Internet at http://dnb.ddb.de/.

Cover design by Clear Point Designs

The paper in this book meets the guidelines for permanence and durability
of the Committee on Production Guidelines for Book Longevity
of the Council of Library Resources.

© 2008 Peter Lang Publishing, Inc., New York
29 Broadway, 18th floor, New York, NY 10006
www.peterlang.com

Printed in the United States of America

*For my mom and dad*

# Contents

# Foreword

## The Struggle for Deep Change

Schools are deeply conservative institutions. Not capital C conservative, but inertia conservative. Despite changes in the culture, as Larry Cuban (1993) has shown, most of us would recognize the similarity of today's schools to those of our parents and grandparents.

This is true both physically and pedagogically. Despite the criticisms of E.D. Hirsch (1996) and Diane Ravitch (2000), John Dewey's progressive pedagogy does not define the norms and practices of schooling (Goodlad, 1984; Powell et al., 1985). In fact the test-driven curricula that have been the school system's response to the mandates of the No Child Left Behind legislation have become increasingly narrow, skills driven, and, in Ellen Langer's (1997) terms, mindless.

Most of us in and out of education don't recognize how pervasive this is. Our own experience during thousands of hours of Pre-K through college classes have implicitly developed for us a set of tacit beliefs and unconscious norms of the way things are spozed to be (Herndon, 1968; Mayher 1990). Even reformers usually propose innovations that function comfortably within these norms that remain unrecognized and unchallenged.

There have, of course, been exceptions to this—most notably Paulo Freire (1970/2000)—people who have influenced a growing cadre of thinkers and doers who dare to challenge the tacit assumptions, beliefs, and practices underlying the commonsense pedagogy of most schools. To that valiant band must now be added the contributors to this volume who provide both critical theory and critical enactments of what a critical literacy path to school reform might look like.

They straight on confront the social crises of our time—racism, sexism, and homophobia—with critiques that draw on a deep commitment to social justice. Recognizing that deep reform must go beyond individuals to the unjust social arrangements that surround and control us, they provide both powerful analyses and practical responses to what their analyses have uncovered. And, above all, they insist that all of the decisions that affect schools and schooling are embedded in a complex network of social forces and that unless those are understood by teachers and students alike, no meaningful change can occur.

It is not easy to perform the level of cultural, political, and personal critique that must be the driving force behind the kinds of reforms they are arguing for. The implicit norms that all of us have internalized during our years in school blind us to the toxic effects they have on children and teachers, indeed on the whole culture, as these practices persist from generation to generation. It is particularly difficult for those of us who have been successful in the traditional system to recognize how it particularly disenfranchises poor children, the racial and ethnic minorities, and, in complex and sometimes contradictory ways, both boys and girls.

But schools are not just for those who have traditionally been the winners in the fixed game of choose your parent wisely. Schools must be and ostensibly are committed to education for all. Indeed the rhetoric of No Child Left Behind, artfully stolen and distorted from the slogan of the Children's Defense Fund, and the language of most school vision or mission statements testify to their professed commitment to fair, equal, and meaningful education for all.

Freirian critiques reveal the hollowness of those words, however, and make it clear that schools can't function as engines of social justice without a substantive theoretical and practical overhaul. This will be no easy task. The ideas critiqued here run deep, the inertia of the schools is profound, and the capacity of the status quo to defend itself is formidable.

Nevertheless if you aren't satisfied with the educational system you know, and particularly if you are not satisfied with the role you have been assigned to play within it, the challenge presented by this text is one you must accept. If you do so, you and the schools you work in will never be the same.

John S. Mayher
Professor of English Education
New York University

# References

Cuban, Larry (1993). *How Teachers Taught* (2nd Ed.). New York: Teachers College Press.

Freire, Paolo (1970/1990). *Pedagogy of the Oppressed.* London: Herder & Herder/New York: Continuum.

Goodlad, John (1984). *A Place Called School.* New York: McGraw-Hill.

Herndon, James (1968). *The Way It Spozed to Be.* New York: Simon and Schuster.

Hirsch, E.D. (1996). *The Schools We Need and Why We Don't Have Them.* New York: Doubleday.

Langer, Ellen (1997). *The Power of Mindful Learning.* Reading, MA: Addison-Wesley.

Mayher, John S. (1990). *Uncommon Sense: Theoretical Practice in Language Education.* Portsmouth, NH: Boynton/Cook Heinemann.

Powell, Arthur, Eleanor Farrar, David K. Cohen et al. (1985). *The Shopping Mall High School.* Boston: Houghton Mifflin.

Ravitch, Diane (2000). *Left Back: A Century of Failed School Reforms.* New York: Simon and Schuster.

# Acknowledgments

I would like to thank Diane Caracciolo, Robert Linné, Diana Feige and Michael O'Loughlin for the feedback and sage advice; Tracy Lederman, who helped me in the beginning stages of the book; all my contributors; and Martin Kempner for his work with the youth of New York City. And a special thank you to my sister-in-law, Fan-Ching Lin, and Sophie Appel for all their help formatting the book.

# Introduction

*Laraine Wallowitz*

## Critical Literacies Defined

Critical pedagogues believe that education should provide all students the opportunity to question, discover, and transform their futures. The principles and practices of critical pedagogy are designed to help students become critical thinkers/readers/consumers/producers of the word and the world. They learn to separate themselves from—and deconstruct—the values, institutions, and ideologies that shape them. Broadly stated, critical pedagogy interrogates power structures in American education in order to challenge the status quo and enact social justice for underserved populations. Critical theorists assume that teaching is a highly political act and that all knowledge is socially, politically, and culturally constructed.

Consequently, educators must be aware of the ways they are preserving existing power relations by privileging what Freire calls the "banking system of education," wherein teachers deposit knowledge into students' heads as if it is uncontested fact. The "hidden curriculum" (Giroux & Purpel, 1983), or the unintentional messages and consequences received by the banking method, has led to the marginalization of poor, minority, and learning -disabled students. Thus, education has become (or continues to be) a vehicle for socialization and social control (Anyon, 1980; Fine, 1991; Finn, 1999).

Within the broader framework of critical pedagogy, critical literacy is a vehicle through which educators teach for social justice. Critical literacy aims to challenge the status quo by disrupting commonplace notions of socially constructed concepts such as race, class, gender, and sexuality. It allows for a multitude of viewpoints, highlights sociopolitical issues located in texts, and promotes social justice through political activism (Lewison, Flint, & Van Sluys, 2002, p. 382). The critical reader understands that *how* we read is as important as *what* we read and asks questions about the construction of texts/knowledge and power relationships: Who is the intended audience? What is the hidden agenda? How does the text reflect and shape notions of power and privilege? What is included? What is excluded? How is the text trying to position the reader? As such, critical literacy interrogates texts in order to identify and challenge social constructs, ideologies, underlying assumptions, and the power structures that intentionally and unintentionally perpetuate social inequalities and injustices. It is important that we question the production of knowledge and search for the hidden agendas in school curricula, governmental legislation, corporate policies, and mass media.

Additionally, critical literacy redefines literacy to include print and non-print texts and the attitudes, behaviors, and values that accompany each discourse event, or the way of using language associated with any given genre, culture, or vocation. Literate students in a postmodern world, wherein reality is understood to be socially and culturally constructed and all understanding highly contextualized, must be "able to engage in a range of literacy practices drawing upon different sets of skills and processes suited to those particular practices" (Stevens & Bean, 2007, p. 18). Thus, the teachers and students must learn how to read the "word and the world" (Freire and Macedo, 1987; Gee, 1990).

This book is designed to expand the notion of literacy from simply teaching skills, decoding the printed word, and increasing fluency to one that incorporates reading, writing, and thinking about content-specific texts such as paintings, primary sources, media, word problems, and textbooks from a critical literacy perspective. If teachers only rely on traditional texts to inform their understanding of reading, writing, and literacy instruction, we ignore other equally important, nontraditional texts, such as TV, advertising, music, clothing, film, art, Internet, and other sign systems students negotiate and subvert everyday. We also argue that the narrow definition of literacy—reading and writing the printed word—has often resulted in excluding marginalized populations by invalidating their home literacies and cultural identities. As researchers have discovered, there are a multitude of "hidden literacies" (Finders, 1997) students use to make sense of their world and resist the ways society has positioned them. We are suggesting a more inclusive and expansive notion of text offered by traditional literacy across the curriculum programs. Today's literacy teachers should think in terms of multiple literacies.

The chapters in this volume are informed by the theory and perspectives of critical pedagogues inspired by the work of Paolo Freire. Over three decades ago, Brazilian educator Paulo Freire articulated a philosophy of education for peasants in his book *Education for Critical Consciousness* (1974). In his approach to literacy, Freire used generative words situated in everyday events of the workers to teach them to decode and dialogue about the social, economic, and political inequalities of the reality in which they lived. While the workers learned to read the word, they were also learning to "perceive themselves in dialectical relationship with their social reality" in order to create change (p. 34). Freire also critiqued the "banking method" of education, where students were trained to adapt to their world of oppression. Education, he argued, should not be an exercise of domination; banking education "treats students as objects of assistance" (p. 83). Instead, education should be about liberation, for "people to come to feel like masters of their thinking by discussing the thinking and views of the world explicitly or implicitly manifest in their own suggestions and those of their comrades" (1973, p. 124).

Further, Freire replaced the banking concept of education with what he called "problem posing," a theory of teaching intended to "unveil reality" by raising student consciousness. Through the act of "unveiling reality," students learn to think about their world critically; by recognizing reality as socially constructed and undergoing constant transformation, they learn that to live fully is to intervene in their reality, thereby becoming active subjects in their own lives. Thus students both "read their world" and "write their world." Freire defined his vision in *Pedagogy of the Oppressed* (1970):

> Problem-posing education bases itself on creativity and stimulates true reflection and action upon reality, thereby responding to the vocation of persons as being who are authentic, only when engaged in inquiry and creative transformation. In sum, banking theory and practice, as immobilizing and fixing forces, fail to acknowledge men and women as historical beings; problem-posing theory and practice takes people's historicity as their starting point. (p. 84)

Hence, problem-posing education places the student at the center of the curriculum and teaches people how to advocate for themselves.

Freire's ideas added an important facet to literacy instruction—that of critique and transformation. His influence reached educators in the United States and led to a burgeoning of the critical literacy movement presently being adapted in English classrooms as an alternative approach to decoding analytic and New Criticism practices. Since then, many scholars in the fields of poststructuralism, Marxism, discourse analysis, and critical theory have worked with and extended Freire's vision.

In addition, important work has been done applying critical literacy in secondary classrooms. There are many useful articles on teachers' putting critical pedagogy into practice. The editors and authors of Rethinking Schools have produced copious publications in the fields of mathematics, science, English, and Social Studies education. Secondary teachers around the world have been influenced by works of other scholars such as Frankenstein (1998) and Stevens and Bean (2007), and particularly by the work of Australian educators (and Chalkface Press) who have written several books in the areas of gender and the critical interrogation of literature. In this time of standardization and scripted teaching, it is important to continue working on critical pedagogical practices.

This collaborative book aims to extend the dialogue on content area and critical literacy by eliciting the experiences of scholars and teachers across the United States who apply critical literacy in their content areas, thereby grounding the theory in the everyday realities of public and private school teachers. The chapters will address questions such as these: What does a critical literacy classroom look like? What various texts are used? What strategies do teachers employ to encourage students and teacher candidates to recognize how texts construct power and privilege? How do teachers incorporate both standards and critical pedagogy? How do educators inspire activism in and out of the classroom? And how can literacy continue to be used as a vehicle for resistance?

Our goal is for content-area teachers to use literacy to liberate and empower students both in and outside the classroom by respecting the literacies students bring to school, teaching students to question the power relationships embedded in texts, and rewrite their worlds for a more just society.

## Politicizing Education

No teaching is neutral. Choosing to create a classroom free from controversial topics does not situate the teacher as impartial or objective. Nor does it ensure that all students feel comfortable in their classes. Many teachers fear imposing their own agendas on their students and follow the state-mandated curriculum, thereby unwittingly imposing someone else's agenda. In this case, teachers become conduits for conservative political plots intending to maintain the status quo. The "safer" our classroom spaces, the more we silence students for whom school seems foreign, hostile, and irrelevant. It is our jobs as educators to teach in the "contact zone" (Pratt, 1991), the place where ideologies clash and move our students out of their comfort zones. It is in that space that the real teaching occurs. A "pedagogy of discomfort" (Boler, 1999) propels students and teachers into social action and prepares citizens in a democracy to understand multiple points of view. We can no longer afford to assume that our values, beliefs, and attitudes are universal; recognizing that no one lives outside ideology, and that all knowledge is contextual, is imperative in a time of globalization, colonization, and standardization.

As such, the role of the teacher in a critical literacy classroom is hard to define as this pedagogical approach is not completely teacher or student centered. Many progressive educators suggest that students should learn and discover new understandings free from the influence of the teacher. While student-centered teaching has merit, a critical pedagogue must sometimes intervene and problematize a student's thought process or point out the assumptions underlying his/her thinking. That is not to say that teaching should be didactic; there are times when the instructor can act as guide or instigator, particularly when students are having trouble moving out of their comfort zones. Also, comments meant to marginalize, such as "fag" or "bitch," are opportunities to problematize the contextual nature of language. Remaining neutral—or silent—in the face of discrimination always condones the behavior of the oppressor. Instances in the classroom when students enter into the "contact zone" are opportunities to discuss the power of words, lead by the teacher or the students. Thus, the teacher's role is always changing: at a moment's notice s/he is a guide, a facilitator, a devil's advocate, and/or a learner. However, one behavior is imperative—self-reflection. Critical pedagogues continually self-reflect (on their own and with their students) and critically read their own classrooms as spaces of unequal power relationships, conflicting ideologies, resistance, and possibility.

The book is divided into three sections: problematizing literacy learning; curricular and pedagogical possibilities; and enactments of critical literacies. The contributions are intended for both pre-service and in-service teachers either familiar or unfamiliar with critical literacy. The lessons, units, and programs are authored by former and practicing secondary teachers who offer their own understanding of critical literacy as it applies to grade 7-12 settings, recognizing the dynamic nature of critical pedagogical practices. Critical literacy classrooms are under constant revision and reflection; there is no one way to apply critical literacy, nor is there a formula for beginning to teach for change, which makes critical education both exciting and untidy. A good place to begin, however, is to recognize, for ourselves and along with our students, the ways in which the language and texts of our disciplines shape our identities, values, opportunities, and belief systems and maintain the existing social order (Shor, 1992). From there our classrooms can move toward becoming spaces of resistance, using literacy as a way to interrogate and rewrite our reality for a fairer world.

## Problematizing Literacy Learning

The first section of the book will define critical literacy, particularly how it differs from critical thinking, and provide a theoretical basis for the implementation of critical literacy in secondary school settings. Chapter 1, by Cara Mulcahy, considers the relationship between critical thinking and critical literacy. She argues that critical literacy is a mindset, a way of viewing and interacting with the world—a philosophy rather than a set of methods or skills. It is important that educators understand the epistemological distinction between teaching for critical thinking versus teaching toward critical literacy so that the two terms do not become synonymous, leading to the depoliticalization of critical pedagogical practices. In chapter 2, Kurt Love interrogates popular views of science as they are presented in textbooks in order to support teachers in providing their students with opportunities to problematize course materials. By using the core principles of critical literacy in conjunction with critical and feminist lenses to reexamine science textbooks, aspects of the "hidden curriculum" can become evident and potentially engage both teachers and students in more democratic processes in interacting with nature, nutrition, ecology, and technology.

In chapter 3, Liz de Freitas argues that mathematics education has much to gain from embracing social justice pedagogy by examining strategies in critical mathematics education that use math curriculum as a critical tool in addressing the ethical dimension of problem solving. She considers the notion of "real life" application as a possible site for ethical reflection by paying particular attention to classroom discourse. She finds that in traditional secondary mathematics classrooms, the ethical exclusion in real world math problems creates a discourse of certainty that serves the status quo by creating the public perception that math is objective and valueless. In chapter 4, Tracy Hogan and John Craven expose the roots of power that give science authority in order to confront the stereotypical image of science as a culturally neutral, unbiased, objective, rational enterprise. The authors promote an understanding of science as a human endeavor—that is, a social enterprise imbued with human desires, motivations, and struggles so as to enhance the reader's capacity to take a critical literacy stance toward the forces of science impacting global communities.

## Curricular and Pedagogical Possibilities

In section two, *Curricular and Pedagogical Possibilities,* the authors describe critical literacy curriculum and pedagogy in various high school settings, both during and after school. Curricula include workshops, programs, instructional units, and lessons designed to help students recognize, resist, and disrupt societal inequities.

Rachel Mattson, in Chapter 5, argues against antihomophobia education that focuses on tolerance, visibility, and acceptance. Instead, she uses Civil Rights leader Bayard Rustin as a vehicle for teaching high school students that homophobia not only affects the queer community but also works alongside other oppressive forces, such as sexism and racism, meant to maintain the status quo. Queer pedagogy, as opposed to tolerance education, invites a critique of norming in general and recognizes the complex relationships connecting gender, race, and heterosexism.

In chapter 6, Lisa Hotchtritt suggests using graffiti art in grades 7-12 in order to ground art education in the lives of students. High school curricula that heavily rely on traditional elements and principles to the exclusion of contemporary artists indirectly teach students to value the Western canon and stifle creativity and critical thinking. Instead of reproduction and repetition, she recommends an issue-based approach to art education wherein students can use art as a means of dealing with the complexities of their lives.

Chapter 7, by Jane Bolgatz, explores the intersections between state-mandated historical thinking skills and the tools of critical literacy in the context of test-driven global studies instruction. This chapter specifically describes a unit on Joan of Arc as an avenue through which social studies students can learn required content about medieval Europe as they question how historians come to conclusions and how teachers can make thoughtful decisions about sources, all the while participating in compelling instruction that meets the heterogeneous academic needs of all students.

In chapter 8, Bruce Castellano discusses his Increase the Peace program, a student-led initiative aimed at teaching students to combat prejudice and bullying and to accept individual differences. Started in a public high school in New York seventeen years ago, Increase the Peace is an antiviolence, human rights program that trains high school students to teach their peers about difference, prejudice, and bullying reduction. This curriculum-based program has worked successfully with many teachers regardless of their years of experience or tenure in the public school systems.

## Enactments of Critical Literacies

The third section, *Enactments of Critical Literacies,* includes stories of teachers implementing critical literacy into their middle and high school classrooms and after-school programs. The chapters include students' voices and negotiations with critical literacies, providing a unique window into the complex enactment of social justice pedagogy with young people. Chapter 9 describes Laraine Wallowitz's efforts to incorporate critical literacies into a New York City public high school with a predominately African American population; she does this using Toni Morrison's novel *The Bluest Eye* and other print and nonprint texts in order to problematize representations of "beauty" constructed by literature, advertising, music, and the media. In chapter 10, Rita Verma maintains that educators of world language have a unique opportunity to foster critical inquiry with their students as they learn the intricacies of language. World language instructors tend to focus on the skill and drill of memorizing vocabulary and verb tenses, thus separating the life, history, and culture behind the words. As a result, educators miss valuable opportunities to engage in critical discussions. She presents case studies from secondary-level Spanish classrooms in New York that illustrate how prejudice and social justice, language and power, and critical analysis of the global political landscape become integrated into the daily classroom curriculum.

In chapter 11, Carlin Borsheim and Robert Petrone describe a semester-long curriculum wherein they use canonical and nontraditional texts to develop within themselves and their students "critical habits of mind" (Shor, 1992). They seek to understand how the secondary English classroom might work to help adolescents manage and consume the multiplicity of texts in their lives both within the schools and outside, through the explicit teaching of critical literacies designed to foster in the students the dispositions, habits of mind, and skills to understand, question, challenge, and transform the status quo. In the final chapter, Alice Pennisi focuses on students as participants in a "visual critical literacy" project that transforms student disengagement into engagement and considers the curricular implications of dealing with socio-political issues in an art context. The chapter describes young artists—who as members of Voices of Women (VOW), a collaborative young women's art group—become empowered through art making. She shows how art can be used as a means for adolescent girls to explore notions of identity and establish an individual narrative voice.

The contributions included in this volume provide a range of ideas for implementation in various public secondary school settings across the United States. This book is intended for practitioners and scholars who are familiar, or unfamiliar, with critical literacy. It is our intention to show how critical literacy is a possibility in the current climate of standardized testing and scripted teaching. A critical literacy approach to teaching offers teachers and students a new paradigm of thinking about the word and the world that empowers, engages, and challenges the American populace to resist the social forces that regulate and control and to imagine a more just reality for everyone.

# References

Anyon, J. (1980). Social class and the hidden curriculum of work. In *Journal of Education, 49* (3), 381–386.

Boler, M. (1999). *Feeling power: Emotions and education.* New York: Routledge.

Finders, L. (1997). *Just girls: Hidden literacies and life in junior high.* New York: Teachers College Press.

Fine, M. L. (1991). *Framing dropouts: Notes on the politics of an urban public high school.* Albany, NY: SUNY Press.

Finn, P. (1999). *Literacy with an attitude: Educating working-class children in their own self-Interest.* Albany, NY: SUNY Press.

Frankenstein, M. (1998). Goals for a critical mathematical literacy curriculum. In Menkart Lee & Okazawa-Ray, Eds., *Beyond heroes and holidays: A practical guide to K-12 anti-racist, multicultural education and staff development.* Washington, DC. Network of Educators on the Americas.

Freire, P. (1974). *Education for critical consciousness.* New York: The Crossroads Publishing Company.

Freire, P. (1970/1997). *Pedagogy of the oppressed.* New York: Continuum.

Freire, P., & Macedo, D. (1987). *Literacy: Reading the word and the world.* South Hadley, MA: Bergin and Harvey.

Gee, J. P. (1990). *Sociolinguistics and literacies: Ideology in discourses.* London: Taylor & Francis.

Giroux, H.A., & Purpel. D.E. (1988). *The hidden curriculum and moral education: Deception or discovery?* Berkeley, CA: McCutchan Publishing Corp.

Lewison, M., Flint, A.S., & Van Sluys, K. (2002). Taking on critical literacy: The journey of newcomers and novices. In *Language Arts, 70* (5), 382–392.

Myers, M. (1996). *Changing our minds: Negotiating English and literacy.* Urbana, IL: NCTE.

Pratt, M.L. (1991). Arts of the contact zone. In *Profession, 91,* 33–40.

Shor, I. (1992). *Empowering education: Critical teaching for social change.* Chicago: University of Chicago Press.

Stevens, L.P., & Bean, T. W. (2007). *Critical literacy: Context, research, and practice in the K-12 classroom.* Thousand Oaks, CA: Sage Publishers.

# Recommendations for Further Reading

Barrell, B.R.C., Hammett, R.F., Mayher, J.S., & Pradle, G.M., Eds. (2004). *Teaching English today: Advocating change in the secondary curriculum.* New York: Teachers College Press.

Bigelow, B., &, Peterson, B. (2002). *Rethinking globalization: Teaching for justice in an unjust world.* Milwaukee, WI: Rethinking Schools.

Bigelow, B., & Peterson, B. (1998). *Rethinking Columbus: The next 500 years.* Milwaukee, WI: Rethinking Schools.

Christensen, L. (2000). *Reading, writing, and rising up: Teaching about social justice and the power of the written word.* Milwaukee, WI: Rethinking Schools.

Comber, B., & Simpson, A., Eds. (2001). *Negotiating critical literacies.* Mahwah, NJ: Erlbaum Assoc.

Delpit, L. (2006). *Other people's children: Cultural conflict in the classroom.* New York: New Press.

Edelsky, C. (2006). *With literacy and justice for all: Rethinking the social in language education.* NY: Routledge.

Foss, A. (2002). Peeling the onion: Teaching critical literacy with students of privilege. In *Language Arts, 79,* 393-403

Gutstein, E. (2006). *Reading and writing the work with mathematics: Toward a pedagogy for social justice.* New York: Routledge.

Gutstein, E., & Peterson, B. (2005). *Rethinking mathematics: Teaching social justice by the numbers.* Milwaukee, WI: Rethinking Schools.

Heath, S.B. (1983). *Ways with words: Language, life and work in communities and classrooms.* Cambridge: Cambridge University Press.

Lankshear, C. (1997). *Changing literacies.* Philadelphia: Open University Press.

Lankshear, C., & McLaren, P.L. (1993). *Critical literacy: Politics, praxis, and the postmodern.* Albany, NY: SUNY Press.

Lund, D.E., & Carr, P.R. (Eds.). (2008). *Doing democracy: Striving for political literacy and social justice.* New York: Peter Lang.

Mellor, B. (1989). *Reading Hamlet.* Urbana, IL: NCTE.

Mellor, B., O'Neill, M., & Patterson, A. (1987). *Reading stories.* Urbana, IL: NCTE.

Mellor, B., & Patterson, A. (1996). *Investigating texts.* Urbana, IL: NCTE.

Mellor, B., Patterson, A., & O'Neill, M. (1991). *Reading fictions.* Urbana, IL: NCTE.

Moon, B. (1990). *Studying Literature.* Urbana, IL: NCTE.

Shor, I., & Pari, C. (1999). *Critical literacy in action: Writing words, changing worlds/A tribute to the teachings of Paulo Freire.* Portsmouth, NH: Boynton/Cook.

Wallowitz, L. (2004). "Reading as resistance: Gendered messages in literature and media." In *English Journal, 93,* 26-31.

Wolk, S. (2003). Teaching for critical literacy in social studies. In *The social studies, 94* (3), 101-107.

# SECTION 1

# PROBLEMATIZING LITERACY LEARNING

# Chapter 1

# The Tangled Web We Weave: Critical Literacy and Critical Thinking

*Cara M. Mulcahy*

Critical literacy and critical thinking are sometimes confused with one another even though they have different goals and educate for different purposes. Therefore, it is important that educators are aware of how the two differ in order disrupt the conservative monopoly on the educative practices of secondary teachers. This chapter begins with a preliminary discussion of the terms "critical literacy" and "critical thinking," followed by an examination of the ways critical literacy and critical thinking compare to one another, particularly on issues such as fair-mindedness, problem solving, point of view, and questioning. The chapter concludes by considering the importance of acknowledging the differences between critical literacy and critical thinking and addresses the necessity for including critical literacy in the teaching of content area literacy.

## Literacies and the Content Area

William S. Gray, a pioneer of content area reading, is recognized for coining the phrase "Every teacher is a teacher of reading" (Gray as quoted in Vacca, 2002, p. 186). As we enter the twenty-first century, it may be more accurate to say every teacher is a teacher of literacy. In recent years the term "content area reading" has been replaced with the term "content area literacy." Content area literacy no longer applies only to reading and writing but "refers to all the literacies in students' lives—whether in school or out of school—and the myriad forms that today's texts can take, whether textbook or trade book, e-mail, electronic messaging, or Internet sites" (Moss, 2005, p. 48). Similarly, literacy is no longer viewed as merely a set of skills one must master, but as a set of practices, beliefs, and values as well as a way of being in the world. Therefore, as we engage in the teaching of content area literacy, we need to be cognizant of the kinds of literacies we are teaching toward. Critical literacy distinguishes itself from other kinds of literacy in the way it addresses issues of power, social injustice, and transformative action.

## Critical Literacy Defined

Critical literacy is a mindset; it is a way of viewing and interacting with the world, not a set of teaching skills and strategies. From a pedagogical perspective, critical literacy is a philosophy that recognizes the connections between power, knowledge, language, and ideology, and recognizes the inequalities and injustices surrounding us in order to move toward transformative action and social justice. In order to do so, critical literacy examines texts in order to identify and challenge social constructs, underlying assumptions and ideologies, and power structures that intentionally or unintentionally perpetuate social inequalities and injustices. Furthermore, it examines the way in which texts use language to position readers, transmit information, and perpetuate the status quo. Critical literacy aims to delve deeply into the sociopolitical and sociocultural issues embedded in texts in order to identify the root causes of social inequities. By employing critical literacy, one questions the construction of knowledge and searches for hidden agendas in school curricula, governmental legislation, corporation policies, and the media.

Critical literacy separates itself from literacies such as functional, informational, cultural, and progressive literacy in that it works toward praxis. Praxis, as defined by Freire (1970), combines reflection and action in order to transform society. In this way, critical literacy is transformative. Such transformation attempts to eradicate social injustices and inequalities so as to create better social conditions for all. Grounded in critical theory, it recognizes that while literacy can be used to empower oneself, it can also be used as a means to control society. Thus, analyzing a text or being asked to think critically does not mean that one is engaging in critical literacy. Similarly, merely embedding a selection of critical questions and terminology into one's discourse does not necessarily mean one is teaching toward critical literacy.

Much has been written on the differences between critical literacy and critical thinking, and although many caution of the dangers in using the terms interchangeably, confusion continues.

## Unraveling Critical Literacy and Critical Thinking

Here I shall rely upon Paul and Elder's (2005) framework for critical thinking and Lewison, Flint, and Van Sluys's (2002) definition of critical literacy to frame my discussion of the differences and similarities between the two concepts. As defined by Paul and Elder (2005), a critical thinker is skilled in the following three dimensions: analytic, evaluative, and creative thinking. In addition to forming analytical, evaluative, and creative thinkers, critical thinking is also a process whereby a person reflects upon his/her own thinking process so as to create clear, well-reasoned ideas for the benefit of him/herself and others.

Paul and Elder (2005) identify eight elements of critical thought that, when used in combination, allow us to be critical thinkers in accordance with the above understanding. These eight elements are:

1. Purpose, goal, or end in view: Whenever we reason we do so with an objective in mind, with an end goal we wish to reach.

2. Questions at issue (or problems to be solved): As we begin to reason, there is usually a question or a problem that needs to be solved.

3. Point of view or frame of reference: As we engage in reasoning, we do so from a specific standpoint or perspective. This point of view is constructed by our mind.

4. The information we use in reasoning: Whenever we reason we do so about some phenomena.

5. The conceptual dimensions of our reasoning: Certain ideas and concepts created by the mind are used when we reason.

6. Assumptions: To begin reasoning, we must have a starting point. To establish a starting point, we must take some things for granted.

7. Our inferences, interpretations, and conclusions: As we reason, we create inferences in an attempt to understand the issue at hand.

8. Implications and consequences—where our reasoning takes us: The process of reasoning leads us somewhere new. Reasoning is not static. Implications and consequences are creations of our reasoning and they affect our thoughts and actions.

Once again the emphasis here is on one's ability to rationalize one's inner dialogue and thought process with the goal of being able to evaluate one's thinking, feelings, and actions in a disciplined manner.

Critical literacy, on the other hand, can be described as having four dimensions: (1) disrupting the commonplace, (2) interrogating multiple viewpoints, (3) focusing on sociopolitical issues, and (4) taking action and promoting social justice (Lewison, Flint, & Van Sluys, 2002). These four dimensions relate closely to Freire's notion of a liberating education, which allows one to problem-pose, engage in dialogue, and examine the world in a way that uncovers social oppressions and encourages people to understand ways in which their world can be transformed. Unlike the "banking" approach to education whereby students are seen as receptacles or bins to be filled and "in which the scope of action allowed to the students extends only as far as receiving, filling, and storing the deposits" (p. 72), critical literacy aims to actively engage the students in their learning and reading of texts by addressing these four dimensions of critical literacy.

Through problem posing, critique, and transformation, students are taught to question social constructs such as race, gender, ethnicity, and sexuality and the ways in which texts position them as readers, consumers, and sociopolitical beings. By suggesting that readers learn to interrogate texts from multiple viewpoints, consider sociopolitical issues, and disrupt commonplace notions of gender, race, and class, critical literacy scholars changed our relationship to the text and the world from unidirectional to dialectical.

## Goals and Purposes

The goal of teaching critical thinking is to help students focus on developing their ability to reason, analyze, evaluate, and create in a way that is disciplined and that expresses their thoughts, feelings, and actions in a rational and clear manner. The goal of educating toward critical literacy, however, is to uncover the inequalities that exist within society, identify the root causes that may be perpetuating the inequalities, and to take social action so as to create a more just and equal society. Immediately one can begin to understand that critical literacy is concerned not only with the individual and one's ability to think rationally, but also with societal issues that reach beyond the individual—issues relating to social injustice, social inequalities, and unequal power relations. Shannon quoted in McDaniel (2004) points out, critical perspectives push the definition of literacy beyond traditional decoding or encoding of words in order to reproduce the meaning of text or society until it becomes a means for understanding one's own history and culture, to recognize connections between one's life and the social structure, to believe that change in one's life, and the lives of others and society are possible as well as desirable, and to act on this new knowledge in order to foster equal and just participation in all the decisions that affect and control our lives. (p. 171)

Similar to critical literacy, proponents of critical thinking, too, are concerned with how a person thinks, feels, and acts. However, critical thinking appears to be more concerned with just the individual, with developing "a powerful inner voice of reason" (Elder & Paul, 1998, p. 300) and in this respect is unlike critical literacy that also considers the impact of thinking in relation to societal matters. This can be evidenced more clearly when Paul and Elder (2005) state:

Without the active knowledge that Critical Thinking empowers, we are unlikely to be personally transformed by our learning. Without the cultivation of our intellectual capacities such as fairmindedness, we are unlikely to notice our inconsistencies and contradictions. We are apt to uncritically conform in many domains of our personal lives. (p. 22)

Clearly then, while advocates of critical literacy would agree it is important that we not "uncritically conform" in our personal lives, critical theorists would argue that it is just as important that we not uncritically conform at a societal level as well.

In order to reach beyond the individual realm and move to the societal realm, critical literacy advocates contend that it is not enough to identify facts or argue against "demonstrably false beliefs" (Burbules & Berk, 1999). One must also examine the larger impact of those facts and false beliefs at the societal level. For example, on completing a policy analysis of *Reading First* (the federal initiative in reading that was signed into law in 2002) from a critical literacy perspective, it became evident that although the goal to have all children reading by grade three is ideal, it is unrealistic (Mulcahy, 2003). Not only does it assume all students develop at the same rate, it discounts the many variables that affect student learning: economic status, cultural background, biased testing practices, auditory processing delays, as well as other physiological and psychological factors. In addition to considering the multiple variables that influence student learning, one also needs to ask who is benefiting from this initiative. Who will be negatively impacted by it? What economic, business, and political interests are being brought to bear on the initiative? Therefore, when engaging in critical literacy one is examining not only the logic and reasoning that is supporting an idea or an argument, one is also challenging the underlying societal factors involved. Burbules and Berk (1999) point out that, unlike critical thinking, critical pedagogy, which has much in common with critical literacy,

> looks to how an issue relates to "deeper" explanations—deeper in the sense that they refer to the basic functioning of power on institutional and societal level. For Critical Pedagogy, it makes no sense to talk about issues on a nonrelational, item-by-item basis. Where Critical Thinking emphasizes the immediate reasons and assumptions of an argument, Critical Pedagogy wants to draw in for consideration factors that may appear at first of less immediate relevance. (p. 9)

Many aspects of the four dimensions put forth by Lewison, Flint, and Van Sluys incorporate cultural and social levels of transformation. Under the dimension "disrupting the commonplace," they explain how critical literacy examines language so as to understand "how it shapes identity, constructs cultural discourses, and supports or disrupts the status quo." Similarly under the dimension "focusing on sociopolitical issues," they explain that redefining literacy is a "form of cultural citizenship and politics that increases opportunities for subordinate groups to participate in society" (p. 383). Lewison et al. are making a connection between the individual, society, and a move to action. One can become critically conscious by developing an awareness of oneself, of one's place in a larger system of networks, and of one's own thinking while at the same time developing a sense of interrelatedness and interconnectivity among social, cultural, and political dimensions.

In addition, at the heart of critical consciousness is the importance of taking action and making change. In fact, for Freire, the two, reflection and action, must occur together. Burbules and Berk (1999) explain it well when they state:

> Critical Pedagogy would never find it sufficient to reform the habits of thought of thinkers, however effectively, without challenging and transforming the institutions, ideologies, and relations that engender distorted, oppressed thinking in the first place—not as an additional act beyond the pedagogical one, but as an inseparable part of it. For Critical Thinking, at most, the development of more discerning thinkers might make them more likely to undermine discreditable institutions, to challenge misleading authorities, and so on—but this would be a separate consequence of the attainment of Critical Thinking, not part of it. (p. 6)

This need for a move to action is not evident in Paul and Elder's framework for critical thinking. Although they talk about creativity and analytic thought as important dimensions, the need for social transformation does not appear to be a necessary component. And while social transformation may result from one's ability to critically examine a given issue, many critical theorists would argue it is more a byproduct of critical thinking than a purposeful outcome.

## Fair-Mindedness and Neutrality

When discussing the importance of developing critical thought, Paul and Elder refer to the development of fair-mindedness as a way to cultivate intellectual capacities. Without fair-mindedness, readers and thinkers can not be objective and recognize their contradictions and inconsistencies. Supporters of critical literacy also believe it important to acknowledge the inconsistencies and contradictions within ourselves and within society. Such inconsistencies and contradictions may be referred to as tensions or binary opposites. However, a difference arises between critical literacy and critical thinking when we examine why fair-mindedness is an important to teach. Paul and Elder underline the importance of fair-mindedness in one's thinking so that we can be transformed by our learning. Without fair-mindedness our inconsistencies and contradictions will prevent us from "critically examining" many domains of our lives. The implication here is that by becoming rational and applying the skills of critical thinking one is empowered. This, again, focuses on the individual, overlooking the social, cultural, and political aspects that surround us. Becoming empowered and changing one's own circumstances may be difficult or impossible without also transforming certain aspects of society. Kincheloe (2005) reminds us, "We cannot simply attempt to cultivate the intellect without changing the unjust social context in which such minds operate" (p. 21).

The belief that one can cultivate fair-mindedness also implies that one can analyze facts or problems in a neutral or unbiased way, thereby creating the belief that information or data can be examined objectively. Followers of critical literacy would strongly disagree. To believe knowledge is neutral overlooks "how sociopolitical systems, power relationships, and language are intertwined and inseparable" (Lewison, Flint, & Van Sluys, 2002, p. 383). Furthermore, due to personal biases, cultivating fair-mindedness may not be possible. In critical literacy, there is no pretense at being objective: All interpretations and analyses are value-laden and tied to the social, cultural, and historical context in which the text was examined. Being aware of our contradictions, inconsistencies, and biases allows us and others to understand how we are positioned and how others might be positioning us with their inferences, interpretations, and conclusions.

Critical theorists do not believe that there is one truth to be found or that reality exists outside of language, culture, and ideology. Instead they acknowledge that many truths may exist and it is only through dialogue and "interrogating multiple viewpoints" that we come to understand and acknowledge the many ways in which truth and knowledge can be grasped. The elements listed under the dimension "interrogating multiple viewpoints" address this aspect of critical literacy. Lewison et al. suggest we reflect on "multiple and contradictory perspectives," use multiple voices to interrogate texts, to pay attention to and seek out "the voices of those who have been silenced or marginalized," to write "counternarratives to dominant discourses," and to "make difference visible" (p. 383).

Acknowledging one's own contradictions and inconsistencies is important. Doing so allows one to become aware of who he or she is and how he or she operates and interacts with the world. Critical literacy, instead of attempting to achieve fair-mindedness, encourages one to make contradictions, inconsistencies, and biases known.

## Inferences

In explaining the element of critical thought that addresses our inferences, interpretations, and conclusions, critical literacy and critical thinking may have much in common. According to Paul and Elder, it is not the information or the data that determines how we arrive at certain understandings. Instead drawing on "the powers of origination of our own minds," (p. 24-5) it is our own concepts and understanding that lead us to infer, interpret, and draw conclusions.

Here both critical literacy and critical thinking can be related to transactional reading theory—that is, the way the text, the reader, and the context interact with one another to construct meaning. When applying transactional reading theory to the notion of drawing inferences, it is understood that one may come away with knowledge that differs from the author's original intent or from another person's analysis of the same text. Inferences are created by combining the reader's background knowledge with information from the text, which in turn creates new meaning. Therefore, there may be many possible inferences to be drawn from any one piece of text. With this understanding, it makes it difficult to say, categorically, that one's inference or reasoning is defective. However, advocates of critical thinking suggest that an inference can be incorrect because of some fault with a person's reasoning, which implies that there is one truth that can be found in the text.

From the standpoint of critical literacy, many possible inferences, interpretations, and conclusions may emerge from an analysis—with no one being more correct than another. Furthermore, one's opinions, inferences, and conclusions are open to debate. Information and data alone are not what cause us to arrive at certain conclusions or interpretations. This we do for ourselves as inferring, interpreting, and drawing conclusions are meaning-making constructions or creations.

## Questioning and Problem Posing

Although asking questions is important to think critically and be critically literate, the purposes for questioning are somewhat different in each case. Critical thinking suggests we pose questions in order to reason through an issue. In the scholarship on critical thinking, Paul and Elder explain that the purpose of setting questions is to be clear about what we are asking in order to find a reasonable answer. They write, "If we are not clear about the question we are asking, or how the question relates to our basic purpose or goal, we will not be able to find a reasonable answer to it, or an answer that will serve our purpose" (p. 23). Questions that guide critical thinking might include: What examples were used to support the author's claim? Do you agree with the author's argument? Does the author include differing points of view?

Critical literacy, on the other hand, proposes we ask questions that interrogate the status quo and challenge commonly accepted social practices. Questioning is not solely for the purpose of ascertaining reasonable answers. Instead, critical literacy questions focus on uncovering inequalities and injustices, and on identifying why and how such inequalities are perpetuated. When "disrupting the commonplace" one problematizes "subjects of study" and interrogates texts by "asking questions" such as how is gender being constructed by this text? Or how does this text reify or disrupt stereotypes? Similarly, when "interrogating multiple view points," one poses questions about the voices included or excluded in the text: Who is missing from this text? Whose story is being told and whose is ignored? And, when focusing on sociopolitical issues, Lewison et al. suggest, one is constantly "challenging the unquestioned legitimacy of unequal power relations" (p. 382): How do I benefit from racism? Sexism? When engaging in critical pedagogy, students need to be problem posing instead of trying to find logical answers, as critical thinking asks us to.

In addition, both critical thinking and critical literacy demand that readers problematize assumptions inherent in texts. If our assumptions go unquestioned, we disallow the possibility of realizing alternative ways of being in the world. Holding to our assumptions without question leads to a passive acceptance of the status quo:

> All reasoning must begin somewhere, and must take some things for granted. Any defect in the starting points of our reasoning, any problem in what we are taking for granted, is a possible source of problems. Only we can create the assumptions on the basis of which we will reason. We (i.e. create) our minds' starting point. (p. 24)

Our assumptions, if unquestioned, can lead to problems in our reasoning. Critical literacy educators, too, would argue that false or misleading assumptions are problematic as they can lead to an unquestioning acceptance of the status quo.

While Paul and Elder acknowledge our assumptions may be a "possible source of problems," Lewison et al. encourage us to challenge commonly held assumptions, particularly those about race, class, gender, and sexuality. Accepting that our assumptions may be problematic allows us to reconceptualize the "every-day' through new lenses." In so doing, we challenge unquestioned power relationships and interrogate popular culture and media to uncover how we are being positioned and constructed by television, video games, comics, and the like (p. 383).

## Multiple Viewpoints

The importance of being aware of one's point of view is common to both critical literacy and critical thinking. Both recognize that points of view are human constructions. However, critical thinking warns readers against "defects in our point of view and frame of reference" as a possible "source of problem in our reasoning" (Paul & Elder, p. 24). It acknowledges that one's own point of view may be too narrow, imprecise, and contradictory. Again, as with other elements of thought discussed by Paul and Elder, the word "defect" suggests that something may be wrong with an individual's point of view. It further suggests that there is a correct point of view or frame of reference from which we should begin reasoning, while critical pedagogues maintain that there is no one correct position from which to construct meaning.

Critical literacy advocates ask readers to move beyond individual point of view to incorporate the importance of understanding multiple viewpoints. In so doing critical literacy attempts to put readers in the shoes of others viewing a situation from other perspectives. This is important as it allows readers to see that many possibilities may exist. It further reinforces the notion that there may not be one truth, but many possible ways of understanding the truth. Critical literacy invites students to read from many different perspectives and to always keep in mind whose voices are being heard and whose are missing, because who is missing from texts is as important as who is included.

In sum, the purpose of interrogating multiple viewpoints in critical literacy is not to find fault with a certain person's or group's point of view but to understand more fully the many perspectives from which people view the world. Who is to say an individual's point of view is defective? It is defective according to whom? Critical literacy understands that language, thoughts, beliefs, and actions are influenced by society and that our attitudes and understandings are often constructed by the context in which we operate. Therefore, one person's point of view is going to differ from another's depending on the context in which they operate.

## The Importance of Critical Literacy for Content Area Literacy

In the field of content area literacy, a paradigm shift is underway from a "cognition and learning paradigm" that emerged in the 1970s and remained popular through the 1980s to a "social constructivist paradigm" of the 1990s. With this shift came "an emphasis on understanding the sociocultural underpinnings of teaching and learning in content classrooms" (Vacca, 2002, p. 193). Because critical literacy focuses on social transformation as well as individual transformation, integrating critical literacy into the teaching of the content areas allows us to further this paradigm shift toward a transformative and liberating education.

Another advantage of integrating critical literacy with content area literacy is that, apart from encouraging students to connect classroom learning with their everyday lives, it also allows for students to make connections across the disciplines, something that is often overlooked by a fragmented approach to the curriculum. While critical thinking often focuses on issues "item-by-item," critical literacy strives to make students aware of the interrelatedness and interconnectiveness of the world:

> Hence, Critical Thinking tends to address issues in an item-by-item fashion, not within a grand scheme with other issues. The issues themselves may have relations to one another, and they may have connections to broader themes, but those relations and connections are not the focus of investigation. What is crucial to the issue at hand is the interplay of an immediate cluster of evidence, reason, and arguments. For Critical Thinking, what is important is to describe the issue, give the various reasons for and against, and draw out any assumptions (and only those) that have immediate and direct bearing on the argument. This tends to produce a more analytical and less holistic mode of critique. (Burbules & Berk, 1999, p. 55)

In contrast to critical thinking, critical literacy encourages students to examine how the issues under examination may connect to one another and to broader themes. Making such connections is important because it discourages students from viewing things in isolation from one another and instead encourages them to understand the far-reaching impact any issue may have on the larger society.

In keeping with this sentiment, while critical thinking is crucially important in supplying students with the skills to analyze arguments and ideas presented to them in their texts, critical literacy challenges students to identify issues such as gender bias, cultural bias, omissions of narratives by marginalized groups from texts, and re-write the text to represent a more complete picture. Thus, critical literacy pedagogy is transformative and accepts nothing less than social and political equality for all American citizens by educating students to upset the status quo.

In conclusion, although both critical literacy and critical thinking are important for students, it is necessary that educators be aware of how they differ and understand that the two ideas are not synonymous. Failing to disentangle critical literacy and critical thinking from one another could lead to a neutralization of critical literacy. McLaren (1998) cautions us of this. He argues, taxonomies promoting critical thinking have allowed neoconservatives and liberals to "neutralize the term critical by repeated and imprecise usage, removing its political and cultural dimensions and laundering its analytic potency to mean 'thinking skills'" (p. 161). To avoid such a fate, critical pedagogues must persist in making the distinction between critical literacy and critical thinking.

# References

Burbules, N.C., & Berk, R. (1999). Critical thinking and critical pedagogy: Relations, differences and limits in critical theories in education. In T.S. Popkewitz & L. Fendler (Eds.), *Critical Theories in Education* (pp. 45–65). New York: Routledge.

Elder, L., & Paul. R. (1998). The role of Socratic questioning in thinking, teaching, and learning. *Clearing House,* 71(5), 297–302.

Freire, P. (1970). *Pedagogy of the oppressed.* New York: Herder & Herder.

Kincheloe, J.L. (2005). *Critical pedagogy.* New York: Peter Lang.

Lewison, M., Flint, A.S., & Van Sluys, K. (2002). Taking on critical literacy: The journey of newcomers and novices. *Language Arts,* 79(5), 382–392.

McDaniel, C. (2004). Critical literacy: A questioning stance and the possibility for change. *The Reading Teacher,* 57(5), 472–481.

McLaren, P. (1998). *Life in schools: An introduction to critical pedagogy in the field of education.* White Plains, NY: Longman.

Moss, B. (2005). Making a case and a place for effective content area literacy instruction in the elementary grades. *The Reading Teacher,* 59(1), 46–55.

Mulcahy, C.M. (2003). Emergent federal government policy on literacy in the USA. *Irish Educational Studies,* 22 (Autumn), 91–100.

Paul, R., & Elder, L. (2005). *The thinkers guide to the nature and functions of critical & creative thinking.* Dillon Beach, CA: Foundation for Critical Thinking

Shannon, P. (1995). *Text, lies, & and videotape: Stories about life, literacy, & learning.* Portsmouth, NH: Heinemann.

Shor, I. (1992). *Empowering education: Critical teaching for social change.* Chicago: University of Chicago Press.

Vacca, R.T. (2002). Making a difference in adolescents' school lives: Visible and invisible aspects of content area reading. In A.E. Farstrup & S.J. Samuels (Eds.), *What research has to say about reading instruction* (pp. 184–204). Newark, DE: International Reading Association.

Vasquez, V.M. (2004). *Negotiating critical literacies with young children.* Mahwah, NJ: Lawrence Erlbaum Associates.

# Chapter 2

# Being Critically Literate in Science

*Kurt Love*

Louis Pasteur's famous quote "Science knows no country, because knowledge belongs to humanity, and is the torch which illuminates the world" demonstrates the widely accepted notion that science is universal and objective. The work of a scientist is generally seen as neutral, unbiased, and transcendent of culture, and science as disconnected from culture, history, gender, race, class, place, economics, and politics. Teaching science tends to take on the same characteristics and follow the same path. However, understanding nature is a process that looks different throughout history, in different places, and in different cultures. For example, science in Western, industrialized cultures has been constructed through patriarchy, classism, elitism, and influenced by capitalism and politics. Yet, teachers, curricula, and textbooks portray science as distinctly separate from any social or cultural relationships. This false construction begets and concentrates power in the form of authority in science-based knowledge. If a person claims that a type of knowledge is "scientific," a host of assumptions, whether explicit or covert, are attached to that statement. This process is one to which teachers and textbooks currently pay little attention, and its omission leads to the positioning of science knowledge as privileged and uncontested by the general public.

## Critical Literacy Components

As you've seen in the previous chapter, asking students to be critically literate entails multiple actions while reading; critical readers are consciously active in the process of questioning the author's agenda and purpose for writing the text. Critical readers analyze the author's discourse and metacognitively attend to their own processes of incorporating information and acting in ways that reshape and mold it with their thoughts, prior knowledge, and identity. Finally, critical readers are moved to action in their social and cultural positions to disrupt hegemony and to conserve cultural practices that resist loss of power and community.

By performing the aforementioned actions, critical readers are disrupting the power of the one-way, sender-receiver model of reading. In the latter relationship, the author maintains power because the reader views the author as the knower, while the reader positions him or herself as lesser-than and simply "banks" information submissively (Freire, 1970). Thus, readers who passively receive information from texts without questioning the author's intentions and purposes are trapped in a subordinated power position.

If we are to ask our students to become critical readers, teachers must be critical readers and thinkers themselves. Yet, the practice of teaching is becoming more and more controlled by government policies and pressures to create assimilative uniformity. Teachers are increasingly expected to repro-gram children to be docile, democratically timid vessels for regurgitation in order to prevent social agitation. Similarly, teachers are expected to be ideological mirrors of the dominant discourses and ideologies. Policymakers have found that placing intense pressure on standardized tests (which are reflective of the dominant group's ideologies) keeps teachers from straying away from accepted discourse and into critical positions that might challenge the power structure. In this sense, standardized tests may be intended to ideologically control teachers more than the kids they teach. Controlling the teachers is a fairly effortless task because of the constant fear that is created in the teaching community about closing schools and/or losing jobs if teachers deviate for the authoritarian-designed course. In other words, teachers who do not succeed in having their students ideologically march at a certain rhythm, pace, and frequency can be reprimanded, cited, and even removed from teaching. This presence of fear forces teachers (who are typically not radical) to perpetuate ideologies that they may even be against.

Politicians, state departments of education, education programs in colleges and universities, parents, and even students are demanding that teachers increase their numbers of students who pass state-authored tests; as a result teaching is monolithically becoming a practice of "teaching to the test." Teachers, who generally do not have access or authorship rights to the tests, are forced to teach in ways that strongly favor "learning-as-regurgitation" methods. In this setting, teachers are receiving many consistent messages that knowledge and language are static, linear, monocultural (or in the case of science, acultural), and neatly packaged. Teachers are not encouraged to problematize content, critically question its roots, or challenge assertions in state and district curriculum standards. The environment for teaching is itself becoming more and more hostile to critical education, pushing teachers away from the very practices that the authors in this book are espousing are vital to developing critical readers, which is essential for a strong and healthy democratic society. The languaging processes in education are literally steering teachers toward greater levels of compliance and colonization. As teachers, we need to resist this kind of movement, at least in part, by becoming more critically literate ourselves.

At the heart of the process of becoming critically literate is understanding the relationships between power and knowledge. The process of constructing knowledge is not a "neutral" process as it is popularly viewed in Western, industrialized societies. There exists no moderate body of "knowledge-constructors" who test and search for every bit of bias for extraction before it "goes to press" so that the public is exposed to bias-free information only. Every text, every piece of knowledge, and every concept is grounded in the politics, history, culture, and power relationships of its time. A simple, yet powerful demonstration of this is seen in science textbooks of the early and middle decades of the twentieth century. Whenever student images were used in the textbooks, White males were shown as active (seemingly performing experiments by their use of lab equipment), while others were shown as either passive (as it often was with females) or altogether absent (as it was with non-Whites) (Bianchini, 1993). These textbooks strongly suggested that only White males had the ability to become career scientists.

## Power/Knowledge Relationship

Teaching and knowledge are deeply connected to root power relationships. I view the relationship in my own teaching practice as a two-directional process where each is continually influencing the other. As I teach about a topic, I attend to the power relationships that exist within the topic by providing space for multiple voices and experiences of the students and for analyzing how their value systems and personal histories shape and reshape knowledge. I am much less concerned with my students having to memorize concepts in science and am more interested in providing opportunities for them to critique, ponder, question, and reject concepts. I approach teaching in this manner for two main reasons. First, if students can actively engage with a concept by critiquing, pondering, questioning, and/or rejecting it, I feel comfortable that they have more than a functional understanding of the concept. Critical readers cannot engage in the processes of critical reflection without fully engaging in the text. Performing critical actions shows quite readily that students have understanding beyond the fundamentals of the content. Second, I view knowledge creation as an entirely human-dependent process. If that is the case, then it means that culture, history, race, gender, sexual orientation, time, place, class, and an infinite amount of other nuances are attached to knowledge. Therefore, knowledge cannot be static or neutral; it is fluid, temporal, and a function of place—being reorganized, perpetuated, and lost.

Furthermore, the constant degradation of global ecology due to years of colonization and, more recently, globalization is also an ongoing threat to diverse knowledges. Vandana Shiva (2000; 2005) describes the continual reduction of diverse knowledges as being directly connected to the limiting and homogenizing of biodiversity. Just as diverse knowledges diminish as colonization continues through the ongoing process of global Westernization, a simultaneous and equally culturally destructive process is occurring because the destruction of biodiversity (often via Western, corporate practices) pushes earth-based cultures toward dependency upon Western industry and technology. That is, globalization causes destruction of the environments that diverse peoples with diverse knowledges rely upon for sustenance as well as history, tradition, and culture. When an environment is destroyed, so are the cultures of the people who depend upon them.

Yet, certain knowledges are not included in science textbooks and curricula because knowledge is connected to power. Textbooks and curricula largely exclude the teachings of Vandana Shiva, along with many other feminists, ecofeminists, and eco-justice theorists because they challenge the power of the science canon. "School knowledge" remains topical, based on fact "bits" disconnected (seemingly) from ecological and economic issues and focused on getting teachers to march to the same drumbeat. In other words, schools are generally not in the business of producing radical students who challenge systems of power. Schools are sites where assimilation is the first priority, usually to produce "productive" docile workers.

Who benefits from the school's production of acquiescing adults who remain loyal to the corporate-state? Corporations and governments that do not want the masses to question their methods, which could very easily lead to turning over power to the disenfranchised.

Therefore, schools generally reflect the ideologies of the dominant group (Ballantine, 2001). Schools are organized to produce people who believe that the state and corporations are acting on their behalf, which, in effect, reinforces the perceived legitimacy of the state and corporate ideologies. The benefit, then, is the production of a mass of docile students who become socially and politically docile workers. To produce passive people who will not challenge the power structure, "school knowledge" must be uniform, standardized, homogenized, and uncritical. Historical figures need to be described as infallible heroes (Loewen, 1996), and science must be portrayed as value-free to demonstrate and justify the corporate-state's current ideologies as just and fair. To do this, students are largely not exposed to any in-depth analysis that utilizes critical, feminist, or eco-justice perspectives in their assignments, readings, or in the teachers' lectures. There may be the occasional topical analysis that looks critical, but it serves the purpose of doing just that, giving the illusion that the masses have the freedom to question power imbalances so that they feel free. Of course, exceptions do occur when teachers, students, and/or administrators consciously choose to disrupt power structures, which is a process that begins with becoming critically literate.

Therefore, it is imperative that teachers learn theories about how knowledge and power operate if they are inclined to be critical and help their students mediate the power structures, especially of government, corporations, patriarchy, and technological centrism (viewing technology as dominant over the priorities of nature). Teachers often focus heavily on practice and less on theory, as if one can function without the other. However, when one's practices are consciously informed by the theories of how societies and cultures operate, the practices are more likely to serve as both emancipatory (resisting concentrated power by government and corporations) and ecologically just (revitalizing the cultural commons [described below]). Thus, the greatest action that a teacher can do is to help students disrupt power imbalances, promote peace, and create ecological sustainability.

## Critically Viewing "Science Knowledge" with Feminist Theory

Feminist theory has provided a wealth of deep analysis and critique of how Western science upholds patriarchy and represents masculine ways of thinking. Sadly, mainstream culture seems to have stigmatized feminists and feminist theorists, stereotyping them as militants or "complainers" who have no connection with the "real world." However, feminists have shown that those in power positions (often males or patriarchical females) greatly affect reality construction, which ultimately affects individual practices, institutions, collective actions, and perceptions of history. Also, there is no one version of feminism. Feminisms have many different foci: gender roles, political processes, race, class, and/or women in developing nations. Still, understanding feminist critiques is, in part, vital to understanding those imbalances that prohibit peace and ecological sustainability.

Feminists have given a great deal of attention to describing how the scientific method creates hegemony between each other and human-over-nature relationships. For example, feminists have historically led the critique on science and science education pointing out that the power that is in the scientific method is often due to how the language of science operates and concentrates power. Since westerners made the argument over 400 years ago that the scientific method is "objective," when a scientific study is reported, it is assumed to be credible if it adhered closely to the scientific method. As described in more detail below, this one word falsely carries with it much power. Critical literacy is the process of questioning how a word or a concept is commonly used and potentially creates worldviews and ideologies that trap us into hegemonic actions.

Many feminist scholars also question to whom science belongs. As is the case in other subject areas, White, European, middle- and upper-middle-class males have benefited from the "story" of science because they have "historically" been the creators. The history of science includes two concepts that can be problematized in the classroom setting. The first is "objectivity," and the second is "neutrality." Both are closely connected to one another, and they are the foundation for constructing science's authority in Western and Westernized (previously earth-based cultures that changed via the colonizing practices of the West) societies. In effect, both objectivity and neutrality legitimize White and male positional views of science.

Critical readers of science will notice immediately and repeatedly that authors claim that the scientific process of investigation is "objective." Objectivity is when bias is removed from investigation and from the reporting of information, claims, assertions, processes, and conclusions. Feminists have asked, "To what extent is objectivity possible?" Is it possible to be completely separate from one's self when observing, writing, reporting, and constructing questions for the investigation? How does one go about not being one's self? Starting with the notion that knowledge is entirely a human-based action, when is it possible to remove the "human experience" from creating knowledge? Being objective is like saying that we can remove ourselves from ourselves and somehow exist nowhere or perhaps everywhere.

Donna Haraway (1988) describes being "objective" as a process by which a partial truth is portrayed as a whole truth. She calls the claim to objectivity a "god-trick." One would have to be separate from the human experience and view it from a different plane like a god to attain a whole truth. As a consequence, bias is inescapable and always present. When a person is doing an investigation, it is that person's worldview that presents assumptions about nature, social interactions, and systematic processes that inform how that person creates questions for investigation, performs investigations, and reports the investigations. For instance, a person entrenched in a European culture believes that nature is something that can be isolated into variables and tested through manipulation of those variables. A contrasting view from Native Americans states that nature is deeply interconnected, and we are all located in relationships with nature. Therefore, isolating and testing "variables" of nature is antithetical to the organization of nature and an inappropriate, if not impossible, task. Native Americans focus on the relationships and interconnected happenings in nature rather than on atomizing and reducing nature to irreducible parts like that of a machine.

Furthermore, worldviews and ideologies are represented in differences in language. Language creates reality perception (and vice versa). Gregory Bateson (1972) stated that language is like a roadmap because they both select and hide information. For example, the English word "sun" is defined in Western cultures as a physical body at the center of the solar system that provides energy to the planets of the solar system. Similarly, Earth is described as a physical object in the solar system. Language usage focuses on the physical properties and the operations of the sun and the earth. In contrast, many Native American tribal languages describe nature in terms of relationships with nature rather than as physical objects:

> So everything is like a big family. We are children of the Great Spirit, children of Mother Earth, children of the sky, and so on. We have that relationship, that kinship that is part of our identity. That is knowing who we are ... we live in a world of many circles and these circles constitute our identity and they go out to encompass every thing that there is in the Universe. That is our kinship. Those are our relatives. The Universe is a family and we have to deal with other things in that Universe with that in mind. (Forbes, 1979, pp. 5–6)

For example, the word for Earth in some Native American languages is derived from or is the same word for "mother." As Cajete (1994) explained, "The geographical and structural orientations of Indigenous communities to their natural place and the cosmos reflected a communal consciousness that extended to and included the natural world in an intimate and mutually reciprocal relationship" (p. 174).

Science content found in science textbooks rooted in Western, industrial culture is largely devoid of relationships outside of the objectified, physical, human-centered views of nature. Children in public schools in the United States are not exposed to multiple views of our relationships with nature in emotional, interconnected, or even spiritual ways. Historically, perceiving nature as an object to be manipulated comes from the dominant, colonizing culture that views nature largely for profit. Native American cultures do not rely on the concept of objectivity because they do not see that separating themselves from nature is possible. Objectivity is not only a false construction but a highly inappropriate one in light of the relationships people have with nature.

In Western, industrial cultures, if one is "objective" during investigations, the results reported are seen as "neutral" and not connected to cultural values or biases. The results are even seen as "Truth." Claiming neutrality (in partnership with objectivity) leads to a construction of knowledge that is representative of Divine knowledge—another "god-trick." Additional sociocultural benefits exist in the form of power. Once neutrality is associated with information, that information is hierarchically placed as universal, superior, and transcending human activity. Sandra Harding (1986) points out that Western scientists have seen science as the path to truth because of their claims of being value free and objective. Yet, the creation of any information is completely human dependent.

How are we to consider thinking of science investigations, then? Feminist theorists have pointed to two possible alternatives. Sandra Harding (1991) suggests that objectivity can be strengthened as multiple voices become included in the investigative process. "Strong objectivity" is when underrepresented peoples investigate and create knowledge. However, this is problematic because it still involves people choosing the underrepresented peoples, which creates yet another privilege for the dominant group.

Donna Haraway (1988) presents a second alternative to objectivity. She suggests that knowledge is "situated" because information always comes from humans and is never free from culture, values, and history. In other words, knowledge-creation is a process that is filtered through the cultures, values, and history of those who are creating the knowledge. Being transparent illuminates the ways in which scientists may be limited in their creation of knowledge. This process openly addresses the ways in which knowledge has been influenced during its investigation, creation, and reporting stages.

Science textbooks do not provide discussions of scientists situated in history, culture, class, gender, race, or sexual orientation when they developed their research questions/philosophies, performed their experiments, and interpreted and reported their findings. Textbooks do not address scientists' value-laden assumptions and assertions, nor do the textbooks provide contrasting situated knowledges from diverse peoples. Western science is presented as the only science. Many examples exist in history of scientists creating conclusions that were tied to the values of the dominant value system of its time. Galileo Galilei, Johannes Kepler, Rene Descartes, and Isaac Newton all described the universe as either a machine or a clock, implying that life is mechanistic, lifeless, and rigorously controlled in its performance. This provided much latitude for scientists to view nature as a large machine with individual parts that can be isolated and inspected. This also encouraged Westerners to view nature as separate from humans. Francis Bacon asserted that science, not the church, had governance over "wonders" and "marvels" (Daston, 1994). Bacon, who was in good favor with nobility and King James I, used his assertion to help the monarchy in its power "tug-of-war" with the church. Bacons' theories provided a rationale for repositioning power away from the church and closer to the monarchy. Charles Darwin, revered by the Victorian elite, used "survival of the fittest" to support the class-driven idea that impoverished people should not reproduce (Rosser, 1986). Additionally, countless scientists have described homosexuality as a disease, women as biologically inferior to men, and Blacks as a different subspecies than Whites (Harding, 1986, 1991; Rosser, 1986).

Each of these scientists cloaked themselves in "neutrality" and "objectivity" when making these assertions. That gives uncritical (and perhaps "unconscious") teachers and students license to do the same and hegemonically perpetuate power relationships with practices of domination and colonization. For teachers and students, Paulo Freire (1973) and Ira Shor (1992) suggest that gaining "critical consciousness" is the focus of an emancipatory education. Connecting individual experiences and meaning with social structures is at the heart of critical consciousness. Again, science textbooks lead students and teachers down a different path. Their push for memorization of facts and assimilation into the dominant worldview of nature (i.e., humans disconnected from nature, nature objectified for purposes of experimental manipulation, and nature for-profit only) explicitly directs students and teachers without opportunity for uncovering the power relationships that exist within that knowledge.

Critical readers and feminists also ask, "Whom does this worldview serve?" The majority of scientists in modern-day, Western, industrial cultures rely upon either corporate or government funding for their research. Is teaching science in ways that are uncritical of Western science servicing corporations' and governments' desires? Looking at the bigger picture, local, state, and national governments have mandated and approved standards and curricula. Since the 1970s, teachers have increasingly come under the control of standardized tests and closely aligned curricula. Politicians and government officials have used the word "accountability" so frequently that the popular movement of closing down schools is becoming more accepted. Additionally, students, teachers, administrators, and politicians commonly view the purpose of education as a way to support corporations and the national growth domestic product. Science is taught and textbooks are written in this context with these pressures.

## Eco-Justice—Commons Practices

To be a critical reader of science, teachers and students also need to problematize the languaging processes in the text or in any form of communication. Language is rooted in metaphorical processes, and these "root metaphors" drive meaning and construct reality. The root metaphors provide organization and structure for communication to occur, but this also means that ideologies are part of the languaging process (Bowers, 2003, 2005a, 2005b, 2006a). Much of this goes unnoticed in everyday communications. For example, technology is often described with words such as "progress" and "advancement." However, this uncritical description of technology as a positive movement for society is quite discriminatory against indigenous cultures, assumes Western superiority, and drives a wedge between humans and nature, making humans the center of existence as they "progress" away from nature.

Science textbooks (as well as other media in the form of videos, Web sites, and science magazines) put technology on a pedestal, often portraying it as transcendent of the human experience. Yet, technology is a direct extension of ideology. Military technologies are extensions of war ideologies and serve as applications of that ideology. The use of robotics on the assembly lines is ideologically grounded in capitalistic practices in search for the greatest profit.

Computers are also part of the same ideology of capitalism as the use and practice of language turns toward value systems that respect the written word over oral traditions and over face-to-face interactions (Bowers, 2006a). More and more colleges are offering online courses in place of in-person classes because monetary profit takes priority over interpersonal processes of learning. Teachers from pre-school through high school are trying to find more ways for students to become techno-savvy without critically looking at what languaging processes are affected as they become increasingly technologically dependent.

Another problematic root metaphor in science is "individualism." This is tied to competition and profit, as well as to a human-centered (or human-over-nature) perspective. Science textbooks often turn scientists into individual heroes or intellectual "capitalists." James Watson and Francis Crick are revered as superheroes for the description of the structure of the DNA molecule. Yet, Rosalind Franklin—who developed the first x-ray crystallographies of the DNA molecule, which James Watson so coyly played politics to possess—received no mention during Watson and Crick's receiving of the Nobel Prize, even though Franklin's photographs were integral for them to figure out the DNA molecule. This kind of competitive behavior is parallel to the business practices of Microsoft and Apple, especially in the beginning stages of the development of the personal computer. The same competitive and profit-driven practices are present with pharmaceutical companies. In this context, the competitive individual is a corporation in the business of competitive investigations tied to billions of dollars of profit.

Becoming critically literate in science education requires understanding the power relationships embedded in science knowledge. An area of pedagogical work called eco-justice not only includes language and power relationships as they are tied together in metaphors, but also includes looking at how industrialization (and technology-based cultures) reduces the cultural commons of a society. The current industrial cultural practices work to maximize profit at the expense of the health of the environment and the people. Seeking this kind of profit also means privatizing practices that were once communal, such as growing food in common locations, or having access to basic, life-sustaining resources, such as clean, fresh water. The cultural commons are, or have been, linked to ecological sustainability (such as small, local farming practices that both feed the community and leave a negligible ecological footprint), to art (such as murals on buildings and public performances), to crafts and craft knowledge, as well as to food preparation and health practices.

Because privatization and competition are so pervasive in the West, they seem both natural and morally appropriate, making it initially difficult to imagine the possibility of cultural commons. The cultural commons— which exist because of centuries or even, and in many cultures (especially indigenous cultures), thousands of years of knowledge and traditions—are increasingly being replaced by the most temporal and nomadic forms of knowledge life cycles. The knowledge that was once used to perform the task is then lost because of the technology that automates the task with minimal human action. For example, many of our foremothers and forefathers in the U.S. were quite skilled in working with the land to regularly produce food and predicting weather based on many elements besides looking to the clouds. As we in the U.S. have become more reliant on technology and experts who interpret data, recent generations of people are far less capable of understanding how to cultivate the earth and read the signs to predict weather. These knowledges that were once considered "common sense" are quickly becoming extinct knowledges in the West.

In effect, living experiences in the West are not tied to thousands of years of knowledge about the rhythms and cycles of nature; rather, they are being reinvented in the name of maximizing profit. Living experiences are continually thinning to that of consuming rather than producing, technology in place of nature, media instead of interrelationships, and individuals before community. Living experiences are being reduced to consumerism, with the constant reminder that the very next product that we buy will make us (as seen in daytime television advertisements) *Cheer, Shout, Snuggle,* and be *Whisk*(ed) away with a *Bounty* of *Joy* and *Zest.* However, bringing these fantasies to *Life* only *Depends* on whether or not we *Total*(ly) "buy" into the idea that products can actually link the material and the emotional.

Science curricula and science textbooks are deeply connected to the industrial culture's use of the all-powerful individual who succeeds by consuming. The major push in science education is through the use of inquiry methods in problem-based learning. Inquiry methods center the individual as the producer of knowledge, and problem-based learning positions nature as an object for manipulation. Therefore, the human dominates and manipulates nature, reinforcing that humans are paramount and nature can and should be separate and objectifiable. This is the rationale that allows for our industrial culture to view maximized profit (not sustainability of environment and human health) as the ultimate goal. Both capitalism (derived from competitive individualism) and consumerism (or individuals causing depletion) ignore that living experiences are tied to ancient earth-based knowledges and the existence of cultural commons and commons-based practices. In the presence of strong cultural commons and ancient earth-based knowledges, capitalism and consumerism are minimized to levels that maintain sustainability of environment and health, as opposed to monetary profit for the sake of the few at the expense of the health of the planet.

## Taking Action

The old adage "we teach how we've been taught" reminds today's teachers that we must be creative and continually adjust our classroom practices. Currently, critically teaching science is not common in secondary classrooms, but with some reflective thought and imagination, change can occur. The major steps involve questioning putative objectivity and neutrality, rethinking how we teach the history of science, including voices from multiple perspectives (including those of women and different cultures), and connecting with our cultural commons.

### Questioning Common Ideologies of Science

Despite the common belief that science appears as the least likely place for critical work, critical literacy is both possible and necessary. Included here are several ways in which to teach students to be critically literate in science. First, begin by grounding science in culture and history. To do this, invite students to question the intentions of the author: Is this text trying to portray itself as neutral, disconnected from history and culture? Is the author pushing technology as unequivocally good? Is there a dilution of controversy? Consider the background of the authors. Authors who take a critical approach will often position themselves in culture and history, and acknowledge the ways in which class, race, and gender affect the production of knowledge. Therefore, if authors are not reflexive about the cultural and social conditions in which they write, they are more than likely not approaching their work critically.

Second, focus on the ideologies that were used to develop the text. What ideologies underpin this text? Is it rooted in capitalism? Individualism? Anthropocentrism (human-centered worldview)? Human-nature dualities?

Third, focus on creating space for multiple viewpoints. Is the science exclusively described from a Western, industrial culture point of view? What voices are missing in the text? Is there an attempt to include differing paradigms in understanding nature? Are there indigenous knowledges that address similar concepts in nature that can be used as a counter-text? What issues emerge when a feminist lens is applied to the reading?

Fourth, what actions can students engage in to better understand the differing voices, community practices, and intergenerational knowledges that exist in their communities? And how can use intergenerational knowledges to resist the destruction being done to our planet?

## A Multicultural Science

A critical teacher who is helping students to become critically literate in science can start by discussing women's contributions to science. (Marie Curie is often the "token" woman). The "Wings of Discovery" is a group that has an extensive collection on women's contributions to science research and knowledge. Additionally, Clifford Conner's book *A People's History of Science* documents those scientists of different races, cultures and socioeconomic backgrounds who have made uncountable contributions over thousands of years to science, ecology, navigation, engineering, and health.Of course, being critically literate in science means more than acknowledging the contributions of women and marginalized groups. Doing so might be considered an "add-on" approach, which still positions White, European males as the norm with occasional contributions from "other" peoples.

At the core of being critically literate in science is acknowledging that understanding and investigating nature does not occur exclusively through the sense of vision or secondarily through the other four senses. Clifford Geertz (1973) suggests that having a deep knowledge occurs when we engage in developing "thick descriptions." Thick descriptions are those that make explicit what is generally taken-for-granted information and, because of this status, can go unnoticed and thus ignored as a part of critique and critical reflection. Chet Bowers suggests that students from early elementary through college can engage in activities that incorporate developing deep understandings of ecology and culture by using thick descriptions. Activities could include comparing local farms to cities, zoos to wildlife refuges, and social interactions via different media such as instant messaging versus in-person communications.

These activities have similar processes that are inherent in science investigations, such as observations, analysis of data, and communicating conclusions. Science lessons readily lend themselves to students exploring and generating thick descriptions because of the use of observation and inquiry. Having students develop their own investigative questions, especially those that compare different environments, strengthens students' abilities to potentially analyze their own social relationships, histories, and privileges, as well as making deeper connections between their cultures and relationships with nature. Teaching science can be an empowering experience for students, especially if the questions that they investigate are not just limited to the "hard" or traditional sciences (biology, chemistry, physics, and earth sciences). The social sciences (sociology, anthropology, and cultural studies) all rely on similar processes of investigation and the communication of those findings. Critically literacy is strengthened when students have frequent opportunities to employ research methods to understand both natural and sociocultural phenomena and relationships.

## Revitalizing the Cultural Commons in our Communities

Critical readers do not depend on what Noam Chomsky (1992) called the social condition of "expertocracy," whereby the general masses give up their power to the "experts" who become the decision makers. The last and most powerful stage of being a critical reader involves taking action toward social (and ecological) justice. Chet Bowers (2006b) discussed what schools are already doing in order to revitalize the public commons through science education.

> In a few elementary and middle schools students are introduced to what is now called "slow food". That is, they are learning to care for vegetable gardens, to prepare meals that utilize the vegetables from the school gardens, and to share the food with the needy in the community. In other middle and high schools spread throughout the country, and located mostly in rural areas, students are learning environmental stewardship through involvement in community-centered environmental problem solving. Students are working with other members of the community in addressing such issues as restoring the local watershed, promoting more ecologically sound approaches to waste disposal, mapping the green areas of the community, and so forth. (p. 27)

In the lengthy quote above, Bowers describes several ways in which students are engaging with community members, elders, and their peers in order to connect with nature, protect the environment, and resist large corporations by democratically participating in local environmental decision making and producing food in local gardens. These actions are grounded in the ancient knowledges of the nonindustrialized, non-Western cultures, as for thousands of years they were ecologically sustainable and largely uninvolved in systems that relied upon money.

Bowers argues that critical teachers need to take care when attempting to emancipate their students because, although power is unequally organized and worth disrupting, there are many aspects of intergenerational knowledges from cultures all over the world (including indigenous peoples in colonized areas such as the United States, Canada, Australia, and Africa) that have healthy relationships with the environment and cultural practices that strengthen communities. Bowers argues that it is a colonizing action to label nonindustrialized, non-Western cultures and societies as "backward." Many aspects of the "backward" cultures have ecologically sustainable practices that are grounded in traditions. Traditions, Bowers argues, are not oppressive by default, which is why Bowers states that every culture must decide what needs to be conserved in order to protect the environment and community processes (Bowers, 2006a).

The current commons-based projects in Detroit demonstrate Bowers's argument for conserving and revitalizing the cultural commons. Over 30,000 people are involved in the creation and maintenance of over 500 community gardens. This situation has provided many opportunities for children to interact with elders to learn about traditional ethnic recipes, traditions connected to food preparation, and familial traditions. Additionally, spaces that were once empty lots with trash and sites for criminal activities such as drug-related crimes are being reduced in number as these become the sites for the community gardens. The educational aspects connected to the community gardens are numerous. Students learn about plants and their needs, soil types, soil nutritional levels, plant life cycles, food preparation, and cultural history. Many gardens in Detroit are specific to ethnicities. There are African, Korean, Puerto Rican, Filipino, and Italian gardens, each with their respective plants and herbs that characterize their styles of cooking (Bowers, 2006a).

In addition to gardening, craft making involves a great deal of scientific knowledge. During the early stages of the Enlightenment Period, scientists often studied the work of ironsmiths, coopers, tanners, and other craft-workers to understand how they made their products. However, craft-workers did not welcome the scientists' inquiries and investigations mainly because the secrets of their craft would then become public knowledge and would decrease their profits in the marketplace (Conner, 2005). Yet, science courses generally do not ask students to learn a craft. This is isolated to the vocational education courses such as woodworking and automobile maintenance, or to art courses such as photography, drawing, or painting. Teachers can make connections with craft-makers in the local community and setup mentorship relationships with their students as part of the learning experience. Making crafts involves local production and local relationships (as well as potential global customers via the use of the Internet to sell the product). Teaching science can include making connections to craft experts in the community to teach science fundamentals of materials, physical properties, force and motion principles, botany, farming, animal care, sound and light principles, and chemistry.

## Conclusion

Being critically literate in science can be a challenging task due to the popular views of science as being neutral, universal, and objective. However, teachers can readily engage their students in critically viewing and questioning the power structure and knowledge-construction processes of science by beginning with the following: problematizing the history of "science" as defined by White, Western males; showing how science-based knowledge is socially constructed and highly contextualized; and engaging students in community-based projects that revitalize the public commons. The process of learning science does not have to be isolated from the current practices of the teacher as the authoritative figure, delivering "packages" of facts that are disconnected from culture, society, and meaningful purpose (aside from the exclusive reason of passing evaluations). Science education can be a process of questioning the text and of acting in ways that develop healthier ecological conditions and stronger community relationships.

# References

Ballantine, J. H. (2001). *The sociology of education.* Upper Saddle River, NJ: Prentice Hall.

Bateson, G. (1972). *Steps to an ecology of mind.* New York: Ballantine Books.

Bianchini, J. A. (1993, April). *The high school biology text book: A changing mosaic of gender, science, and purpose.* Paper presented at the American Educational Research Association, Atlanta, GA.

Bowers, C. A. (2003). Can critical pedagogy be greened? *Educational Studies: A Journal of the American Educational Studies Association, 34*(1), 11-37.

Bowers, C. A. (2005a). How Peter McLaren and Donna Houston, and other "green" Marxists contribute to the globalization of the West's industrial culture. *Educational Studies: A Journal of the American Educational Studies Association, 37*(2), 185-195.

Bowers, C. A. (2005b). *The false promises of constructivist theories of learning: A global and ecological critique.* New York: Peter Lang.

Bowers, C. A. (2006a). *Revitalizing the commons: Cultural and educational sites of resistance and affirmation.* New York: Lexington Books.

Bowers, C. A. (2006b). Transforming environmental education: Making the renewal of the cultural and environmental commons the focus of educational reform. From http://www.cabowers.net/pdf/TransformingEE.pdf.

Cajete, G. (1994). *Look to the mountain: An ecology of indigenous education.* Durango, CO: Kivaki Press.

Chomsky, N. (1992). *Deterring democracy.* New York: Hill and Wang.

Conner, C. D. (2005). *A people's history of science: Miners, midwives, and "low mechanicks."* New York City: Avalon.

Daston, L. (1994). Baconian facts, academic civility, and the prehistory of objectivity. In A. Megill (Ed.), *Rethinking objectivity* (pp. 37-63). Durham, NC: Duke University Press.

Forbes, J. (1979). *Traditional Native American philosophy and multicultural education.* Los Angeles: American Indian Studies Center, University of California.

Freire, P. (1970). *Pedagogy of the oppressed.* New York City: Continuum.

Freire, P. (1973). *Education for critical consciousness.* New York: Seabury.

Geertz, C. (1973). *Interpretation of cultures.* New York: Basic Books.

Haraway, D. J. (1988). Situated knowledges: The science question in feminism and the privilege of partial perspective. *Feminist Studies, 14*(3), 575-599.

Harding, S. (1986). *The science question in feminism.* Ithaca, NY: Cornell University Press.

Harding, S. (1991). *Whose science? Whose knowledge? Thinking from women's lives.* Ithaca, NY: Cornell University Press.

Loewen, J. W. (1996). *Lies my teacher told me: Everything your American history textbook got wrong.* New York: Touchstone.

Rosser, S. V. (1986). *Teaching science and health from a feminist perspective: A practical guide.* New York: Pergamon Press.

Shiva, V. (2000). *Tomorrow's biodiversity.* New York: Thames & Hudson.

Shiva, V. (2005). *Earth democracy: Justice, sustainability and peace.* Cambridge, MA: South End Press.

Shor, I. (1992). *Empowering education: Critical teaching for social change.* Chicago: University of Chicago Press.

# Chapter 3

# Critical Mathematics Education: Recognizing the Ethical Dimension of Problem Solving

*Elizabeth de Freitas*

## The Concrete

Freire (1970/1998) advocated for a critical pedagogy that was grounded in the "present, existential, concrete situation" (p. 76). He envisioned a teaching praxis that began with the lived experiences of students, accessing their emotional and ethical ties to the situations in which they struggled for voice and equity. Pedagogy that dwells on the social injustices of a given context can trigger student "moral outrage" (Iyer et al., 2004, p. 356) and increase student participation. The emotion that fuels outrage, unlike that which underpins guilt, can become a source of political agency in the service of the disadvantaged (Leach et al., 2002). When outrage is buttressed with strong problem-solving skills, students are able to envision how they are implicated in the experiences of others, and how they might go about redressing the situation for the benefit of all.

Mathematics education often seems bereft of ethical principles that might fuel moral outrage, but it does, in theory, furnish students with strong problem-solving skills. These skills are both quantitative and qualitative insofar as students master procedural and conceptual knowledge and learn when and how to apply that knowledge in various contexts. In the language of school mathematics, the "concrete situation" to which Freire refers might be considered the "real life" application. "Real life" applications have the potential to tap student lived experience and trigger ethical reflection. Most examples of "real life" applications, however, are less concerned with citizenship and social justice and more concerned with enhancing mastery of mathematical skills. In this chapter, I examine the notion of "real life" applications as possible sites for ethical reflection. I discuss problems with the "real" in mathematics education and show how these are based on faulty cognitive theories of knowledge transfer. I then consider alternative visions of mathematics application and suggest that attention to classroom discourse and the craft of mathematics offer ways of introducing the ethical into school mathematics.

## Critical Mathematics Education

"Critical mathematics education" is an attempt to reconceive school mathematics as a site of political power, ethical contestation, and moral outrage. Critical mathematics education refers to a set of concerns or principles that function as catalysts for reconceiving and redesigning the lived experience of school mathematics. These concerns or principles are meant to target issues of political agency in society through an examination of mathematics education. The approach addresses political issues in relation to teaching and learning mathematics, confronts the problems of access and opportunity according to skin color, gender, and class, and examines the cultural reinscription of power through applications of mathematics in society (Skovsmose & Borba, 2004, p. 207). Various proponents of critical mathematics education have pursued this agenda in different ways: designing new mathematics curricula that address social justice issues (Gutstein, 2006; Tate, 2005), studying the role of mathematics teacher disposition toward social justice pedagogy (de Freitas, in press; Rodriguez & Kitchen, 2005; Zevenbergen, 2004), deconstructing the instructional strategies unique to school mathematics that inhibit increased participation (de Freitas, 2004; Walshaw, 2005), generating a sociopolitical ethics of mathematics education (Skovsmose, 2005; Valero, 2004), and offering visions of alternative teaching practices (Brown, 2001). Although many of these authors define their unique approach in different terms, one can trace a collective movement in the research community that takes form in relation to the Freirian concept of the critical. As a paradigm for student-centered teaching practice, critical mathematics education springs from Freire's critical agenda and offers educators and researchers a wide range of methodologies for exploring the concerns listed above.

It is not, however, a panacea. Gutstein (2008) remarks that the challenges to critical mathematics education often seem insurmountable when one is faced with the stalwart institutional practices that currently structure school mathematics and policy. Mechanisms of cultural reproduction that continue to sustain systemic inequity in/through education cannot simply be named and then easily abolished. Despite the efforts of many in the last century, studies continue to reveal correlations between socioeconomic status and mathematics achievement and indicate that little progress has been made regarding these patterns of inequity (Gates, 2006). Studies of mathematics teacher practice continue to show that the vast majority of mathematics teachers are still teaching skill and drill in ways that serve only a select set of students (Confrey & Kazak, 2006).

Because application problems rely on a shared understanding of the "real," they tend to produce large differences in measured achievement between social classes (Cooper, 2001, p. 256). Applications and "realistic" tasks have proven to be the most problematic, or rather the most revealing, in terms of differentiated cultural performances (Cooper & Dunne, 2004). Empirical work on assessment items has shown that students' confusion about the border between the "real" life, or the "everyday" realm, and the mathematical is correlated to socioeconomic position, gender, and ethnicity (Cooper, 1998a, 1998b). In other words, when students are asked to complete an application, their actions will be conditioned and constituted by their sociocultural position. Studies have shown that students who are designated working class are three times more likely to solve a "realistic" problem with a "realistic" answer (taking into account subjective and ethical issues) and fail to read the code of the problem as one demanding a mathematical solution (Cooper & Dunne, 2004, p. 71). Since these "realistic" applications are a reflection of reform movements in mathematics that attempt to move away from the esoteric and toward more "meaningful curriculum," it seems crucial that we unravel the ways that they may *not* address our aim of increasing mathematics participation in schools. Instead, they may demand an even more esoteric performance by introducing another level of code based on one's own enculturation into the discursive practices of school mathematics.

Skovsmose and Borba (2004) are careful to suggest that the critical approach must always attend to the "what if not" of school mathematics, that it must investigate the possible—think the otherwise—and explore "what could be" (p. 211). They argue that researchers and educators must imagine alternatives that trouble the current situation by actively and creatively generating visions or descriptions of a mathematics education that is more inclusive, more playful, and more relevant. The approach is profoundly hopeful and imaginative and offers educators a positive (and critical) means for professional development. "It confronts what is the case with what is not the case but what could become the case" (p. 214).

One way of practicing critical mathematics is to revise what is offered through the mainstream curricula using the concerns mentioned above as a guide. Consider, for instance, the "real" life applications generated by The Consortium of Mathematics and its Applications (COMAP) (www.comap.com), which is a nonprofit organization dedicated to enhancing mathematics instruction through emphasis on modeling. The term modeling is used to refer to the practice of "real life" problem solving through the use of mathematical applications. In practice, modeling is used to "understand, predict and control events in the real world" (Dossey et al., 2002, p. 13). Like any good application problem, modeling problems do not necessarily pre-scribe the kinds of tools or methods that might be appropriate in obtaining a solution. A good application problem refrains from supplying instructions or specifying the best tools for the job. After all, deciding whether a particular method is suitable or not should be part of the problem-solving process. This decision process or reflective deliberation—the stage when one reflects on the suitability of the mathematical methods to the given problem—is one place where ethical reflection might enter the application of mathematics.

Textbooks too often specify the appropriate tool to be used for the given problem and leave out the crucial ethical moment of reflecting on whether the means suit the ends. COMAP comes close to creating this moment of ethical reflection, since they create curriculum that aims to capture the messiness of "real life" problems and each year sponsor a series of contests for students at various levels. These contests involve one messy problem and no scripted solution technique. Teams of four high school students from all over the world have thirty-six hours to create a solution and submit it to COMAP via the Internet.

Unfortunately, since its inception, COMAP's high school mathematical modeling contest problems are almost always without ethical or political context.[12] The messiness of these problems pertains to the complex and difficult physical aspects of the "real" world but avoids the ethical messiness of student agency and political action. I don't mean to detract from this other kind of messiness, but rather to point to the infrequency of problems that are couched in political or ethical issues. Successful students—such as those who select to participate in the COMAP contests—are trained to read the "real" or "realistic" application task as one without ethical significance. For instance, the 2006 contest problems, although wonderfully challenging, were woefully disconnected from the complexity of the ethical world. Consider this problem about a "South Sea Island Resort":

> A South Sea island chain has decided to transform one of their islands into a resort. This roughly circular island, about 5 kilometers across, contains a mountain that covers the entire island. The mountain is approximately conical, is about 1000 meters high at the center, appears to be sandy, and has little vegetation on it. It has been proposed to lease some fire-fighting ships and wash the mountain into the harbor. It is desired to accomplish this as quickly as possible.
>
> Build a mathematical model for washing away the mountain. Use your model to respond to the questions below.
>
> • How should the stream of water be directed at the mountain, as a function of time?
>
> • How long will it take using a single fire-fighting ship?
>
> • Could the use of 2 (or 3, 4, etc.) fire-fighting ships decrease the time by more than a factor of 2 (or 3, 4, etc.)?
>
> • Make a recommendation to the resort committee about what to do.
>
> (COMAP, http://www.comap.com/highschool/contests/himcm/2006problems.html)

The problem is a "fake" problem and is easily recognized as unrealistic from an environmental perspective. Moreover, the driving principle behind the application is profit, as is often the case in school mathematics. If the mountain of sand were actually washed into the surrounding water, one could well imagine that the cost to marine life would be unimaginable. The problem refuses to address any of the environmental or political issues that might be relevant to the context. Rather, the problem hails the student as businessman or engineer and demands that the best solution be one acceptable to a resort committee. It is conceivable that a team response might take into consideration the environmental damage of flattening the island, since the task does not prescribe the method of solution and thereby allows for distinct answers, but the guiding questions would dissuade one from pursuing this aspect of the problem. The code for determining the preferred kind of solution is found in the statement: "It is desired to accomplish this as quickly as possible."

In order to make this problem more "critical," while still inviting mathematical application, one could ask students to consider the problem from multiple perspectives, each of which having different desired solutions. One could add a few statements regarding the environmental impact of the task, such as: "A ring of coral reef with 1 km diameter surrounds the island. Every cubic meter of sand deposited on the reef kills 1 square meter of coral." Students could then be asked to create two models, one favoring the resort committee interests and the other favoring an island environment committee. The problem would begin to access the ethical dimensions of applying mathematics in this context. In designing the task as a debate about the contested value of each alternative action, and in attending to the ways that particular solutions will serve particular segments of society, the students are enacting critical mathematics practices. Another approach might involve rewriting the code statement: "It is desired to accomplish this as quickly as possible while minimizing the damage to the local environment." This minor change in the statement forces the students to recognize the ethical conse- quences of their desired efficiency. By introducing the conditional into the statement, the best solution is still the one that maximizes the speed of completing the task, but within the constraints of ethical action.

This sort of modification can be achieved by teachers on a daily basis by revising typical textbook questions so that they address the student in terms other than profit and consumerism. For instance, pre-service teachers in my *Critical Literacy in Mathematics and Science Education* course are given a set of "real" life applications and asked to re-write these in ways that address "citizenship, environmentalism or social responsibility." For many pre-service teachers, their first inclination is to simply attach humanitarian goals to the problem, without altering any of the information. In the following example, most pre-service teachers simply added a sentence that declared Kim's intention to raise money for charity, instead of for profit.

> Kim is having a sale at his store and wants to advertise. He had decided to promote his sale through radio and TV. He wants to have his ad broadcast at most ten times and does not want to spend more than $2400. For a thirty-second spot, the TV station charges $300 dollars. The radio station charges $200 dollars for a thirty-second spot. The TV station has roughly 8,000 viewers, while the radio station has 6,000. Kim wants to know how many times he should run the advertisement in each of these me- dia outlets to maximize the number of times the advertisement is heard.

After discussing the mathematics involved in this problem, I then offered another more radical version, pointing out that the mathematical skills were the same in both.

Kim is in charge of a homeless shelter in an impoverished community. The shelter is a big space – like a gym, with movable walls – and it totals 2,400 square feet. She accepts applications for a 6 month period. She has space for two kinds of applicants:

(1) individual applicants and (2) family applicants. A family requires 300 square feet whereas an individual only requires 200 square feet. She can accept no more than 10 applicants in total, due to the time it takes to process the applications.

$X \geq 0$

$Y \geq 0$

$X + Y \leq 10$
$300X + 200Y \leq 2400$

These inequalities (also supplied in the first version) summarize the constraints on how many individuals and families she can accept. She knows that when she houses people they are likely to put money back into the local community and improve services generally. These are people who are often on the edge of poverty and they need a step up before they can get back into regular housing. Based on research she has done over the firs year of the Shelter being open, she has noticed that families tend to put back $8000 into the community where individuals put back $6000 (based on a six month period).

If Kim hopes to maximize the amount of money that is put back into the community, how many of each kind of applicant should she accept?

With continued exposure to the practice of re-writing problems, pre-service teachers became more adept at modifying textbook questions, and also became more critical of the "real" as it was presented in applications. At the end of the semester, the following problem was given and pre-service teachers were asked to modify it:

Sampson's dog, Cecil, is tied to a post by a chain 7 meters long. How much play area Does Cecil have? Express your answer to the nearest square meter.

(Serra, 2008, p. 451)

Although some of the new versions of the problem indicated that pre-service teachers were still struggling with the critical agenda of the course, and some indicated that they hadn't yet grasped the proper grammar required to convey the appropriate mathematics (For instance, one student wrote "The students are going to clean up the garbage on an area of the beach. If they start at the life guard chair and walk out 7 meters, how much area will they clean?"), most pre-service teachers produced alternatives that pushed the problem into areas of social justice and environmentalism. Below are two such examples:

1.  Mr. Smith from the Institute of Natural Disasters visited the epicenter (center)of an earthquake in California. The furthest reports of activity were from 16 miles away. Mr. Smith was told to report the area of damage to the Disaster Relief Board of California. With this information, they could estimate the amount of volunteers and money needed to help local families rebuild houses; provide food and shelter and other necessities. What is the area in square miles for the effects of the earthquake? Express your answer to the nearest square mile.

2.  Crude oil leaking from the hull of an oil tanker is spreading in a circular plume  on the surface of the water. Within 5 minutes of the hull being punctuated, the plume has reached a buoy located 7 meters from the ship. How large is the area of contamination after just 5 minutes of leakage? After 10 minutes, the plume is 14 meters from the ship. How large is the area of contamination now? After 15 minutes, the plume is 21 meters from the ship. If you extrapolate using this information, how large an area will be contaminated with crude oil after 30 minutes? What does this ay about hwo quickly clean-up needs to get underway in order to minimize damage to the environment?

Despite this new critical focus, applications of this sort require further critique because they continue to honor the mathematics as politically neutral (Valero, 2004, p. 14). Moreover, the modified versions tend to incorporate more "everyday" language and will doubtless prove even more challenging for students who are ill-equipped for the code switching required in completing "real life applications within school mathematics. In the next section, I discuss the ramifications of honoring mathematics as politically neutral, and I look more carefully at problems inherent to the discourse of mathematics.

## Ethical Filtration

According to Ernest (2001), "Critical mathematics education aims to empower learners as individuals and citizens in society, by developing mathematical power both to overcome barriers to higher education and employment and thus increasing economic self-determination, and by fostering critical awareness and democratic citizenship via mathematics" (p. 288). Note that the mathematics itself is seen as a neutral tool that might be used for good or evil. Ernest's vision assumes that there is nothing inherent to the mathematics itself (that being the various semiotic practices that comprise the *doing* of mathematics) that might compromise such democratic applications. He lists possible applications that are grounded in democratic and social justice ideals: surveys and analysis of statistics on the homeless, property values, patterns in petrol use, corporate profits, and gender and racial bias. These excellent ideas for curricula, however, are often reduced, through the application of a mathematical model, to extremely inadequate and often unethical representations of the "real" experiences of those under study.

*Rethinking Mathematics* (Gutstein & Peterson, 2005) is a collection of practical examples and reflective essays that attempts to offer teachers concrete instances of social justice mathematics curricula, including activities that explore the cost of war and poverty and the connections between race, privilege, and inequity. Again, these activities are compelling and powerful classroom applications, and I have used them in my own classrooms. But the act of simplifying the contextual factors to allow for a mathematical application often creates a problem that is less "realistic" and dangerously naïve. Recognizing the risks in application—even when guided by inclusive democratic goals—is crucial if we are to develop a more far-reaching critical mathematics.

Application is a complex concept that involves content mastery and emphasis on the five NCTM[3] process standards (problem solving, reasoning and proof, communication, connections, and representation). Applying mathematics to the "real" world requires recognizing both the messiness of life contexts and the limitations of the mathematical tools to adequately represent or model such messiness. Reflecting on whether a given application is suitable or not is a crucial aspect of all application. Unfortunately, mathematics "in action" (Skovsmose, in press) often entails an "ethical filtration" whereby the agent (be it a student, an engineer, or someone else) reduces the complex ethical and political situation to a set of abstract parameters that are then combined into a simplifying model primarily used for prediction. According to Skovsmose, ethical filtration is built into the practice of mathematics in action, that is to say, the act of stripping away the contingent and the subjective are inherent to mathematical problem solving. For instance, Skovsmose recounts how a group of students were given the assignment "Family support in a micro society," in which they were shown portraits of 24 families and asked to formulate ethical principles for distributing child benefits. They were then asked to determine a set of parameters and an algorithm for child benefit distribution.

> In the process of turning the verbally-formulated principles for distribution into functional algorithms, the students experienced how the original principles needed to become simplified. At times the principles were almost ignored when mathematics was brought into operation to do the distribution. The students experienced the general phenomenon that when mathematics is brought into action, a new discourse takes over. The ethical principle, which might have guided the initial considerations, becomes substituted by the technical administration of the system. This is an ethical filtration, and it is a common consequence of bringing mathematics into action. (Skovsmose, in press)

It's crucial to consider this ethical filtration process as something that derails attempts at critical mathematics. Moreover, one can see that mathematics education *actually* teaches students to enact ethical erasure so as to successfully generate solutions that seem unambiguous. Aside from the preponderance of applications in textbooks that are blatantly unreflective ("Your task is to find the best location to build the new gas station so as to maximize your profit."), one can see in the Skovsmose example, that even those tasks with a political or ethical principle underpinning their design involve a recontextualizing practice of abstraction that sacrifices the ethical in order to achieve *one* solution. It is hard to imagine how moral outrage might be sustained in a mathematics classroom where ethical filtration is ultimately operative.

Since ethical issues are often the source of our sense of agency and action, one can draw connections between the process of ethical filtration in mathematics education and the process of disengagement in school mathematics. Textbooks fail to offer students controversial problems to which they might apply mathematical skills, and teachers often don't have the alternative resources to introduce current issues into the curriculum. Students perceive mathematics as disconnected from the world of language and politics precisely because these textbooks offer such a limited sense of contextual relevance (Dowling, 1998). This disconnection serves the status quo because it creates a public perception that mathematics belongs to an abstract realm of dispassionate ability. Recent research on student identity in mathematics suggests that successful high school mathematics students perceive their success in terms of conformance, compliance, and lack of agency (Boaler & Greeno, 2000; Povey et al., 2004; Walshaw, 2004). Many students perceive school mathematics as a site of complete erasure where identity and agency are sacrificed. This perception is not simply a reflection of frustrated students who have given up on mathematics; Boaler and Greeno (2000) interviewed successful students in high school mathematics and found that a significant majority believed that success in mathematics was simply about following rules and denying personal agency. In the eyes of many educators, this research seems to suggest that "traditional math is bad for society" (Gutstein & Peterson, 2005, p. 14). This may sound extreme to some readers, but the target is not the math itself, but the way it is enacted in classrooms through discursive practices and power relations.

## Knowledge Transfer

Applying mathematics to "real life" situations has traditionally been theorized as a form of transferring knowledge from one context to another (Abreu, 2002, p. 329). The concept of knowledge transfer comes from cognitive theories of learning that posit developmental models of skill acquisition (p. 330). According to this approach, application and problem solving are theorized as higher-level skills that involve transferring more basic skills—skills that have successfully been unsituated and internalized—to new and unfamiliar situations.

Challenges to the concept of knowledge transfer have come from ethnographers who have studied the context-dependent nature of cognition (Greenfield & Lave, 1982), arguing that cognition and skill acquisition cannot be abstracted from the sociocultural context, that doing mathematics is a deeply embodied cultural practice, and that applications of knowledge are complex social enactments of identity. Applications of school mathematics are not at all straightforward, nor, it seems, are they at all frequent in the lived experiences of students. In their famous study of "street mathematics" and tailoring, Greenfield and Lave concluded: "It appears that neither schooling nor tailoring skills generalize very far beyond the circumstances in which they are ordinarily applied" (p. 199).

Cobb and Yackel (1996) theorized student learning in classrooms according to layers of collective discursive norms: social norms, sociomathematical norms, and classroom mathematical practices. They defined sociomathematical norms as "normative understandings of what counts as mathematically different, mathematically sophisticated, mathematically efficient, and mathematically elegant" (p. 461). Other sociocultural researchers have built on these situated theories of learning and have developed new ways of making sense of mathematics education as a cultural practice (Lerman & Zevenbergen, 2004). These researchers read the mathematics classroom through a discursive lens, studying the ways that identities are constituted in the classroom through discursive practices and enactments of power relations.

Reading "application" as a cultural practice—instead of a transfer of knowledge—allows researchers to ask new questions about the ethics of application. In application problems, there is always a presumed distinction between the new and the familiar content, and one can hear different modalities (of affect, certainty, and authority) as teachers and students speak through their process of problem solving in the unfamiliar situation. Attention to the language of uncertainty in problem solving, such as hedging or equivocation (such words "maybe," "probably," "almost," "wonder," "sort of"), is an important "think aloud" teaching method that models the process of conjecture and specula- tion. Conjecturing and speculating require a language of uncertainty – a form of communication that is deliberative, in process, tangential, inconclusive. "Hedges," for example, are frequently used (Rowland, 2008).

In contrast, many associate the domain of mathematics with precision, exactness, and definitive answers. There is no humility in the language of certainty, no moment to introduce the "what if not" conjectures that help students reflect on the consequences of their actions. I believe that "think aloud" methods of modeling humility can help students embrace/celebrate a language of uncertainty as they enter into an application problem. Sustaining that humility as one considers possible solution strategies can be achieved through continual attention to the language of epistemic authority. Presenting application problems in terms of hesitation, hedging, and ambiguity, and asking students to model their responses on this same language, will teach students to contexualize their solutions in terms of their own authority and social position. Reflecting on the language of uncertainty allows us to reflect on the ethical dimension of our problem solving, to reflect on the implication of our proposed solutions. Although think aloud strategies point to the process of deliberation and thereby locate or situate the problem solver in a particular context – with a corresponding particular agenda – such discursive practices do not represent the tightly packed noun phrases and concise phrasing found in mathematic textbooks. The task of bridging these two radically different registers remains a daunting challenge for both educators and researchers.

## Conclusion: Mathematics as Craft

The word "application" comes from Latin where it means "a joining to, an attaching of oneself to" and similarly the word "apply" means "to attach to, to devote oneself to" to "lay, fold or twist" or "to plait, to braid, to intertwine" (http://www.etymonline.com/index.php). These definitions suggest that application is a process of merging oneself with that which is outside of oneself. This subjection of oneself to the task at hand, this folding of self into other, is what makes application a form of ethical action. "Joining" is an ethical action that brings the world together with shared concerns. Accordingly, applications are always ethical and material—we are implicated in our applica- tions in ethical and material ways. We enter the situation when we apply our knowledge to it, we interfere when trying to understand the other, we trace our own interests onto the contexts to which we apply our tools.

de Abreu (2002) suggests that we abandon the language of knowledge transfer and speak of a "tool kit"—a collection of community skills—that would be in circulation to a lesser or greater extent in mathematics classrooms. The tool kit would be comprised of various numeracy strategies, methods of spatial reasoning, notation and vocabulary proficiency, and, of course, instruments to be used when decoding applications and "realistic" problems. The tool kit metaphor promotes a "craft" vision of doing mathematics education, suggesting that instruction be seen as apprenticeship in communities of practice and as leading to mastery of these tools ("to plait, to braid, to intertwine") and ultimately to full membership in the community. de Abreu (2002) quotes Resnick, Pontecorvo, and Saljo (1997) in arguing that the concept of tool is appropriate in the mathematics context:

> The concept of tool is expanded ... beyond the conventional view of a tool as a physical artifact. Not only physical artifacts but also concepts, structures of reasoning, and the forms of discourse that constrain and enable interactions within communities qualify as tools. Vygotsky ... originally distinguished tools from signs, or language. However, subsequent influential developers of theories of socially situated cognition ... have suggested that many kinds of thinking, as well as physical actions, are carried out by means of tools. (p. 3)

As a metaphor, the tool kit effectively positions mathematical skills in the public domain, and demands that we envision learning as a material and cultural process of enacting particular kinds of performances. It shifts our attention away from the issue of inner ability, and focuses on identity and culture. It is worth noting that the tool kit doesn't include any instruments for ethical reflection on the use of the tools. This is left to the individual. The ethics of craft are often about doing "good work" with passion and attention to detail. But I would like to suggest that in some instances, when craft is sufficiently central to the power structure of culture (for instance, in the case of medicine or, for that matter, education) there must be a code of ethics about how (and whether) one should apply the tools. In medicine, various ethical oaths have historically guided the application of powerful medical knowledge and tools. The medical oath is mean to remind doctors (and those that submit themselves to their care) that medical power/knowledge must be in the service of those in need to assistance. We characterize medicine as a "caring profession," but isn't the issue of care implicated in all uses of power? Why wouldn't such an oath accompany the application of any powerful tool in the world?

The NCTM introduced their "equity principle" as an ethical oath for teachers, to remind them that their role was to ensure that all students should have the opportunity to learn "powerful mathematics." In this chapter I have argued that we need another ethical principle to accompany the mastery and application of powerful mathematics. Why not consider the tool kit of powerful mathematics to be akin to the doctor's medical leather bag? The application oath might simply demand that the mathematical agent (be it a student, a teacher, or someone else) must reflect on the ethical consequences of her/his mathematical actions in the "real" world and seek to serve others in need of assistance through the use of these powerful tools.

# Notes

This chapter was published in the *International Electronic Journal of Mathematics Education,* Volume 3, Number 2, July 2008.

1. There are the usual questions related to elections and fair representation, but aside from these, COMAP seems committed to keeping the high school problems apolitical. The COMAP "math serve" contest was introduced as a means of bridging mathematics applications and community service, but this contest was closed due to lack of interest.
2. National Council of Teachers of Mathematics

# References

Adler, J. (2001). *Teaching mathematics in multilingual classrooms.* Dordrecht, The Netherlands: Kluwer.

Boaler, J., & Greeno, G. (2000). Identity, agency, and knowing in mathematical worlds. In J. Boaler (Ed.). *Multiple perspectives on mathematics teaching and learning.* London, UK: Alex Publishing. 171-199.

Cobb, P., & Yackel, E. (1996). Sociomathematical norms, argumentation, and autonomy in mathematics. *Journal for Research in Mathematics Education,* 27(4): 458-477.

COMAP, http://www.comap.com/highschool/contests/himcm/2006problems.html. Accessed on June 12, 2007.

Confrey, J., & Kazak, S. (2006). A thirty year reflection on constructivism in mathematics education. In A. Gutierrez & P. Boero (Eds.). *Handbook of research on the psychology of mathematics education: Past, present and future.* Rotterdam, ND: Sense Publishing. 367-402.

Cooper, B. (1998a). Assessing National Curriculum Mathematics in England: Exploring children's interpretation of Key Stage 2 tests in clinical interviews. *Educational Studies in Mathematics* 35(1): 19-49.

Cooper, B. (1998b). Using Bernstein and Bourdieu to understand children's difficulties with "realistic" mathematics testing: An exploratory study. *International Journal of Qualitative Studies in Education* 11(4): 511-532.

Cooper, B. (2001). Social class and "real life" mathematics assessments. In P. Gates (Ed.). *Issues in mathematics teaching.* New York: Routledge/Falmer. 245-258.

Cooper, B., & Dunne, M. (2004). Constructing the "legitimate" goal of a "realistic" maths item: A comparison of 10-11 and 13-14 year olds. In B. Allen & S. Johnston-Wilder (Eds.). *Mathematics Education: Exploring the culture of learning.* New York: Routledge/Falmer. 69-90.

Davis, P. (2008).*Applied* mathematics as social contract. *Philosophy of Mathematics Education Jounral* 22 (November). http://www.people.ex.ac.uk/PErnest/pome22/index.htm

de Abreu, G. (2002). Mathematics learning in out of school contexts: A cultural psychology perspective. In L.D. English (Ed.). *Handbook of International Research in Mathematics Education.* Mahwah, NJ: Lawrence Erlbaum Associates. 323-354.

de Freitas, E. (2004). Plotting intersections along the political axis: The interior voice of dissenting mathematics teachers. *Educational Studies in Mathematics* 55: 259-274.

de Freitas, E. (2008a). Troubling teacher identity: Preparing mathematics teachers to teach for diversity. *Teaching Education* 19(1).

De Freitas, E. (2008b). Mathematics and its other: Dislocating the feminine. *Gender and Education* 20 (3). 281-290.

Dossey, J.A., McCrone, S., Giordano, F.R., & Weir, M.D. (2002). *Mathematics methods and modeling for today's mathematics classrooms: A contemporary approach to teaching grades 7-12.* Pacific Grove, CA: Brooks/Cole.

Dowling, P. (1998). *The Sociology of Mathematics Education: Mathematical myths/ Pedagogic Texts.* London, UK: Falmer Press.

Ernest, P. (2001). Critical Mathematics Education. In P. Gates (Ed.). *Issues in mathematics teaching.* New York: Routledge/Falmer.

Ernest, P. (2004). Postmodernity and social research in mathematics education. In P. Valero & R. Zevenbergen (Eds.). *Researching the socio-political dimensions of mathematics education: Issues of power in theory and methodology.* New York: Kluwer Academic Publishers. 65-84.

Freire, P. (1970/1998). *Pedagogy of the oppressed.* M.B. Ramos (Trans.). New York: Continuum.

Gates, P. (2006). The place of equity and social justice in the history of PME. In A. Gutierrez & P. Boero (Eds.). *Handbook of research on the psychology of mathematics education: Past, present and future.* Rotterdam, ND: Sense Publishing. 367-402.

Greenfield, P., & Lave, J. (1982). Cognitive aspects of informal education. In D.A. Wagner & H.W. Stevenson (Eds.). *Cultural Perspectives in Childhood Development.* San Francisco: Freeman. 181-207.

Gutstein, E. (2006). *Reading and writing the world with mathematics: Toward a pedagogy for social justice.* New York: Routledge.

Gutstein, E. (2008). Building political relationships with students: An aspect of social justice pedagogy. In E. de Freitas & K. Nolan (Eds.). *Opening the research text: Insights and in(ter)ventions into mathematics education.* New York: Springer Verlag.

Gutstein, E., & Peterson, B. (2005). *Rethinking mathematics: Teaching social justice by the numbers.* Milwaukee, WI: Rethinking Schools.

Hersh, R. (2008). Ethics for mathematics. *Philosophy of Mathematics Education Journal* 22 (November). http://www.people.ex.ac.uk/PErnest/pome22/index.htm

Iyer, A., Leach, C.W., & Pedersen, A. (2004). Racial wrongs and restitutions: The role of guilt and other group-based emotions. In M. Fine, L. Weis, L.P. Pruitt, & A. Burns (Eds.). *Off white: Readings on power, privilege, and resistance, second edition.* New York: Routledge. 345-361.

Leach, C.W., Snider, N., & Iyer, A. (2002). Poisoning the consciences of the fortunate: The experience of relative advantage and the support for social equality. In I. Walker & H.J. Smith (Eds.). *Relative deprivation: Specification, development and integration.* New York: Cambridge University Press. 136-163.

Lerman, P., & Zevenbergen, R. (2004). The socio-political context of the mathematics classroom: Using Bernstein's theoretical framework to understand classroom communications. In P. Valero & R. Zevenbergen (Eds.). *Researching the socio-political dimensions of mathematics education: Issues of power in theory and methodology.* New York: Kluwer Academic Publishers. 27-42.

Lorde, A. (1984). *Sister outsider.* Freedom, CA: Crossing Press.

Morgan, C. (2006). What does social semiotics have to offer mathematics education research? *Educational Studies in Mathematics* 61: 219-245.

Mukhopadhyay, S. & Greer, B. (2001). Modeling with purpose: Mathematics as a critical tool. In B. Atweh, H. Forgasz, & B. Nebres (Eds.). *Socio-cultural research on mathematics education: An international perspective.* Mahwah: Lawrence Erlbaum.

Povey, H., Burton, L., Angier, C., & Boylan, M. (2004). Learners as authors in the mathematics classroom. In B. Allen & S. Johnston-Wilder (Eds.). *Mathematics education: Exploring the culture of learning.* New York: Routledge-Falmer. 43–56.

Resnick, L.B., Pontecorvo, C., & Saljo, R. (1997). Discourse, tools and reasoning. In L.B. Resnick, C. Pontecorvo, & R. Saljo (Eds.). *Discourse, tools and reasoning: Essays on situated cognition.* New York: Sringer and Nato Scientific Affairs Division. 1–20.

Rodriguez, A.J., & Kitchen, R.S. (Eds.) (2005). *Preparing mathematics and science teachers for diverse classrooms: Promising strategies for transformative pedagogy.* Mahwah, NJ: Lawrence Erlbaum Associates Publishers.

Rowland, T. (2008). Key note lecture. International Conference on Equity and Discourse: Creating equitable discourse in the mathematics classroom. May 16, 2008, Rochester, NY.

SEAC (Schools Examinations and Assessment Council). (1993). Pilot Standard Tests: Key Stage 2, London: SEAC/University of London.

Serra, M. (2008). *Discovering geometry: An investigative approach.* Emeryville, CA: Key Curriculum Press.

Skovsmose, O. (2005). *Travelling through education: Uncertainty, mathematics, responsibility.* Rotterdam: Sense Publishers.

Skovsmose, O. (2008). Mathematics Education in a knowledge market: Developing functional and critical competencies. In E. de Freitas & K. Nolan (Eds.). *Opening the research text: Insights and in(ter)ventions into mathematics education.* New York: Springer Verlag.

Skovsmose, O., & Borba, M. (2004). Research methodology and critical mathematics education. In P. Valero & R. Zevenbergen (Eds.). *Researching the socio-political dimensions of mathematics education: Issues of power in theory and methodology.* New York: Kluwer Academic Publishers.

Tate, W.F. (2005). Race, retrenchment, and the reform of school mathematics. In E. Gutstein & B. Peterson (Eds.). *Rethinking mathematics: Teaching social justice by the numbers.* Milwaukee, WI: Rethinking Schools. 31–40.

Valero, P. (2004). Socio-political perspectives on mathematics education. In P. Valero & R. Zevenbergen (Eds.). *Researching the socio-political dimensions of mathematics education: Issues of power in theory and methodology.* Norwell, MA: Kluwer Academic Publishers Group.

Valero, P., & Zevenbergen, R. (Eds.). (2004). *Researching the socio-political dimensions of mathematics education: Issues of power in theory and methodology.* New York: Kluwer Academic Publishers.

Walshaw, M. (2004). A powerful theory of active engagement. *For the Learning of Mathematics.* 4–10.

Walshaw, M. (Ed.) (2005). *Mathematics education within the postmodern.* Charlotte, NC: Information Age Publishing.

Zevenbergen, R. (2003). Teachers' beliefs about teaching mathematics to students from socially disadvantaged backgrounds: Implications for social justice. In L. Burton (Ed.). *Which way social justice and mathematics education?* London: Praeger Publishers.

# Chapter 4

# Disempowering the Authority of Science: Preparing Students for a Public Voice

*Tracy Hogan and John Craven*

*Eternal Vigilance is the Price of Liberty.*

*Wendell Phillips, abolitionist and advocate to the oppressed, 1852*

It may be argued that there are largely two conflicting epistemological paradigms shaping the world today: religion and science. Both currently hold powerful sway over the lives and livelihood of millions around the globe. Both are driving cultural forces that impact educational, economic, health and welfare, and political policies worldwide. While influences of religion on society and culture date back to some of the earliest records of humankind, it may be persuasively argued that science has profoundly and most dramatically changed the cultural landscape over the last few centuries. Specifically, the rhetoric and applications of knowledge (i.e., technology) produced by scientific communities now exert powerful global change forces that shape the development of norms, values, and lifestyles across broad communities. Thus, it follows that science and technology are intricately linked to the fabric that defines individuals and their development as self in society. For these reasons, science, as much as religion, can be characterized as source of power and authority in society.

Science can be dually conceived as process and product. That is, the scientific enterprise is both a way of knowing (producing knowledge about the observable world) and the collective body of that knowledge. The American Association for the Advancement of Science (1993) defines science as "an intellectual and social endeavor-the application of human intelligence to figuring out how the world works" (p. 3). Practitioners, historians, and philosophers of science argue that the enterprise of science offers society a powerful and robust way of knowing and understanding the phenomenological world. The pundits of science hold the endeavor as a liberating alternative to the dogmatic frameworks found in religion.

However, there are oppositional viewpoints suggesting that science seems to be headed down a path of exclusivity, elitism, and unquestionability (beyond reproach). This irreproachability is noted by Dingle (1972), who wrote:

> It is ironical that, in the very field in which Science has claimed superiority to Theology, for example—in the abandoning of dogma and the granting of absolute freedom to criticism—the positions are now reversed. Science will not tolerate criticism of special relativity, while Theology talks freely about the death of God, religionless Christianity, and so on. (p. 5)

Some take Dingle's thesis on the state of science as an extremist's position. Indeed, one must also recognize the likelihood that within the scientific community there are purists who hold that the epistemological enterprise of science is completely separate from its politicalization. However, it should be argued that the scientific enterprise, as a cultural activity, and its practitioners (scientists) are not immune to the forces that shape all other aspects of human activity (See Horgan, 1996). In fact, in recent years there have been very contentious debates on the exclusivity and marginalization occurring in science (See Harding, 1991; 1998).

At a time when concerns about the dogmatism of science seem to be growing, there also appears to be a mounting number of instances in the American society in which the perceived "authority" and the hegemonic forces associated with positivism (a philosophical perspective of science that ignores subjective experience and idealizes objectivity) are being exploited in an effort to control the beliefs and actions of others; manipulate values held by individuals and society; censure knowledge and information; control which questions can and should be asked; and dictate modes of inquiry. For example, over the past years media outlets have printed several expositories detailing the degree to which the integrity of scientific reports to the public have been compromised to suit the political and economic interests of those in the White House (Kennedy, 2004). Those censured or edited reports to the public not only influenced policy and funding decisions, they also restricted access to information and knowledge needed by those making very important personal, social, and lifestyle decisions. More worrisome are the influences these carefully constructed, "scientific-based" messages have on people's behavior and thoughts (for more on such threats read Schwartz, 2007). While we recognize that there are those in the field who will argue that editorializing and censuring is a political process and not a scientific one, we take the position that a "cherry-picking" of facts, figures (statistics), and scientific interpretations can and does occur in this process. This is known as "bias" in science. As Collingridge and Reeve (1986) report,

> Bias receives a psychological characterization, being a distortion produced by some vested interest in drawing conclusions from the available data, or in deciding just what data is available. Bias may be avoided by ensuring that the scientific experts advising policymakers have no interests in the outcome of the policy, one way or another. (p. 10)

The threat of bias is exacerbated when politics and science are economically linked. The probability that scientists with vested interests in continued funding will demonstrate some form of bias in the selection and interpretation of data is surely to increase when, for example, a government with a particular political agenda funds those research programs. Moreover, when policymakers (for their own purposes) take advantage of disagreements among scientific experts by deciding which interpretations will be disseminated to the public, they usurp the public's right to debate and diversity. In other words, they restrict the pool of people deciding what is and is not scientific. It is important to note that the term "scientific" is often a euphemism for "truth" when used by policymakers to convince public opinion.

By recognizing the significant influence of science and technology on the development of self and society (i.e., its "power") *and* by understanding the potentiality of scientific dogmatism, it becomes incumbent upon an engaged citizenry to take a critical literacy stance to understand, question, and challenge those aspects of the scientific enterprise (rhetoric and praxis) that are working against inclusivity and open democracy. In this chapter, we envision critical literacy as a liberating habit of mind to question authority in society. Our conception, grounded in both Critical Theory and Critical Discourse Analysis (See Rogers, Malancharuvil-Berkes, Mosley, Hyui, & Joseph, 2005), compels us to confront the ways in which the scientific discourse is used both for and against social justice.

Toward this end we deem it vital to explore the construct of science as authority in society and to examine some practices of the scientific community that perpetuate the myth of objectivism and rationality. It is imperative to expose science as an imperfect, fallible human enterprise so as to empower individuals to question the image of science they believe (and/or are led to believe) exists. We also hope to help develop a sensitivity on the part of the reader to the ways in which *appeals to the authority of science* (see Walton, 1997) are used to shape the beliefs, opinions, way of life, and status of people around the world.

The aim of this chapter, therefore, is twofold. First, we want to expose the roots of power that give science authority. And second, we want to confront the stereotypical image of science as a culturally neutral, unbiased, objective, rational enterprise. In its stead, we intend to promote an understanding of science as a human endeavor—that is, a social enterprise imbued with human desires, motivations, and struggles. In doing so, we hope to enhance the reader's capacity to take a critical literacy stance toward the forces of science impacting global communities. This need becomes all the more necessary at a time when the communities face increasingly complex issues deeply rooted in science and technology.

## Science as Authority

If, as thus far claimed, science serves as an "authority" in culture, it is reasonable to question the source of that authority. Exactly what is it that empowers science? The response to this question is several-fold. First, science has been remarkably successful in producing knowledge about the way the phenomenological world (that is, the physical/observable world) operates; and in today's world, knowledge is equated to power. Second, people often perceive sources of knowledge in terms of authority. Often these perceptions are associated with forms of compliant behavioralism. And third, there is a tendency of the human mind to hold beliefs about knowledge (i.e., epistemological orientations) and naïve conceptions of science that propagate science as authority.

### Science and Knowledge

With regard to the first point, scientists have indeed made vast contributions to the knowledge base shedding important light on the way the world works. The knowledge produced by scientists and the scientific enterprise is powerful because it provides robust causal explanations for common phenomena such as changes in seasons on earth, the rise and fall of tides, the movement of objects in space and on earth, and innumerable geological processes. Perhaps more importantly, scientific knowledge allows one to make and test predictions about future events (climatological forecasts are a good example here). Predictability in an all too often hostile world fulfills a basic human need for comfort and hope. At the same time, the ability of scientists to predict phenomena such as solar eclipses, volcanic eruptions, hail storms, and floods often borders on the mysterious (if not miraculous) for those uninitiated in the sciences. Similarly, the knowledge produced by the methods of science has helped pave the way for the development of pharmaceuticals and medicinal practices that cure the ill and "restore life" to thousands every day (again, a mysterious, if not mystical, power). The "mysticism" of science is all the more apparent in the field of quantum mechanics and string theory wherein unobservable entities may exist in twenty or more dimensions (See Greene, 2005; Smolin, 2007).

Whereas a few hundred years ago safe passage across an ocean was unfathomable, today NASA scientists send spacecrafts to pinpoint destinations deep in outerspace to survey planets and take "pictures" of the universe moments after its birth from the Big Bang. The source of these abilities—scientific knowledge—makes those possessing that knowledge superior to those without it. Naturally, it is through a process of negotiation and consensus within the scientific community that determines what knowledge is or is not scientific (See Ziman, 1968). Scientific knowledge, therefore, is less a matter of right versus wrong, and more a matter of majority rule—who is out and who is in.

Thus, the community of people trained in the sciences, creating the knowledge, and thereby "owning" that knowledge becomes, by default, a figure of authority in society. Conversely, it is understandable why people turn to science for answers to questions regarding such things as safety, security, and health. From this perspective, it is those without the knowledge (without the power) who give science its authority. And, although ratings of science-based TV and other media reveal a deep public interest in science, it has been generally shown that the public does not understand how science works.

## Public Perceptions of Science

Consider, for example, the survey of public perceptions of science, which is one important task of the National Science Board (NSB). The NSB is a congressionally funded agency charged with overseeing and establishing the policies of the National Science Foundation. The president of the United

States and Congress use the National Science Board as the advisory body for matters relating to science and engineering research and education (National Science Board, 2007). Recently, the NSB (2006) found that most Americans do not understand the process of science, the nature of scientific inquiry, and the enterprise of science. This lack of understanding, in turn, creates an environment consisting of a majority of American citizens who are unable to differentiate between science and pseudoscience. In fact, a Gallup poll (Moore, 2005) revealed that over three quarters of those surveyed believed in at least one paranormal event such as ESP (extra sensory perception), haunted houses, and/or astrology as a scientifically based phenomenon.

There are many other indicators that reveal that the public either does not understand the enterprise or, perhaps worse, holds deeply flawed views. One such example includes a benchmark study revealing the scientific conceptions children held (Chambers, 1983). Specifically, over 4800 children were asked to "draw a scientist" (Draw a Scientist Test: DAST). The drawings were analyzed as representations of the characteristics of scientists as perceived by the children. These characteristics included clothing (i.e., lab coat), facial hair growth (i.e., beard, mustache, sideburns), glasses, representations of knowledge (books), research (lab equipment), technology, and descriptors of science including formulas and/or the periodic table. By the second grade, Chambers found that the stereotypical scientist (defined by at least three or more characteristics present in the picture) had emerged. Furthermore, while almost half of the participants were females, fewer then 1 percent of the drawings portrayed this gender.

Since the initial DAST study, researchers have examined views of scientists across age groups, gender, and cultures (Fung, 2002; Newton & Newton, 1992; Thomas, Henley, & Snell, 2006; Fort & Varney, 1989) and found results similar to Chambers's (1983). For example, Thomas et al. (2006) set out to determine if stereotypical views of a scientist (i.e., white male) continued into early adulthood. The DAST (Chambers, 1983) was administered to a group of undergraduates. Their findings were consistent with previous research, in that over 83 percent of the total drawings were that of male scientists, over half drawn as chemists, and a mean number of approximately three of the stereotypical characteristics were included in the drawings.

Collectively, the draw-a-scientist studies reveal a common conception of a scientist as a white male wearing a white lab coat. Not surprisingly, there have been numerous studies on the image of the white lab coat itself as a symbol of authority (See Blumhagen, 1979; Ikusaka, Kamegi, Sunaga, Narita, Kobayashi,

Yonenami, & Watanabe, 1999; Rehman, Nietert, Cope, & Kilpatrick, 2005). In one recent study, Brase and Richmond (2004) found that doctors wearing white laboratory coats were perceived as more authoritative than those in simple formal clothing. One possible interpretation of these perceptions is that patients are induced by either some type of fear or (and) respect.

## Science and Cognition

A fear of science and the incomprehensibility of the scientific way of thinking, one that is quite unnatural according to Wolpart (2000), most likely is another contributing factor in the empowerment of science as authority. It has been found that fear of authority begins quite early in life. Researchers examining the development of reasoning abilities across the lifespan have found that while children reason differently through moral and ethical dilemmas, young children look to figures of authority to guide their decisions (see Kohlberg, 1976; Gilligan, 1982). In many instances, children respond to a dilemma such as whether or not it would be appropriate to steal a medicinal drug for a loved one when one cannot afford to buy the drug outright in terms of authority (i.e., police) and consequences (i.e., jail). As individuals age, one might suppose that adults would reason through both ethical and moral dilemmas through a set of more complex principles and ideals. However, there is abundant research showing that adults continue to seek an authority's guidance in their decision-making processes (Perry, 1970; Kitchener & Fischer, 1990; Kitchener, Lynch, Fischer, & Wood, 1993; King & Kitchener, 1994; Schommer, 1990).

As Plato wrote in "The Allegory of the Cave" and Freire wrote in *Pedagogy of the Oppressed*, a "fear of freedom" is all too often a condition of humankind. It follows that this fear "may equally lead them to desire the role of oppressor or bind them to the role of oppressed" (Freire, 1997, p. 28). It may also follow, then, that a fear of science, to some extent, imparts authority to science. And it is this fear that may all too often prevent many people from questioning the rhetoric of that authority. Apparently, as Sir Francis Bacon wrote, it is true that knowledge is power. But, if knowledge is not power, they are certainly married (see Collingridge and Reeve, 1986).

This reliance on "knowledge" authorities has roots in mainstream cognitive theories specifically studied through the lenses of both developmental and epistemological predispositions of the human mind. According to Goldman (1993), epistemology is defined, in part, as a person's beliefs concerning the origin and nature of knowledge. For example, one person might believe that knowledge comes from authority and what authority says is absolute. On the other hand, a different person might view knowledge as an accumulation of information from different sources and individuals and use the "best" evidence to determine what is right and/or wrong.

Research into the epistemological orientation of individuals dates back some fifty years ago when Piaget (1950) used the term *genetic epistemology* (Hofer & Pintrich, 1997) to define his model of intellectual development. At that time, developmental psychologists began to examine relationships between the intersection of philosophy and psychology. William G. Perry, Jr. (1970) began exploring students' epistemological development throughout their college experience. He developed an instrument called the *Checklist of Educational Values* (CLEV) that was based on authoritarian personality research (Adorno, Frenkel-Brunswik, Levinson, & Sanford, 1950) and Stern's Instrument of Beliefs (Stern, 1953). Perry was interested in how students respond to the academic and social environments found within their university; he assumed their responses would be different depending on their personalities. Through the administration of the CLEV instrument and follow-up interviews, Perry argued that college students view their world not so much through their personality as through a developmental process based on how they view the world.

Perry's scheme consists of nine positions moving from a dualism approach where authority commands absolute truth to the ninth position of developing commitments in a relativistic environment (viewing knowledge within context, through multiple views and with uncertainty). While research findings support this scheme, there is scant evidence suggesting that the latter levels of thinking are found among people to any significant degree. In other words, college-level students often fail to integrate knowledge delivered by others and through one's own reflective practice (i.e., accepting the norm without questioning other possibilities).

Connections can be made between Perry's work and research on the relationship between the perceptions of science held by individuals and how those perceptions influence belief systems, reasoning abilities, and decision-making processes related to endeavors associated with science. Unfortunately, those connections have been used for self-serving, if not nefarious, reasons. For example, the knowledge that both male and female children as well as adolescents perceive scientists as a white male dressed in a lab coat (authority) has been exploited by the media industry. Specifically, the white lab coat is used as a subliminal representation of authority. Advertisers targeting those in need of medical care, including drugs, devices, and procedures, take advantage of this reasoning system (human belief) by consistently featuring middle-aged males dressed in white lab coats offering knowledge. This ploy is carefully crafted in that studies have suggested that adults look to those dressed in white lab coats as symbols of authority in science and medicine. What becomes most disturbing is that people may no longer question credentials, nor the diagnoses or the medical recommendations, due, in part, to the attire of an individual.

## Debunking the Authority of Science

To retract an unwarranted grant of authority to science and reclaim the public's right to a critical voice in matters of policymaking, Collingridge and Reeve (1986) argue that it is necessary to debunk the myths of science and outline the realities of science. According to their treatise, the myths of science include the following: (1) that science yields truth, (2) that experts can be expected to agree, and (3) that science is one (i.e., that there is unity across all disciplines within science). These myths, they argue, contribute to a general belief that the "truths" of science (i.e., scientific knowledge) are completely objective and impervious to the cultural influences. Furthermore, the myths perpetuate a confidence that purely reasoned policy can be based on purely reasoned science.

The reality of science, according to Collingridge and Reeve (1986), is that (1) science yields guesses rather than truths, (2) disagreement among experts is both natural and necessary, and (3) there are many forms of science. Given such realities, policy should not be based on science.

If, as laid out above, knowledge is power and science produces knowledge, it follows that controlling science results in the control of power. And power struggles are ubiquitous within the scientific enterprise. For those in the "know," there is a clear pecking order in which "science" is more powerful than others. Physics, steeped in mathematics and, today, appearing to many as being more mystical than scientific, is at the top of the pyramid of power. Below the sublime power and superiority of the physicists, are lower orders including chemistry and biology. Below that, there are earth scientists. Further yet, we leave the realms of "hard" sciences and enter the realm of "soft" sciences (what some at higher levels might call pseudosciences). These include psychology, sociology, anthropology, and the like.

Regardless of these differing levels of power within the domain of science, each branch is itself immersed in a culture of politics, policy, and economics.

This immersion removes the enterprise of science from a pure, objective praxis to one that is subjective, contextually bound, and culture laden. For example, people (from scientific as well as nonscientific communities) from around the world have been arguing for years that worldwide climate change is certainly occurring and that detrimental effects are being felt globally. The effects of global warming impact both societal and geographic features of countless countries. It is widely recognized that climate change is a naturally occurring, cyclic event. However, since the industrial revolution, there appears to be an increase in atmospheric carbon dioxide (a heat-trapping gas) resulting from human activity, specifically through the emissions of fossil fuels. To many scientists, there is compelling evidence suggesting that global warming is occurring at an unprecedented rate. The data includes such things as speed of glacial ice melting (glacial retreat), the rise of sea levels, and the shifting of plant and animal communities worldwide. Despite the global debate on climate change, a 2006 poll revealed that only 30 percent of the people surveyed agreed that humans were a primary cause of global warming and that only 49 percent believed that climate change was an issue for concern ("Poll," 2006).

Surprisingly, the "science" of global warming was called into question (Eilperin, 2006). This may have been in part due to interference by the U.S. government. In March 2001, President Bush reported that he, along with his administration, would not sign the Kyoto Treaty, an international accord that set greenhouse gas emission limits. President Bush pointed to several "scientific findings" supporting his stance. However, in the winter of 2007, Congress began investigating reports that scientists who studied climate change were being pressured by the executive branch to downplay (or not report) findings that supported the argument for increasing global temperatures (Herbert, 2007). The investigation concluded that such pressures did indeed exist. Specifically, a questionnaire was sent out to 1600 scientists by the Union of Concerned Scientists and the Government Accountability Project to obtain responses concerning science and political pressures. Of the questionnaires returned, 43 percent of respondents reported that their work was edited to the point where the meaning of their findings was changed, 46 percent of the respondents indicated that administrative requirements negatively affected their work on climate change, and 67 percent indicated that the work-related environment for federally funded climate research was worse now than five years back (Union of Concerned Scientists, 2007). Furthermore, in 2005, Rick Piltz, a senior official in the government office for climate research resigned in protest over the editing of scientific documents for sake of "toning down" findings related to global warming.

A second example highlighting ways in which political forces affect the scientific landscape relates to the roles and responsibilities of the U.S. chief heath educator (i.e., surgeon general). While he or she is a political appointee of the president of the United States, the appointee carries the weight of being the lead spokesperson on health matters within the U.S. government. The main mission of the surgeon general is to advocate on issues that will improve individual overall well-being, highlighting the dangers of smoking, obesity, and alcohol consumption and furthering health education among the general public. However, in July 2007, approximately one year after Dr. Richard Carmona finished his four-year term as the surgeon general, the public was informed of specifics relating to the obstruction of health information by the president's office. Of particular significance is the observation Dr. Carmona made before a House committee: "the administration would not allow him to speak on the scientific and medical aspects of stem cell research, emergency contraception, comprehensive sexual education and prison or mental health issues" (Harris, 2007).

These examples (for others, see Kennedy, 2004; Collingridge and Reeve, 1986) beg the question "What other (scientific) information might be excluded from reports concerning matters of public health and education?" The answer is, disturbingly enough, quite a lot. For example, given that abstinence education programs have become prominent curriculums in many school districts across the country, students and parents should begin to ask whether the lack of information concerning sexual health is due more to a political position rather than to sound scientific findings (i.e., mental and physical health is benefited when knowledge of sex and sexuality is available). Furthermore, the issue of scientific research funding becomes greatly skewed in light of the available information. In that the government power players are setting forth an agenda of abstinence education as the prevailing sex education curriculum; funding for research and programming will surely be reserved for those in moral agreement with the present political force. This has become apparent in that since 1996 the U.S. Congress has allocated over 300 million dollars to fund programs preaching abstinence before marriage. This funding disregards the science in that large-scale research studies have found that abstinence curriculums do not significantly delay the onset of sexual behavior among adolescents (Council on Scientific Affairs, 1999; Beil, 2007).

## Educational Implications

In this chapter we have highlighted the implicit, authoritarian views of science typically held by both students and the general public. We have also explored some of the social and cognitive factors that support such beliefs. Lastly, we have expressed our concerns about the ability of policymakers to exploit both the perceived authority of science and the naiveté of a public ill informed of the realities of scientific enterprise. These points should provide educators with a clear call to action. Specifically, that teachers need to offer opportunities for students to begin cultivating a habit of mind where one questions so-called facts and seeks answers rather than, as Perry (1970) notes, unquestioningly accepting knowledge from authority. We would argue that educators might also question their own beliefs about the nature of science and their epistemological orientations for those beliefs have been shown to have manifestations in classroom practice.

The research into connections between teachers' thinking and classroom practice has a long history (see Calderhead, 1996; Day, Calderhead, & Denicolo, 1993; Kansanen, Tirri, Meri, Krofkfors, Husu, & Jyrhama, 2000). Although there are many gaps in that knowledge base, the research suggests that a teacher's epistemological beliefs about the nature of inquiry, the nature of knowledge, and judgments about reality can influence their practice (Pintrich, 1990). Indeed, Marlene Schommer and Kiersten Walker (1995) may have best summarized the relationship between epistemology and teaching and learning by the following:

> Epistemological beliefs have a critical place in the classroom. These beliefs may help or hinder learning. Furthermore, epistemological beliefs are most likely being modified by classroom interactions. If we want students to be thoughtful, independent thinkers, and yet we teach them lists of facts as if they are immutable, then we may be instilling philosophical systems in students that resist our own teaching objectives. (p. 430)

Furthermore, among science teachers who were studied within an epistemological framework, Gallagher (1991) found that the majority of didactic teachers held an empiricist view of knowledge that emphasized the "scientific method" and the culturally neutral view of science. With these findings in mind, it becomes critical for science teachers—alongside their students—to explore the ways in which knowledge is constructed within scientific communities and the nature of scientific knowledge.

Although science literacy (as articulated by the American Association for the Advancement of Science and the National Science Teachers Association) has been at the forefront of the national agenda for many decades, the qualities and characteristics associated with those who are science literate only marginally address habits of mind that are fundamental to critical literacy. We would argue that there is a fundamental difference, for example, between critically analyzing data and taking a critical stance against the potential political and economical motives behind scientific claims. Based upon that data, skepticism as it relates to science literacy is limited to the evaluation of claims and data connected to scientific inquiry—it has not widely been connected to evaluating the political, social, and economic forces behind research agendas and scientific messages coming out of inquiry communities. Furthermore, science literacy has failed to address those cultural aspects of the enterprise that by design or unintended consequence result in the marginalization of others. One purpose of this chapter is to confront this disparity by calling for an expanded view of what it is meant to be science literate.

Thus, we argue that individuals (teachers, students, and the broader public) need to cultivate a skeptical mind wherein one questions, for example, the source of information and the political and/or economic forces driving the dissemination of the information. In this process, one also searches for the untold story, considers the ways in which information may be used to control or marginalize others, and seeks opposing viewpoints. To develop understandings about the nature of science and the epistemology of scientific knowledge, it has been argued that students must engage their own epistemological orientations and beliefs about scientific proof, logic, and justification (e.g., Craven, Hand, & Prain, 2002; Lawrence, Hand, & Prain, 1998). Furthermore, when students experience learning that combines experiential and text-based approaches in a classroom that has them interacting socially in partnerships and small teams, they are more able to fully engage in conceptual learning (Guthrie, Anderson, Alao, & Rinehart, 1999).

To foster the development of critical literacy in science, students should be offered opportunities to investigate origins of scientific information, explore possible biases in the data and/or findings, and become critical consumers of scientific news. For example, print media (Craven & Hogan, 2000; Jarman & McClune, 2007) have been found to be fruitful avenues for adolescents to examine their own epistemological orientations while questioning the validity of scientific news. This was highlighted in the authors' 2001 study of sixth (n=108) and eighth grade (n=94) students enrolled in a public, urban middle school who participated in an inquiry unit to determine if students were successful in shifting their conceptions of the nature of scientific knowledge from a mostly naïve approach to a robust, deeper understandings. The pedagogical approach of this unit was informed by an interactive-constructive instructional design (Shymansky, Yore, Treagust, Thiele, Harrison, Waldrip, Stocklmayer, & Venville, 1997) that entailed engaging the prior knowledge of the student, exploring a problem (or several problems), challenging and proposing alternative ideas, consolidating new ideas into existing understanding, and evaluating the understanding in one or more of the engage, explore, and consolidate phases.

Specifically, the approach required students to (1) draw upon their tacit knowledge of what science is by self-selecting samples of scientific and pseudo-scientific writings from the print material, (2) articulate the defining attributes of science using the selected writings, (3) justify (i.e., argue) their selections and rationales, and (4) come to consensus with other students on the qualities and characteristics that make something scientific. A brief description of the stages in the activity is as follows:

### Stage 1. Individual Writing Exercise.

Search printed material available to the public (e.g., newspapers) to find an example of something "scientific" and "pseudoscientific." Cut each example out and create a poster that explains why you (*the student*) decided one was scientific and the other pseudoscientific. Somewhere on the poster, list the qualities and/or characteristics that you have identified. Finally, graphically connect the qualities and/or characteristics to actual points in the printed article that illustrates it.

### Stage 2. Individual Argument and Justification.

Working in groups of three to four students, each student is to present their individual poster creation to the others in the group. Each student must explain the qualities and characteristics she/he identified for each type of sample of writing and defend the illustrations cited in the text that exemplify the qualities and characteristics. When all students have presented their work to the group, each student is to find another group of students and repeat the process.

### Stage 3. Cooperative Argument and Justification.

Working in groups of three to four students, the group must generate a list of qualities and/or characteristics that make the pieces of writing from their posters either scientific or pseudoscientific. Complete consensus had to be reached with all members agreeing on the categorization of the writing piece, the qualities and/or characteristics that make them so, and the exemplars from the text that specifically illustrate them.

Analyses of the teacher journal reflections and evaluation of the completed posters revealed significant shifts in the sixth graders understandings of the creative ventures within scientific work (i.e., human imagination informs scientific knowledge, creativity is expressed in scientific laws, theories and concepts), while eighth graders made significant shifts in their abilities to describe the enterprise of science. That is, they moved away from naïve conceptions of scientific knowledge toward the more complex understandings that scientific knowledge may contain error or change over time, and that scientific ideas may become outdated over time.

However, it is important to note that findings from this developmental study of both sixth and eighth graders' perceptions of science showed remarkable congruency and thus would suggest that the views of sixth graders are tenaciously held and remain steadfast through several years of schooling. Clearly, educators need to consider certain factors if they want to challenge students to tackle questions such as "How do we know?," "What evidence is there to support ...?, " and "What makes something scientific?" These factors address the cognitive abilities of the learner as well as the nature of the science curriculum that they have experienced. If, for example, students have not consistently taken part in a science curriculum that places value and emphasis on critically evaluating the sources of data as much as the data itself, then we should not be expecting students to understand the multiple dimensions of the nature of science. As Maxine Greene (1987) reminds us "it is not unusual for teachers and students to master the terminology in a given field, while retaining a 'naive' view of the experience or phenomena to which knowledge in that field refers" (p. 496).

Thus, we propose a gathering of curriculum ideas to be explored in the K-12 science classroom to challenge such naïve views. Table 1 includes a set of prompting materials that may offer a learning avenue to both improve and continue a cultivation of students' habits of mind, specifically questioning and arguing the status quo. The table highlights sample activities that could be implemented in the classroom where students are provided the necessary opportunities to improve their critical literacy skills. The questions accompanying the suggested prompting materials are only beginning points—a more thorough and complex discussion will most likely evolve from each of these activities. However, these ideas do offer teachers of science a springboard to begin developing an age-appropriate critical literacy curriculum.

Table 1 Critical Literacy Activities in the Science Classroom

| *Prompting Materials* | *Critical Questions* |
|---|---|
| Text articles representing the entanglement of science and politics (i.e., global warming, stem cell research, bioengineering of food supply, nuclear power). | How is the science being distorted? |
| | Is what is being portrayed as scientific accepted widely by the scientific community? What are the opposing viewpoints? |
| | Who is benefiting from this issue/argument? |
| | Are specific groups of people being denied access to the information? |
| | Who is regulating whom? |
| Multimedia clips (i.e., infomercials) | Who is the target audience and why? |
| | What are the audience demographics? |
| | What are the characters trying to get the audience to do? |
| | Is the science being used to change behavior or being used to direct peoples' actions in a specific way? |
| Science-based television shows (i.e., fictional or nonfictional formats to examine the portrayal of science). | What evidence is used to build the argument? |
| | Are multiple perspectives of the topic introduced? |
| | Who is responsible for producing the show? |
| | Are the claims being put forth on the broadcast testable? |
| Opposing Viewpoints Texts (these texts present two sides of an argument. For example, one essay may be arguing for the benefits of cloning while another against it). | How do you begin to tease out the science versus the political claims? |
| | Who are the authors of each essay and what is their background (i.e., employment, political influence, credentials, etc.). |
| | Are scientific findings distorted? |
| | Who stands to benefit from each side? |
| | What groups of people are being ignored on either side of the argument? |

*Continued on following page*

| Prompting Materials | Critical Questions |
|---|---|
| Curriculum materials produced by trade organizations. | Why was the curriculum funded? Were the materials developed to counter negative perceptions? |
| | What type of picture is presented of these agencies? |
| | How does the funding agency benefit? |
| | How was the curriculum evaluated? Using what criteria? |
| | Who stands to benefit? Who loses? |
| | How have the materials been prepared to complement the agencies'/organizations' mission? |
| Computer simulation programs based on scientific concepts. | To what degree is the simulation accurate in terms of the scientific process? |
| | Are multiple perspectives of the science included within the simulation? |
| | What groups are being represented in the programs? |
| | Are there biases perpetuated in the simulation by the program designers and/or developers? |

Although the critical literacy approach to teaching appears to be gaining momentum in schools across many disciplines, we conclude by stating the importance of continuing the search for instructional approaches in a field (science) where concepts are traditionally taught as a rhetoric of conclusions (Schwab, 1962)—our approach is aimed at causing shifts in students' conceptual understandings of the nature knowledge and the cultural biases inherent in the scientific enterprise.

# References

Adorno, T. W., Frenkel-Brunswik, E., Levinson, D. J., & Sanford, R. W. (1950). *The authoritarian personality.* New York: Harper and Row.

American Association for the Advancement of Science. (1993). *Benchmarks for science literacy.* New York: Oxford University Press.

Beil, L. (2007, July 18). Abstinence education faces an uncertain future. *New York Times.* Retrieved on August 20, 2007, from http://www.nytimes.com

Blumhagen, D. W. (1979). The doctor's white coat. *Annals of Internal Medical Journal, 91,* 111-116.

Brase, G. L., & Richmond, J. (2004). The white-coat effect: Physician attire and perceived authority, friendliness, and attractiveness. *Journal of Applied Social Psychology 34*(12), 2469-2481.

Calderhead, J. (1996). *Teacher beliefs and knowledge.* New York: Simon & Schuster.

Chambers, D. W. (1983). Stereotypic images of the scientist: The draw a scientist test. *Science Education, 67,* 255-265.

Collingridge, D., & Reeve, C. (1986). *Science speaks to power: The role of experts in policy making.* New York: St Martin's Press.

Council on Scientific Affairs. (1999). *Report of the Council on Scientific Affairs.* [Action of the AMA House of Delegates 1999 Interim Meeting, CSA Report 7-I-99]. Chicago, IL: American Medical Association.

Craven, J., Hand, B., & Prain, V. (2002). Assessing explicit and tacit conceptions of the nature of science among pre-service elementary teachers. *International Journal of Science Education* 24(8), 785-802.

Craven, J. & Hogan, T. (2000, April). *Elementary students constructing the nature and language of science.* Paper presented at the National Association for Research in Science Teaching Annual Conference, New Orleans, LA.

Day, C., Calderhead, J., & Denicolo, P. (1993). *Research on teacher thinking: Understanding professional development.* Washington, DC: Falmer Press.

Dingle, H. (1972). *Science at the crossroads.* London: Martin Brian & O'Keeffe.

Eilperin, J. (2006, April, 6). Climate researchers feeling heat from White House. *Washington Post,* p. A27.

Fort, D. C., & Varney, H. L. (1989). How students see scientists. *Science and Children, 26,* 8-13.

Freire, P. (1997). *Pedagogy of the oppressed: New revised 20th anniversary edition.* New York: Continuum Publishing Company.

Fung, Y. H. (2002). A comparative study of primary and secondary school students' images of scientists. *Research in Science & Technological Education, 20*(2), 199-213.

Gallaher, J. (1991). Prospective and practicing secondary school science teachers' knowledge and beliefs about the philosophy of science. *Science Education,* 75(1), 121- 33.

Gilligan, C. (1982). *In a different voice: Psychological theory and women's development.* Cambridge, MA: Harvard University Press.

Goldman, A. I. (1993). *Philosophical applications of cognitive science.* San Francisco: Westview Press.

Greene, B. (2005). *The elegant universe.* New York: Vintage Books.

Guthrie, J. T., Anderson, E., Alao, S., & Rinehart, J. (1999). Influences of concept-oriented reading instruction on strategy use and conceptual learning from text. *Elementary School Journal, 99*(4), 343-366.

Harding, S. (1991). *Whose science? Whose knowledge? Thinking from women's lives.* Ithaca, NY: Cornell University Press.

Harding, S. (1998). *Is science multicultural? Postcolonialisms, feminisms, and epistemologies.* Bloomington: Indiana University Press.

Harris, G. (2007, July 11). Surgeon general sees 4-year term as compromised. *New York Times,* p. A1.

Herbert, H. J. (2007, January 29). Congress begins tackling climate issues. *The Associated Press.*

Hofer, B. K., & Pintrich, P. R. (1997). The development of epistemological theories: Beliefs about knowledge and knowing and their relation to learning. *Review of Educational Research, 67*(1), 88–140.

Horgan, J. (1996). *The end of science.* Reading, MA: Helix Books.

Ikusaka, M., Kemegi, M., Sunaga, T., Narita, N. Kohayashi, H., Yonenami, K., & Watanabe, M. (1999). Patient's attitude toward consultations by a physician without a white coat in Japan. *Internal Medicine, 38,* 533–536.

Jarman, R., & McClune, B. (2007). *Developing scientific literacy: Using news media in the classroom.* New York: Open University Press.

Kansanen, P., Tirri, K., Meri, M. K., Husu, L., & Jyrhama, R. (2000). *Teachers' pedagogical thinking: Theoretical landscapes, practical challenges.* New York: Peter Lang Publishing.

Kennedy, R. F. Jr. (2004, March 8). The junk science of George W. Bush. *The Nation.* Retrieved August 14, 2007, from http://www.thenation.com/doc/20040308/kennedy

King, P. M., & Kitchener, K. S. (1994). *Developing reflective judgment.* San Francisco: Jossey-Bass.

Kitchener, K. S., & Fischer, K. W. (1990). *A skill approach to the development of reflective thinking.* New York: Karger.

Kitchener, K. S., Lynch, C. L., Fischer, K. W., & Wood, P. K. (1993). Developmental range of reflective judgment: The effect of contextual support and practice on developmental stage. *Developmental Psychology, 29*(5), 893–906.

Kohlberg, Lawrence. (1976). Moral stages and moralization: The cognitive-development approach. In T. Lickona (Ed.), *Moral development and behavior.* New York: Holt, Rinehart & Wilson.

Lawrence, C., Hand, B., & Prain, V. (1998). *Epistemologies of science: Constructing new meaning through writing.* Paper presented at the Annual Meeting of National Association for Research in Science Education, San Diego, CA

Moore, D. W. (2005). Three in four Americans believe in paranormal. *Gallup Poll News Service,* Retrieved August 14, 2007, from http://www.galluppoll.com/content/?CI=16915.

National Science Board (2006). *Science and engineering indicators 2006.* Arlington, VA: National Science Foundation.

National Science Board. (2007). *About the national science board.* Retrieved July 10, 2007, from http://www.nsf.gov/nsb/about/index.jsp

Newton D. P., & Newton, L. D. (1992). Young children's perceptions of science and the scientist. *International Journal of Science Education, 14*(3), 331–348.

Perry, W. G. (1970). *Forms of intellectual and ethical development in the college years: A scheme.* New York: Holt, Rhinehart and Winston.

Phillips, W. (1852, January 28). Speeches before the Massachusetts anti-slavery society. Boston, MA.

Piaget, J. (1950). *Introduction a l'epistemologie genetique.* Paris: Presses Univ. De France.

Pintrich, P. R. (1990). *Implications of psychological research on student learning and college teaching for teacher education.* New York: Macmillan Publishing Company.

Poll: Americans see a climate problem. (2006, March 26). *Time Magazine.* Retrieved July 25, 2007, from http://www.time.com

Rehman, S. U., Nietert, P. J., Cope, D. W., & Kilpatrick, A. O. (2005). What to wear today? Effect of doctor's attire on the trust and confidence of patients. *The American Journal of Medicine, 118*(11), 1279–1286.

Rogers, R., Malancharuvil-Berkes, E., Mosley, M., Hui, D., & Joseph, G. (2005). Critical discourse analysis in education: A review of literature. *Review of Educational Research, 75*(3), 365–416.

Schommer, M. (1990). Effects of beliefs about the nature of knowledge on comprehension. *Journal of Educational Psychology, 82,* 498–504.

Schommer, M., & Walker, K. (1995). Are epistemological beliefs similar across domains? *Journal of Educational Psychology, 87*(3), 424–432.

Schwab, J. J. (1962). *The teaching of science as inquiry.* Cambridge, MA: Harvard University Press.

Schwartz, B. (2007). When words decide. *Scientific American Mind 18*(4), 36–43.

Shymansky, J. A., Yore, L. D., Treagust, D. F., Thiele, R. B., Harrison, A., Waldrip, L. D., Stocklmayer, S. M., & Venville, G. (1997). Examining the construction process: A study of changes in level 10 students' understanding of classical mechanics. *Journal of Research in Science Teaching, 34* (6), 571–593

Smolin, L. (2007). *The trouble with physics: The rise of string theory, the fall of a science, and what comes next.* New York: Mariner Books.

Stern, G. G. (1953). *Inventory of beliefs.* Chicago: University of Chicago Press.

Thomas, M. D., Henley, T. B., & Snell, C. M. (2006). The draw a scientist test: A different population and a somewhat different story. *College Student Journal, 40*(1), 140–148.

Union of Concerned Scientists. (2007, July 30). Investigation reveals widespread suppression of federal climate research. Retrieved July 3, 2007, from http://www.ucsusa.org/news/press_release/investigation-reveals-0007.html

Walton, D. (1997). *Appeal to expert opinion: Arguments from authority.* University Park: The Pennsylvania State University Press.

Wolpart, L. (2000). *The unnatural nature of science.* Cambridge, MA: Harvard University Press.

Ziman, J. (1968). *Public knowledge: The social dimension of science.* New York: Cambridge University Press.

# SECTION 2

# CURRICULAR AND PEDAGOGICAL POSSIBILITIES

# Chapter 5

# Against "Tolerance": Critical Historical Literacy Methods in Antihomophobia Education

*Rachel Mattson*

## Against "Tolerance": Critical Historical Literacy Methods in

## Antihomophobia Education

The 1963 Civil Rights March on Washington is not one of those historical events that Americans have forgotten. Most are familiar with the image of Martin Luther King standing in front of the Lincoln Memorial, delivering what has come to be called his "I Have a Dream" speech. The visual and auditory record of that event is so clearly recognizable that it can be—and is frequently— deployed on the walls of elementary, middle, and high school classrooms, in television shows and movies, in ad campaigns, and elsewhere. Still, the unsurprising fact is that very few Americans actually know much about that speech (which lasted for more than 17 minutes), the March itself, or the historical context in which it was organized. The story of the March—its origins, its goals, and its effect (on the national, international, and local levels)— is a really remarkable saga that reveals a great deal about, among other things, the extraordinary power that ordinary people can possess when they join together in struggle.

But tucked into the story of its origins and the events leading up to the 1963 March on Washington is a tale that illuminates a set of other ideas—ideas about the historical meaning and uses of homophobia and its erasure that raises a set of pressing questions about what we imagine to be the injury inflicted by homophobia and how we might effectively teach against it. This tale centers around the man who is widely recognized to have been the brains behind that historic 1963 March on Washington for Jobs and Justice—Bayard Rustin.

A life-long pacifist and Civil Rights activist, Rustin is among the twentieth century's most important—and most forgotten—political strategists and philosophers. Over the course of his life, he worked tirelessly to dismantle the machinery of racism and war, collaborating with a diversity of organizations (the War Resisters' League, the Southern Christian Leadership Conference, and many others) and serving as a close advisor to a succession of visionary personalities, including Martin Luther King Jr. Indeed, to quote historian John D'Emilio, Rustin, "more than anyone else," was responsible for bringing "the message and methods of Gandhi"—methods that helped make Dr. King's work so distinctively effective—"into the heart of the black freedom struggle" (D'Emilio, 2003, p. 2). As a close advisor to Dr. King, Rustin was among the first Civil Rights leaders to advocate for a massive march on Washington, and he subsequently served as the March's lead organizer. With very little time and a tiny staff, he performed a remarkable feat: conceptualizing the event and coordinating the ground-level, logistical footwork that such an enormous undertaking—the first of its kind—required.

But Rustin was also a gay man who lived in a time when being gay was virtually, in and of itself, a criminal act. And in the days leading up to the March, his homosexuality became a hot topic, one that nearly derailed the entire effort. This is because, in the days leading up to the March, a group of white supremacists used Rustin's homosexuality as a tool in their longstanding campaign to undermine the Civil Rights movement.

What happened was this: In early August 1963 (the March was scheduled for August 28), Strom Thurmond, a Dixiecrat senator from South Carolina, redoubled his attacks on the Civil Rights movement. Using the influence and access he enjoyed as a U.S. senator, Thurmond assembled a stash of documents detailing the personal and political histories of the Civil Rights leadership, focusing his attentions on the man who was quite visibly the event's lead organizer—Rustin. First, Thurmond placed a set of documents in the *Congressional Record* suggesting that Rustin was a communist. But when those materials failed to generate much public interest or scandal, Thurmond made a second attempt to smear Rustin and his work. Several days after his first document dump, Thurmond once again inserted a set of documents into the *Congressional Record*. This time he introduced items—including a *Los Angeles Times* article and a police booking slip—indicating that Rustin was a homosexual and a convicted "sexual pervert." And in this instance, Thurmond's efforts bore fruit. Newspapers across the country carried the story. "Calls Rustin a Convicted Pervert," read the headline in the *Chicago Tribune*, for instance. "Thurmond Bares March Leader's Police Record" (Moore, 1963).[1]

Although these events had a significant effect on Rustin personally, Thurmond's smear campaign failed to dampen the efforts of March organizers. In a remarkable show of unity and clear-headedness, the Civil Rights leadership—including members of the Southern Christian Leadership Conference—spoke out against Thurmond's actions. As Rustin biographer D'Emilio puts it: "Because the accusation was so public, because it was leveled by a white supremacist, and because it came just two weeks before an event on which the movement was banking so much, Civil Rights leaders had to rally to Rustin's defense." We are, they announced, "dismayed that there are in this country men who, wrapping themselves in the mantle of Christian morality, would mutilate the most elementary conceptions of human decency, privacy, and humility in order to persecute other men." Thus the March was held on schedule, and this near-catastrophe largely disappeared from memory (D'Emilio, 2003, p. 349).

These events, I argue in this chapter, offer a good starting place for an effort to rethink the work of antihomophobia education. Standing in opposition to the traditional narratives of the Civil Rights movement and gay history, the story offers an expansive description of the meaning, power, and uses of homophobia in U.S. history. Understanding how, in 1963, a white supremacist U.S. senator used an antigay slur in his attempts to discredit and derail the efforts of the Civil Rights movement—and how, in response, a group of straight, Christian ministers and labor leaders defended the privacy and integrity of their gay colleague and decried the practice of homophobia—requires a complicated investigation and offers an exceptional opportunity for teaching students a range of critical historical literacy skills.

The idea of using Thurmond's attack on Rustin's work in antihomophobia education might appear to be a logical suggestion, one that stays true to the ideals of the movement to teach against homophobia at the secondary level. And in some ways it does: focused on the life experiences of one gay individual, the story (and any classroom lesson that it might inspire) centers on an attack based on hatred of queer people and stigmatization of their sexual desires. Teaching about this event likewise asks students to take queers seriously, and to understand that they have always been part of U.S. life, contributing their talents to a range of fields and endeavors.[2] But in fact, the story—and the strategies that I want to suggest we use in thinking about it and teaching with it—actually poses a critical challenge to some of the premises and traditional methods of antihomophobia education. It suggests, for one thing, that homophobic attacks have the power not only to injure gay men and lesbians exclusively, but also to threaten the liberties of ordinary, even predominantly straight, people. It suggests that homophobia has worked in tandem with other forces—such as white supremacy and electoral power—to uphold a wide range of traditional hierarchies. And it offers an opportunity to teach against not only homophobia narrowly defined, but also gendered and sexual norms broadly stated. In short, it offers the opportunity to understand and teach "homophobia" as an expansive category, one that not only motivates violence against queers but also helps construct a range of identities, masculinities, and femininities, and one that exercises undue control over the behaviors of gay and straight folks alike.

The drive to teach against homophobia broadly defined in this way has not, for the most part, been among the central concerns of antihomophobia educators. Much of the work that antihomophobia educators have developed emphasizes visibility, tolerance, and narrow ideas about the injury of homophobia on adolescent and adult populations. For instance, look at the curricula developed by the organization most active in antihomophobia education, the Gay, Lesbian, and Straight Education Network (GLSEN).[3] Although GLSEN has been a massively important force in making U.S. schools safer for young queers, its curricular resources have often suffered from a narrow conception of homophobia and thus raise troubling questions about the aims and purposes of antihomophobia education. Typical among GLSEN's offerings is one lesson, for instance, that asks students simply to look at a list of well-known "historical figures" who either "had same-sex relationships at some point in their lives and/or transgressed society's gender norms" (GLSEN, January 23, 2003). Then it asks students to briefly consider whether "the connections between their identities and what they gave to the world was openly discussed" in their classrooms. The lesson ends there. Requiring very little in the way of critical thinking, the lesson suggests that the way to fight homophobia is to inform students that gay people existed in history. Tragically oversimplistic, it does very little to help students understand how power works and is unlikely to make these questions engaging or relevant for diverse student populations.

Perhaps even more troubling is another of GLSEN's lessons, one that centers around an incident that occurred during the 2003 U.S. bombing of

Afghanistan (GLSEN, October 30, 2003). In the course of its assault on the countryside, this lesson explains, U.S. Navy personnel were photographed dropping, from the air, a bomb emblazed with the phrase "high jack this fags" (*sic*). When the Associated Press (AP) published this photograph on its Web site, a coalition of gay rights groups launched a series of protests; they criticized the military for homophobia and demanded that the AP remove the photo. "Messages like the one presented in this photograph," argued one activist, "only reinforce the ideas of hatred and division that our nation seeks to defend against. We must not emulate the intolerance of our enemies." In response, the AP removed the photo from its Web site, and the U.S. Navy issued an apology (Dotinga, October 12 and 19, 2001).

Shockingly, however, the GLSEN lesson entirely fails to invite students to discuss what are, to my mind, the most critical among the complicated questions that this incident raises—questions of war, militarism, masculinity, or Afghanistan. On the contrary, it simply asks students to consider how the initial photograph "was handled by the media," and to decide whether they "agree or disagree with" the criticisms made by the gay rights groups opposed to the graffiti on the bomb and the image. "Be sure to emphasize that these are very recent, serious events," GLSEN concludes in a final note to teachers, remarking that "the unchecked bigotry of the soldier, the indifference of the media, and the weak response from the Naval command all perfectly illustrate the insidiousness of anti-LGBT bias in U.S. society." But how can students possibly discuss this incident if they aren't invited to wonder about the inter-workings of U.S. patriotism and masculinity, the war on terror, and the narrow concerns of the gay rights movement? And how can students be expected to ignore the fact that the bomb in question was ultimately let loose on people who have been, for decades, the victims of terror and war as devastating, if not more so, as were the 9/11 bombings? In part because it deploys a narrow definition of homophobia—focusing on the visible use of homophobic slurs and asking for more "tolerance" of gay people—the lesson misses the opportunity to provoke conversations about the complex mechanics of power in U.S. culture and politics; about the relationship between the discourses of masculinity, militarism, and international politics; or about the complex ways that gender and sexual norms function in both national and international contexts.[4]

These failures and lessons demonstrate the real need for complicated discussion about the meanings, presumptions, methods, and intentions of antihomophobia education. What do educators think they will accomplish by insisting that gay men and lesbians be included in the canon or by demanding one-dimensional apologies from the Navy for tolerating anti-gay slurs? What do they hope to accomplish by prioritizing visibility, inclusion, and tolerance? Educators interested in countering homophobia might more profitably attend to the criticisms that scholars of multiculturalism have been developing, for over a decade, about the limitations of tolerance as a social justice goal. Hardly the benevolent force it is often made out to be, tolerance carries with it, to quote philosopher Wendy Brown (2006), "an antagonism toward [difference], as well as the capacity for normalization." Toleration in itself is an "act of power" that, she explains, "disguises power" (Brown, p. 26). Instead of inviting an investigation of the mechanisms of power that create the world we all live in, tolerance-based inquiry invites students to merely learn the codes of politeness and the boundaries of normal. Furthermore, when used by gay men and lesbians, as the queer historian Lisa Duggan argues, demands for tolerance often meet "with very limited success" (Duggan and Hunter, 1995, p. 158).

Instead, antihomophobia education might benefit from some unafraid critical engagement with the insights of queer theory. Indeed, antihomophobia educators are ideally situated to find ways to translate the complicated—but trenchant—ideas that queer theorists have developed into applicable classroom practice. Since queer theories invite students to use a set of critical lenses to investigate everything around them, doing so might open up the terrain upon which we think about the ideal purposes and frameworks for antihomophobia work—and, in fact, for social justice and critical literacy work more generally, since queer theory takes, as its subject, not gay and lesbian identity, but rather various kinds of power relationships and norms. "By shifting the scholarly lens off homosexuality per se ... as the object to be examined," scholar Donna Penn explains, queer theory invites scrutiny of "the production, construction, and investment in the so-called 'normal'" (Penn, 1995, p. 33).

Recent studies of high school culture suggest that this sort of investigation might have far-reaching consequences. In her recently published ethnography—*Dude, You're a Fag*—sociologist C.J. Pascoe (2007) reminds readers that homophobia is "a central mechanism in the making of contemporary American adolescent masculinity" (p. 53). But she also argues that many of the things that we tend to consider as homophobia in a school context are actually gendered disciplinary mechanisms more broadly conceived. As gay-hating as young straight men might be, they are also concerned about their own and their peers' masculinity and are adept at using what Pascoe calls "the specter of the fag" to police each other's behaviors and speech. "Fag talk and fag imitations serve as a discourse with which boys discipline themselves and each other," she explains (p. 54). Pascoe's work suggests the import of social justice education that works against not simply homophobia narrowly defined but also gendered and sexual norms of various kinds. Her work also offers an implicit critique of antihomophobia education as it is currently imagined. Although the boys she studied "knew that they were not supposed to call homosexual boys fags," they continued to believe in a hierarchy that placed queers at the bottom of the totem pole. "Instead of challenging inequity," she concludes, tolerance-based discourses of "gay rights has reinscribed it" (pp. 82–83).

*A lesson:* Complicated and challenging though they are, these ideas can and should, I believe, be used in thinking about new methods for antihomophobia education. And although I am still in the early stages of my work in these areas, I have recently begun to experiment with classroom activities that attempt to do so. These experiments include a set of workshops I co-designed and co-led in 2007 at a public high school (which I will call New York High School) in Manhattan. I was, at the time, serving as the historian-in-residence in NYU's Department of Teaching and Learning, where I spearheaded a series of history education U.S. history-related teacher education projects. As part of this work, I had organized a think tank—a Queer Education Working Group (QEWG)—of scholars, educators, and activists interested in creating a set of frameworks for non-tolerance-based antihomophobia and anti-transphobia education.[5] When we received an invitation from teachers at New York High School to lead a workshop at the school's annual "Antihomophobia Day," the group decided to take the opportunity to design a lesson around Strom Thurmond's homophobic 1963 attack on Rustin and the March on Washington.

Using a collection of primary and secondary source documents from Rustin's life, we designed a lesson meant to get students thinking critically, first and foremost, about the ways in which homophobia can threaten a range of people and interests. Could we get students to consider how homophobia might pose a danger in unexpected ways to even nonqueer people and ostensibly nonqueer "issues"? Deploying the precepts of critical historical literacy—in particular, the drive to teach students to critically read primary source documents for bias and argument and to think about history as a series of debates over meaning—we wanted to give students the opportunity to investigate the question of homophobia alongside other mechanisms of power and other ideas of "normal."

Among the documents we used in this lesson were:

**Photographs.** These specifically included reproductions of two pictures in which Rustin stands next to two immediately recognizable individuals—Martin Luther King Jr. and Malcolm X.[6]

**Photocopies of newspaper articles.** These included, first, a copy of "Calls Rustin a Convicted Pervert," the newspaper article, mentioned earlier, that appeared in the *Chicago Tribune* in August 1963 detailing Senator Strom Thurmond's efforts to discredit the March on Washington by publicizing Rustin's sexuality (Moore, 1963); and, second, the original notice, published in 1953 in the *Los Angeles Times*, of Rustin's arrest on a "morals charge" in Pasadena. "Rustin," the article reads—"a 40-year-old Negro lecturer"—was "arrested by Pasadena police early Thursday in company with two men in an automobile parked near the Green Hotel ... Shortly before his arrest, Rustin spoke on world peace before the American Society of University Women at the Pasadena Athletic Club" (*Los Angeles Times*, 1953).

**Two pieces of writings by Rustin himself.** The first piece was his 1943 letter to the U.S. draft board, in which he declared his conscientious objector status. "I wish to inform you," he wrote, "that I cannot voluntarily submit to an order springing from the Selective service and Training Act for War. There are several reasons for this decision, all stemming from the basic spiritual truth that men are brothers in the sight of God" (Rustin, 1943). The second was an excerpt from Rustin's 1942 essay "Nonviolence vs. Jim Crow," in which he described his efforts to resist Jim Crow on an interstate bus. "It is my sincere conviction," he recalled telling a hostile bus driver, "that the power of love in the world is the greatest power existing. If you have a greater power, my friend, you may move me [to the back of the bus]" (Rustin, 1942).

**An excerpt from John D'Emilio's biography of Rustin.** This is the excerpt in which D'Emilio (2003) describes Thurmond's 1963 attack on Rustin and the Civil Rights movement (p. 348).

We hoped that this diverse collection of documents would enable students to glimpse the complexity of Rustin's experiences and ideas and get a sense of both his political integrity and his commitment to fighting both against racism and for peace as well as the trouble he faced as a result of his sexual desires. We were, of course, presented with a typical challenge: to teach our lesson within the constraints of fifty-minute periods. Additionally, this work was to be wedged into a packed, one-day-long marathon exercise in antihomophobia. Having spent the morning listening to a panel of queer activists talk about their experiences, the ninth and tenth grade students of New York High School would then spend the afternoon shuttling between three or four different practical workshops—among which ours was one.

Because this structure left far too little time for each individual student to consider, at any length, each one of these documents, we organized the workshop around a jigsaw structure. We would divide the class into six small groups, give each group a different document to examine, and then have students break out into a second set of groups—wherein they would describe to each other the original document at which their first group had looked. In that way, every student would have the opportunity to work closely with one document and benefit also from the fact that a range of documents containing a diversity of information about Rustin's life and the 1963 March on Washington had circulated among participants.

In short, the lesson agenda looked like this:

- **Definitions (Ten minutes).** Ask students to throw up their definitions of *racism, homophobia, gender,* and *white supremacy.* Write these ideas on a large piece of paper or chalkboard.

- **Jigsaw Document Analysis (Thirty minutes).** Divide students into six small groups. Give each group a different document relating to Rustin's life and ask each group to analyze their document using the primary document analysis guide sheet we designed for this purpose. After 5–10 minutes, call a break and have each member of each group join a new group, wherein they will have to present their document to this new group. Together the members of these new groups will (using a second guide sheet) try to come up with some theories about the mysterious person at the center of these documents. Who was he? What did he do in his life? What did he believe in? When did he live?

- **Debrief (Ten minutes).** Reconvene the entire class as a group and ask students to share their theories with the larger group. Who was this person? What was he known for? What seems important to you about his story and his life? What, based on his story (or at least the bits that we introduced today), they think about the intersection between homophobia and racism? How does that change the picture of homophobia and racism that we wrote about on the giant paper at the outset?

- **Closeout (Five minutes).** Ask students to discuss what they see as the relationship between homophobia and racism in their school.

Wedged as it was into fifty-minute periods during a one-shot "Antihomophobia Day," our work using this exercise with students at New York High School was not, by any means, perfect. It introduced far too much information for short one-class-period activities, and asked students to use skills that many of them had never been introduced to before—historical thinking skills, interpretive and analytical skills, and leaderless group skills. For several of the students in these classes, meanwhile, these documents were too dense. Although members of each group were able to work together to read the documents, the uneven reading levels and time limits forced some students to take a backseat. Plus, we were asking students to think about both the Civil Rights movement and homophobia in unfamiliar ways. Still, we had some success and learned a great deal. During one of the workshops, for instance, students wondered about Rustin's original arrest and conviction—a conversation that ultimately led to a discussion both about the criminalization of homosexuality and about policing and crime in general. Students began to ask, "who decides what crime is?" Are the police always right? Unexpected as this discussion was, it fit nicely with our original intent to raise questions about the production of norms and about the relationship between homophobia and other forms of power.

## Conclusion

Rustin's life story, historian and biographer John D'Emilio has observed, "reminds us that the most important stories from the past are often those that have been forgotten" (p. 6). Certainly, there is value in recalling Rustin's efforts for its own sake, for the sake of returning credit where credit is due, and for restoring popular historical memory of a set of moments that are so crucial in the history of the twentieth-century United States. But there are other reasons to remember and teach with Rustin's biography. His life story offers radical educators interested in critical literacies an opportunity to help students pick apart the meanings and mechanisms of power. Examining Rustin's life in the context of Thurmond's attack on the March on Washington in particular offers teachers the opportunity to consider, with students, the complexity of both the Civil Rights movement and of homophobia—and to consider the broad questions of how power works and how change happens. It also offers an opportunity for students to consider the ways in which homophobia has functioned historically as a weapon to limit the full expression of all of our personal and political opportunities. Will teaching this story—or others like it—dismantle homophobia and gender norms immediately? No, but it does suggest we might be able to develop methods for teaching against gender and sexual discrimination in ways that ask students to grapple with the complexities of how power works, how change happens, and how each of us relates to these larger historic processes.

  Without diminishing the efforts of those embattled pioneers who have begun to create programs meant to transform the heteronormative climate of secondary schools in the United States, I want to suggest that we need to think differently about what it means to teach against homophobia, and what we hope to accomplish in our efforts therein. Are we simply attempting to replace one set of ideas with another one? I am committed to the idea that historical thinking and queer theories offer important tools for social justice education, and I believe that what we ought to be doing, at least in part, is teaching students to think critically about the world they live in and the categories they deploy on a daily basis—to do this in a way that takes on questions about "normal" as a critical category and to do this in a way that sees the past and present as interconnected and mutually constitutive. If, as sociologist C.J. Pascoe argues, homophobia and hierarchical ideas about masculinity and femininity are central mechanisms "in the making of contemporary American adolescent masculinity," then developing newly effective models for this work carries a great urgency.

# Notes

1. See also D'Emilio (2003), p. 348.
2. Traditional ideas about antihomophobia education tend to stress granting gay men and lesbians visibility. Gerald Unks, editor of *The Gay Teen* does a good job of articulating the thinking behind this idea: "Within the typical secondary school curriculum," he writes, "homosexuals do not exist ... They have fought no battles, held no offices, explored nowhere, written no literature, built nothing, invented nothing, solved no equations ... The lesson to the heterosexual student is abundantly clear: homosexuals do nothing of consequence. To the homosexual student, the message has even greater power: no one who has ever felt as you do has done anything worth mentioning ... The absence from the curriculum of valid information about homosexuality cuts both ways; heterosexual students are given no reasons not to hate homosexuals, while homosexual students are given no reason not to hate themselves" Unks (1995, p. 5).
3. A nonprofit founded in 1990, GLSEN has been at the forefront of school-based antihomophobia work, laboring for years to encourage the establishment of clubs and policies and to develop curricular materials meant to both contest homophobia and support queer students inside the nation's high schools. It has, for nearly 20 years, waged an uphill battle in the face of political attacks, legal challenges, administrative inertia, and often lukewarm support from non-queer-specific progressive educational organizations. See www.glsen.org.
4. GLSEN is not, of course, the only force producing ideas about or models for antihomophobia and antitransphobia education. For a distinct vision, see Kumashiro (2002). The Sylvia Rivera Law Project—a legal services organization serving transgender people—has also sponsored some experiments with different models. In 2004, for instance, the organization held a meeting on the question of Gender Diversity and Children. Aiming not to create new models for teaching against homophobia but, rather, for teaching against the reproduction of gender norms, participants at this meeting created some informational postings and resource lists. For more information, see www.srlp.org.
5. This group, the Queer Education Working Group, consisted of people with a range of identities, skills, and professional locations—including people who identified as gay, straight, queer, and transgendered; public school teachers and literacy coaches, humanities scholars, professors of education, and social justice activists. Special thanks to Laraine Wallowitz, Devin Murphy, and Lezlie Frye, who were my principal collaborators in developing this lesson.
6. The photo of Rustin with Martin Luther King Junior can be found at http://i.cnn.net/cnn/2002/EDUCATION/11/27/rustin.school.ap/vert.story.bayard.ap.jpg; the image of Rustin with Malcolm X appears in Carbado and Weise, eds. (2003).

# References

Brown, W. (2006). *Regulating aversion: Tolerance in the age of identity and empire.* Princeton, NJ: Princeton University Press.

Carbado, D., and Weise, D. (2003). *Time on two crosses: The collected writings of Bayard Rustin.* San Francisco: Cleis Press.

D'Emilio, J. (2003). *Lost prophet: The life and times of Bayard Rustin.* Chicago: University of Chicago Press.

Dotinga, R. (October 12, 2001). "Navy photo shows anti-gay slur on bomb," retrieved February 3, 2006, from PlanetOut.com.

Dotinga, R. (October 19, 2001). "Navy calls bomb message 'inappropriate,'" retrieved February 3, 2006, from PlanetOut.com.

Duggan, L., and Hunter, N.D. (1995). *Sex wars: Sexual dissent and political culture.* New York: Routledge.

The Gay, Lesbian, and Straight Education Network (January 23, 2003). *History Match-up: A GLSEN Lunchbox Resource.* Retrieved February 3, 2006, from www.glsen.org/cgi-bin/iowa/educator/library/record/1643.html.

The Gay, Lesbian, and Straight Education Network (October 30, 2003). *Lesson Plan: What do "faggot" and "dyke" mean?* retrieved February 3, 2006, from www.glsen.org/cgi-bin/iowa/educator/library/record/846.html.

Kumashiro, K. (2002). *Troubling education: Queer activism and anti-oppressive pedagogy.* New York: Routledge.

*Los Angeles Times* (January 23, 1953). "Lecturer sentenced to jail on morals charge."

Moore, W. (1963). "Calls Rustin a Convicted Pervert: Thurmond Bares March Leader's Police Record." *Chicago Tribune*, August 15, 1963.

Pascoe, C.J. (2007). *Dude, you're a fag: Masculinity and sexuality in high school.* Berkeley: University of California Press.

Penn, D. (1995). "Queer: Theorizing politics and history," *Radical history review* (62).

Rustin, B. (1942). "Nonviolence vs. Jim Crow," *Time on two crosses: The collected writings of Bayard Rustin.* San Francisco: Cleis Press, pp. 2–5.

Rustin, B. (1943). "Letter to the draft board," *Time on two crosses: The collected writings of Bayard Rustin.* San Francisco: Cleis Press, pp. 11–13.

Unks, G. (1995). *The gay teen: Educational practice and theory for lesbian, gay and bisexual adolescents.* New York: Routledge.

# Chapter 6

# Grounding Art Education in the Lives of Youth: Using Graffiti Art in the Classroom

*Lisa Hochtritt*

In my teachings at the high school and college levels, I have always been interested in bringing the "outside" into the classroom. I find artistic inspiration in looking at street art and engaging in happenings that occur outside of the confines of school walls. As a college supervisor of pre-service teachers, I visit many classrooms and interact with many art educators. Given my pedagogical predilection to bringing in subjects of interest to my students' outside-of-school lives, I am always intrigued and amazed by what art teachers hang on their classroom walls. In many of the elementary and secondary art education classes I have visited, there is a sameness in the visuality that is common among these educators. The items I see most are factory-produced posters that display the elements and principles of art and design. The frequent prominence of the posters suggest that these particular art characteristics and approaches to talking about art are valued and of great importance to art teachers. I question if students in these classrooms share their teachers' enthusiasm for elements of art such as form, line, and shape and for principles of art such as emphasis, balance, and harmony, and I wonder about the ubiquitous and unbalanced biasness of these visuals.

As Cahan and Kocur (1996) comment about pedagogy that relies heavily on the art elements and principles, "Such approaches also tend to subsume art from every culture and context under narrow formal or technical concerns which are themselves derived from European modernist aesthetic frameworks" (p. xxii). While I am not opposed to learning different types of art vocabulary in elementary and secondary schools, I am in firm opposition to glorifying the Western canon of art that exists within the hierarchical art world to the exclusion of contemporary and nonmajority artists. Gude (2004) explains further:

> When visiting K-12 school art programs, I rarely see meaningful connections being made between these formal descriptors and understanding works of art or analyzing the quality of everyday design...I wonder why what is still considered by many to be the appropriate organizing content for the foundations of 21st century art curriculum is but a shadow of what was modern, fresh, and inspirational 100 years ago. (p. 6)

Art education that emphasizes visual culture and teachers who practice critical pedagogy oppose the long-practiced trend of favoring the elements and principles of art in K-12 classrooms over lessons that have more relevance to young people's lives. Contemporary issues in art and education are finding their way into university classrooms and teacher education courses, but these ideas are relatively slow to funnel back into K-12 classroom art instruction.

The teacher is the gatekeeper for curriculum in the classroom and generally determines the course of study and the themes of the lessons. Yokley (1999) suggests that "many contemporary works of art provide the metaphoric richness that affords opportunity to address issues that affect students' present-day experiences" (p. 24). Yet, I observe the same detached lessons of reproduction and repetition in many classrooms. Some educators argue that they do not include contemporary artists in their teachings because they are not prepared to take on difficult imagery or to explain complicated power issues in a critical way. While others say that political issues have no place in the art classroom (Gaudelius & Speirs, 2002).

Issues-based lessons with social import to youth are at the crux of a contemporary art education model centered on visual culture. As Gaudelius and Speirs (2002) suggest, "Teaching art through an issues-based approach exposes children to issues that give them reason to interact with the world around them as well as look deeply into themselves as the issues connect and intersect with their lives" (p. 4). In this chapter, I challenge the widely held assumption of in-school art that includes only Western artists and antiquated vocabulary. I am advocating for the study and inclusion of youth artwork produced outside of school, such as graffiti art, in the art classroom as a form of cultural production worthy of consideration as a legitimate site of critical literacy and artistic inquiry.

## Graffiti

"Graffiti is a state of mind and a sign of respect."

(Seventh grade male, approximately 12 years old) (Moje, 2000, p. 651)

"Graffiti is a symbol of poverty and hopelessness"

(Adult member of The Philadelphia Anti-Graffiti Network)

(http://www.americanpromise.com/ap4315.htm)

When discussing graffiti, a disconnect exists between youth and adults. As exemplified by the above quotes, young people see graffiti art as important and meaningful, yet most adults fail to see its import. Why is graffiti so attractive to youth? Is it the magnetism of being socially connected to a subculture group, the illegality of the action, recognition by others, or the learning about graffiti art itself that provides the motivation for adolescents to create this art outside of the classroom, or is it a combination of some or all of these elements?

Graffiti art (also known as aerosol art or spray-can art) is prevalent in most urban areas and is usually thought to be the creation of gangs of unsupervised youth. For the purpose of this chapter, graffiti is defined as work that is created by a person or a group of people, usually incorporates a nickname in the image, and is made using spray paint or marker. Graffiti art done by the individual tends to be smaller in size, usually completed very quickly—*tags* (nicknames made using marker or spray paint) and *throw-ups* (outlined tags quickly filled in with spray paint)—with larger pieces (commonly referred to as *masterpieces*) usually executed by a group of writers (a *crew*). The definition of graffiti art in this chapter will include artwork that is created in public spaces on buildings, walls, and mass transit, either authorized and/or unauthorized. For the purpose of this discussion the definition will also be extended to include graffiti created in personal notebooks (*piece books*) in the planning and preparation for graffiti writing on the streets. The adolescents I will be focusing on are high school–aged students (14–18-year-olds), but in some cases, a general discussion of graffiti art will occur that will transcend this age categorization. In these instances, I hope to explore a deeper understanding of the artistic and sociocultural learning processes that are action rather than age specific.

## Historical Perspectives on Graffiti Art

In the beginning there was the word: TAKI 183. A name. A number. And the start of something. Something that, despite the many obstacles and frustrations placed in front of it, has continued, even thrived, for over thirty years, into the new millennium. The genesis of a whole subculture, art form and industry, and, for many, a way of life. (Walmesley, 2005, p. 193)

The evolution of graffiti has covered centuries, but the creation of what we know as "traditional graffiti art" is a relatively new phenomenon. "Graffiti ("scratchings" from the Italian *graffiare*, "to scratch"; the singular is *graffito*) are a form of communication that is both personal and free of the everyday social restraints that normally prevent people from giving uninhibited reign to their thoughts" (Abel & Buckley, 1977, p. 5). Reisner (1971) suggests that graffiti has an ancient and honorable history: from Early Roman times, to the Middle Ages, to the World War II's "Kilroy Was Here," to the modern day public graffiti artists, the tradition of creating art and communicating in a public space continues. Formal graffiti art dates back to the late 1960s and early 1970s, and it was a 1971 article in the *New York Times* that brought the activity of tagging to the attention of the world (http://www.nograffiti.com/Files/history2.htm).

TAKI 183, an adolescent from Uptown Manhattan (Washington Heights), was a foot messenger in NYC and had plenty of opportunity to leave his mark on the streets. TAKI 183 was a nickname: a combination of his shortened real first name, Demetrius, and 183, the street on which he lived. It was believed that he was not the first graffiti writer or even the first king (the best and most prolific graffiti writer), but the first writer to be recognized outside of the newly formed subculture. Cornbread, a young person in Philadelphia, is also recognized as one of the initiators of graffiti. Spurred on by the *New York Times,* article tags from writers JULIO 204, FRANK 207, and JOE 136 started appearing on the streets (http://www.nograffiti.com/Files/history2.htm).

In the other boroughs of New York City, more writers had joined this graffiti-writing movement. The subway system was quickly recognized as a way for writers to connect with each other and gain exposure in all five boroughs (referred to as going *all city*). Writing started moving from the streets to the subways and quickly became competitive. At this early point, the writing consisted mostly of tags. It was the main goal of the writers to put up as many tags as they could in as many places as possible. The more they got their name seen, the more fame and recognition they would gain from their peers. The chance of getting caught was greater on active subway lines, and writers quickly realized that trains could be tagged more safely and efficiently when stopped in the train yards at night (http://www.nograffiti.com/Files/history2.htm).

At a certain point, the proliferation of tags became so commonplace and the walls so saturated that graffiti artists started looking for new ways to be noticed. Making one's tag unique was the first way to set oneself apart from the other writers. Different styles of writing (script and calligraphic) were developed and writers started enhancing their designs with flourishes, stars, arrows, and symbols.

Eventually, writers found that changing the style of tagging and writing was no longer enough to get noticed. The size of the tag increased and the "throw-up" was created. Writers found that the standard spray paint nozzle was too narrow for large letters. Artist ingenuity was engaged and writers experimented with caps from other aerosol products. Thus, the fat and skinny caps were created and they were used for quick fill-ins of larger letters and more precise outlining. Different types of lettering styles—3-D, block, leaning, softie, Wild Style, Bronx style (bubble letters), Brooklyn style (script with lots of flourishes and arrows), and Broadway style (long, slim letters)—were all invented to help the tags stand out uniquely from each other (Mailer, 1974). Masterpieces (large, colorfully elaborate pieces usually done by a group, or crew, of artists) were becoming more common. The people who were responsible for this graffiti art were adolescents looking to make their mark on society, looking for some fame by "getting up" in the city (Castleman, 1982).

## My Interest in Graffiti Art

I taught visual art and video production at the secondary level in a public high school in Northern California. While employed at the high school, I initiated some extracurricular art activities that took place after school and on the weekends and gained a personal interest in the study of young people who create art outside of the regular classroom. With a grant I obtained from a local community foundation in San Mateo, California, I started a comic book-making club, an art car group, and established an annual high school video festival.

During our hours together after school, students had more time to share their personal art-making philosophies with me than they did on regular school days. I was able to talk with them about their art ideas and their process of learning and inquiry through the arts. Informal conversations revealed that they looked forward to their out-of-school art-making activities and clubs, they appreciated the freedom they had to make whatever they wanted to, and they liked hanging out with individuals similar to themselves. Through my work with the students, I became aware of the idea that for many youth, creating art was not about getting a grade in school, but rather about having a place to express themselves. Themes that generally emerged in their work were: reflections on their lives; views of how they thought others saw them; personal topics such as their needs, hopes, desires, and beliefs; issues they were questioning; reactions to current events; memories of their past, or hopes for their future. In general, they liked to create art about themselves. Many times the tone of the piece was confused, violent, or tumultuous and the youth explored issues that some adults would characterize as risqué or problem behavior (i.e., sex, drugs, relationships, suicide). Since this art was created outside of the traditional school day, students felt comfortable taking on difficult imagery and working through personal issues without fear of chastisement. Most of the students said that art making was the one thing they looked forward to. One student even went so far as to tell me, "Art is the only thing worth living for. It's what I get up for in the morning" (T. Jones, personal communication, February 1997).

## Misconceptions about Youth-Generated Artwork

In some educational circles, youth are not seen as possessing the agency to think for themselves or as creators of culture. In fact, as Males (1996) argues, youth are considered a scapegoat generation and blamed for problems that are mostly created by adults. I believe that young people have voices that should be heard and actions that should be studied. Looking carefully at the choices they make, the subcultures in which they belong, and the activities that they prefer can provide meaningful links to youths' inside and outside lives.

Because adolescents spend a lot of time together, it is common to see them gathered in large groups and their dress, language, or attitude lead some community members to conclude that these groups of adolescents are in gangs or preoccupied with illegal activities. But, during my conversations with youth in California about their graffiti-making activities, the topic of gangs did not arise. Frequently mentioned, however, was the idea that the group of youth they hung out with to make graffiti (their *crew*) was considered to be an extended family, a closely knit group of friends. They looked out for each other and they gave each other artistic advice about their pieces. They would often show each other sketches in their notebooks and ask for feedback and suggestions.

Groups of graffiti writers are viewed by its members as a substitute family unit (Cooper & Chalfant, 1984). They are a group with a common artistic goal who do not have many expectations of each other, other than watching each others' backs. In fact, just as in a family, there seems to be a hierarchy of roles. A mentor or master writer will sometimes take on a student to "teach them the ropes." In some instances, the young writer will be expected to steal paint for the mentor (*racking the paint*). In exchange for the act, the mentor may give the student an outline in his/her notebook (*piece book*). This is the place where sketches are tried out with only a small percentage of the designs realized on the city streets. Almost like an initiation process or an ancient atelier practice, the underling will do errands and odd jobs for the teacher in exchange for artistic guidance.

Given these initiation rituals, graffiti has the reputation of being associated with gang activity. However, stories relating gangs and graffiti have been greatly exaggerated (Ferrell, 1996). In reality, only a small percentage of graffiti on the streets is done by gangs marking their territory or proclaiming their presence in a neighborhood. In fact, gang-related graffiti represents only about 20 percent of U.S. graffiti (Walsh, 1996, p. 11). Although many graffiti writers see themselves as part of a collective whole, it is a different kind of gang than we commonly hear about (e.g., the Crips, the Bloods, the Latin Kings). A graffiti gang or crew is a group of artists who look out for each other and provide a place where the individual is able to derive a sense of identity based on the belief of a larger group. The group gains momentum to create graffiti through the collective support of the graffiti writers in the neighborhood. "We're a gang that needs a sense of belonging and a sense of togetherness," says one graffiti writer, Rasta. "It's like a band. You get together and do your thing ... We're just all really tight and cool. It seems like we're close ... It's not like we're gangsters," (as cited in Ferrell, 1996, p. 37).

Authors Clay and Aquila, in a 1994 *Phi Delta Kappa* article, point out that schools and the general public have the tendency to get swept up in the sensationalizing of the gang topic. While they encourage teachers, educators, and parents to familiarize themselves with visual cues relating to gang activity, they caution that it is important to realize that trends can be merely fashion or style rather than indicators of gang involvement. Fashion styles derived directly from the jail cells (large baggy pants with no belts to hold them up and shoes with no laces), supported by the commercialization that capitalizes on youth culture, perpetuates the "gang" ideal. Indeed, graffiti, which was accompanied by the musical form of hip hop and the physical form of break dancing in the 1980s, has now been adapted for suburban and international audiences and conventionalized through marketing and advertising. The contemporary idea of the youth culture has transformed the once subculture into a commonplace ideal.

## The Benefits of Studying Graffiti Art in the Classroom

But, just what do adolescents learn from the act of creating art outside of the traditional classroom and could these actions translate into classroom learning? The husband and wife team of Romotsky and Romotsky (1975), a studio art professor and an English education professor, write about how teachers should understand the values of controversial achievements not normally thought to be appropriate for classroom. They argue these opportunities can offer a key educational device for communicating with students who periodically abandon hope of succeeding in the classroom. They write, "The kid may not be willing to show his skills in the classroom, but he may be acquiring intricate and demanding skills outside of school. These skills are evaluated by peers and have definite social and status values" (p. 13). The authors view the act of creating graffiti as an opportunity to teach non-graffiti writers the skill and artistic intention involved in creating the work.

In 1974, Romotsky and Romotsky explored the didactic possibilities for graffiti at the Downey Museum of Art in Downey, California. They were interested in graffiti art and they were "optimistic about its educational potential" (p. 14). The authors, along with the director of the museum, coordinated an exhibition of graffiti art, a graffiti writing demonstration, and a lecture, all focused on Los Angeles's Chicano graffiti. Three high school students were chosen to participate in the public demonstrations where they "adeptly spray painted gallery walls while onlookers gasped audibly at the intensity, skill and rapidity of the emerging wall coverings" (Romotsky & Romotsky, 1975, p. 14). A reporter from a local television station interviewed the adolescents who explained their process of art making to the audience. The event, "The Street Art Story" established a situation that encouraged an exchange between various segments of the community. The youth were given the opportunity to teach the onlookers about graffiti art, explaining what they do and how they do it. An outcome of this dialogue about graffiti art was a demystification of the process of making the art and the reasons behind its creation. As Romotsky and Romotsky argue, moving the graffiti from the street and into the gallery presented the public with "a context which allowed [them] to respond with comprehension" (p. 35).

Educational implications inherent in this type of art are unquestionably rich and multidimensional, for both the maker and the observer. The Romotskys (1975) suggest:

> To understand ... and even to appreciate the lettering skills devoted to their making is not to sponsor their presence on public walls nor to ignore their defacement implications. Since very real talents, however, are involved in street writing, learning about these graffiti from the youths who inscribe them seems sensible and rational. For when educators can learn more from street writers, then perhaps street writers canlearn more from educators. (p. 35)

The reciprocal learning that takes place in this scenario reflects the dialogical tenets of critical pedagogy. It is important to put aside preconceived notions of art and young people when engaging in a critical discussion about educative practices. The power inherent in the traditional schooling context is omnipotent but, given a strong commitment to diversity and equality, not impossible to challenge.

### A Class Debate: What is Art?

Starting with a simple debate about what constitutes art uncovers hidden assumptions and exposes deeply felt ideas about art. In order to challenge student ideas about the social construction of "art", teachers can follow up with questions such as: What is art? Who decides? Why are some art forms legitimate and others, such as graffiti, criminalized? Who stands to benefit from the criminalization of graffiti art? Asking students to think about where their ideas about art come from lends itself to a critique of representation. How do the media affect the public's perception of art? What is the media's role in presenting art as exclusive and academic? How does such a construction marginalize certain artists and help maintain the status quo?

Guiding the conversation to a discussion about the role of the museum and gallery in defining art is a perfect segue into talking about public art. Art created for display outside of the classrooms, museums, and galleries is known as *public art* and art that is present on the streets, walls, billboards, parks, or even on the sidewalks are all forms of visual communication in the public domain. Robinson, in his book *Soho Walls: Beyond Graffiti* (1990), refers to the streets as "public galleries" (p. 5). It can be argued that art found outside of galleries and on the streets is more accessible and democratic. Why, then, does public art rarely find its way into classrooms as a legitimate subject of study?

The tension between those who believe graffiti is art and those who believe graffiti is vandalism is still felt today; there are separate legions of committed believers on both sides. Much has been written about the topic and students can read articles written from both sides of the debate. Despite the association of graffiti with gang culture, proponents of the art form suggest graffiti creators are fine artists worthy of recognition. Mailer, for example, sees the making of graffiti akin to the great masters' creation of a painting, an art form to be taken seriously. When speaking of young perpetrators of the "crime" of graffiti who are sentenced to community service to clean the graffiti from city walls or subway trains he states, "(In) cleaning the cars, he had been obliged to erase the work of others. All proportions kept, it may in simple pain of heart have been not altogether unequal to condemning Cezanne to wipe out the works of Van Gogh" (Mailer, 1974, p. 44). In these words Mailer is comparing graffiti artists such as Taki 183 to Cezanne, or Julio 204 to Van Gogh. In his mind, asking these artists to paint over the work of another is incomprehensible. What might students make of such a comparison?

Regardless of the means of "getting up," traditional graffiti art has spanned four decades and continues to produce a dedicated legion of adolescents willing to risk their reputations, and sometimes their lives, in the creation of graffiti. Romotsky and Romotsky (1975) argue that young people who participate in the creation of graffiti are "vigorously committed to their task" (p. 12). As committed as youth are to creating graffiti, city authorities are to eradicating it, spending more than $150 million in New York City (Castleman, 1982, p. x) and "four billion dollars nationwide" (Walsh, 1996, p. 3) to remove it. What do students think of the amount of money spent on fighting graffiti art instead of finding a forum for young artists to express themselves?

Graffiti art is a sociocultural experience that holds unique opportunities for adolescents to express themselves; as some researchers suggested, the practice may provide positive ways in which to negotiate through adolescence. I expect that while some of these young people are not successful in regular school, they may exhibit a sophisticated command of the language (verbal and artistic) when used outside of the classroom. Participants seem to be fully cognizant of the social worlds in which they live as they create artwork, not ignorant of influence, but rather interpreting and reinterpreting it to meet their self- and group-identified goals. In essence, these young people are questioning the definition and roles of art in a personalized and meaningful way. Their art practice challenges students to think critically about what art is and what it is used for.

## Graffiti as a Critical Literacy Exercise

One must assume in going forward with this conversation that graffiti art is considered "art." In other words, that art done on the streets is worthy of consideration as "real" art. Marshall (2004) explains that "images in art are critical to deciphering and understanding culture because many of our cultural or social metaphors are investigated and revealed through the arts" (p. 65). Art images created by the public in an unmediated way, images that differ in form from gallery or museum exhibits, can provide clues to contemporary issues and culture.

Working with students to "read" cultural images through the study of signs and signifiers (see, semiotics) is an excellent way to bridge the inside/outside gap in classroom studies. Asking students to simply take into account what they see coming to and from school (looking all around to include items discarded on the ground, messages spray painted on the walls or trash cans, stickers, advertisements, billboards and banners posted on the streets, etc.) and recommending that they keep a written or visual journal can be the first step to making students more aware of the bombardment of images and items that they confront each day, leading to an exercise of critical decipherment, deconstruction, and then personal reconstruction.

Simply recording the items they see, helping them to decipher the messages, and challenging them to see who holds the power in the images is an important lesson for youth to understand. Through critical discussions, reflection, journal writing, and sketching, students can then move on to deconstruct the images with the help of critical literacy prompt questions such as the following: Who is represented in public spaces? Who is being left out? From whose perspective are these images being conveyed? Who is being silenced in these messages? How are men portrayed? How are women portrayed? How are young people portrayed? What kinds of things are being marketed? What is the message that these items are selling? In what ways do you agree or disagree with the intended messages? Then, through additional writing and art making, young people can create their own ads, images, commercials, graffiti art, and stories from issues of personal import or speak back to an image or message that they've been exposed to in their lives.

For example, Forbes (2006) in teaching at an urban public high school, engaged youth in a seven-week unit that examined issues that directly affected them and their neighborhoods. After many initial exercises and discussions about critical media literacy and art in public spaces, she taught them digital imaging skills and Photoshop software. Students then created digital billboards that spoke back to the communities by whom they were most oppressed. Students took on issues of racial profiling, unprotected sex, neighborhood gentrification, stereotyping, and cliques. Teaching through a critical pedagogical lens, as Forbes did, is a way to break down the misconceptions that surround our youth regarding their perceived inability to think deeply and act on topics that affect them.

## Studying Contemporary Artists and Themes

It is important for the youth to become proficient in reading cultural texts and to become more critically literate of that which surrounds them. Adbusters, a Canadian nonprofit social activist and antimedia campaign, is an excellent source for this educational goal. The organization works to reveal power structures inherent in popular media and often humorously redirects the message into the hands of the public by spoofing popular advertisements. Adbusters has a magazine, an activist ad agency, a media foundation, an associated Web site, and teacher lesson plans that directly confront organizations such as the fashion industry, tobacco companies, and fast food restaurants. They remake the ads to humorously and cleverly include facts and information ad agencies leave out. For instance, they took a Nike ad and recreated it to include facts about the sweatshop laborers who make the shoes; they spoofed a milk moustache ad by using the same layout, but introduced elements questioning the use of dairy, advocating instead environmentally friendly soymilk. Using ads the students are already familiar with, such as those Adbusters creates, is an excellent discussion starter and an important critical lesson to include in the classroom.

The *Art: 21—Art in the 21st Century* series is highly accessible to teachers via their Web site (www.pbs.org/art21) and provides excellent resources for the study of contemporary artists. Divided by theme, the series provides background on the artists and associated lesson plans and is accompanied by a book and a DVD. Studying issues surrounding the nature of graffiti art and public art in the contemporary sphere can help to extend the discussion of these forms beyond the simple "art versus crime" debate. For example, artists Margaret Kilgallen and Barry McGee provide excellent starting points for classroom content and graffiti. Both create contemporary art images in public spaces and come from a graffiti art tradition. Their quick and playful street art images have a distinctive style; they're usually site specific, figurative, and nostalgic in quality. Kilgallen and McGee also produce work for museums and galleries that sometimes includes found objects and discarded items that they incorporate into their graffiti-inspired paintings and installations. Golden (2001), writing about Kilgallen and McGee, explains that they "view graffiti as a means of contesting the creeping privatization of public space in American cities. They see all forms of street art as an alternative to the visual barrage of corporate advertising" (p. 32). Much of their artwork, completed on the streets and outside of the gallery or museum, questions accessibility and inclusion/exclusion. Working with these main ideas is an excellent discussion starter in the classroom. After looking at McGee's and Kilgallen's artwork, a teacher can ask the students to identify themes they recognized in the art pieces. Site specificity is an important part of their work and making reference to it, while discussing the visual nature and social issues inherent in the work, is an appropriate bridge into asking the students to share an instance when they have felt excluded (or included) in a situation. This then leads to the topic of access—that is, who is kept out of a certain place and who is let into it—while referencing back to McGee's and Kilgallen's artwork. The lesson and outcomes (be it in Art, English, or Social Studies) can be about the big idea of "access" and can be approached in a number of ways based on the specific subject area.

   Using artists—in this case, artists who thoughtfully challenge the discussion of graffiti, public space, and access—pays homage to the important life experiences that youth bring with them to the classroom. The idea of utilizing artists to discuss a main theme that then leads into personal student references is far different from the idea of an art teacher leading his or her students in an exercise to make their own graffiti tag or to decorate an abandoned car in a graffiti art style. Reproducing artwork that already exists, without discussing the larger social issues behind "how" or "why" it was personally significant for the artist at the time, does very little to teach students about a topic. Social commentary through the arts or writing as guided by a big idea goes deeper than mimicking a style. By making personal an idea that is explored through art and discussion, young people have an opportunity to ground their learning in their own lives.

## Conclusion: Learning Outside of School

Hull and Schultz (2002) discuss how out-of-school contexts and "out-of-school worlds," can be bridged through relevant pedagogy strategies. In the past 25 years, the word "literacy" has been extended to include "events, practices, activities, ideologies, discourses, and identities" (p. 32). It is no longer sufficient to talk about "literacy" in the traditional sense—alternative literacies are becoming common and educators are seeing the need to connect curriculum to students' lives. From an artistic development standpoint, using motivations that engage the student in a topic that relates to their own life and experiences is not new to some, but uncommon in traditional art classrooms. Many teachers are still stuck on teaching only the formal elements of design, art, and color and are either unwilling or unsure about how to include the students' voice in the lesson. Thinking about art teaching in a different way and using alternative teaching methods requires that we look into our students' lives and communities to identify connections that can be made in the classroom, while giving value to the contribution adolescents bring to their own education.

When adolescents feel like they are invisible, in a large classroom, for example, it makes sense that they would try to find recognition elsewhere. In my experience as an art teacher, youth have reported that art provides a forum in which to express oneself and it offers them the chance to be recognized by their peers. In the case of art created in public spaces, and in graffiti art, the act of writing your name around the city and gaining recognition by others seems like an important method of communication for marginalized youth.

Researchers have contributed greatly to the knowledge base we possess in the area of social psychology of graffiti art, and contemporary anthropologists have documented graffiti's colorful history. As Heath (2001) points out, there is a dire need for research that concentrates on the social interactions of peers and the pedagogical implications of learning outside of the traditional classroom. Moje (2000) gives us promising information as to the importance of graffiti in the lives of urban adolescents. Her findings suggest that youth use graffiti to claim their place in the world and to construct their identity using graffiti writings. And writers such as Mailer (1974) and the young artists I interviewed spoke of their public graffiti art practice as a means to make their surroundings more personalized and more beautiful. As Breitbart (1998) reminds us, "One of the clearest demarcations of power, wealth and influence in the urban landscape has always been the ability to invest one's living space with meaning—to literally occupy, define and decorate one's surroundings" (p. 306). Youth taking control of their built environment in the form of graffiti art allows them to do so in a colorful and bold way.

We have much to learn from our youth about engagement with art materials and the alternative methods of literacies they choose to employ during adolescence. The study of visual culture and the images that surround us on a daily basis can no longer be ignored within a classroom context (Freedman, 2003). As this chapter has revealed, there is a need for an updated model of in-school art education that holistically embraces and reflects youths' lived experiences in a personally significant way, something that is not regularly seen in most schools. The inclusion of visual culture, contemporary art, and artists who create outside of the traditionally canonized art world is an important and critical step in upgrading our current art education model. The practice of graffiti art, or a contemporary art practice that includes the rationale of the graffiti art teaching practices, may just be the blueprint for a revised model of principles and elements that positively acknowledges our youths' lived experiences both in and out of the classroom.

# References

Abel, E. L., & Buckley, B. E. (1977). *The handwriting on the wall: Toward a sociology and psychology of graffiti.* Westport, CT: Greenwood Press.

Breitbart, M. M. (1998). "Dana's mystical tunnel." Young people's designs for survival and change in the city. In T. Skelton & G. Valentine (Eds.). *Cool places: Geographies of youth cultures.* London: Routledge.

Cahan, S., & Kocur, Z. (Eds.) (1996). *Contemporary art and multicultural education.* New York: New Museum of Contemporary Art.

Castleman, C. (1982). *Getting up: Subway graffiti in New York.* Cambridge, MA: MIT Press.

Clay, D. A., & Aquila, F. D. (1994, September). Gangs and America's schools: "Spitting the lit"—fact or fad?. *Phi Delta Kappan, 76*(1): 65–66, 68.

Cooper, M., & Chalfant, H. (1984). *Subway art.* New York: Thames and Hudson.

Deiulio, A. M. (1978, April). Of adolescent cultures and subcultures. *Educational Leadership, 35*(7): 517–520.

Ferrell, J. (1996). *Crimes of style: Urban graffiti and the politics of criminality.* Boston: Northeastern University Press.

Forbes, R. (2006). *Becoming activists through art: Urban youth examining community issues through photography.* Unpublished master's thesis, School of the Art Institute of Chicago, Chicago, IL.

Freedman, K. (2003). *Teaching visual culture: Curriculum, aesthetics, and the social life of art.* New York: Teachers College Press.

Gaudelius, Y., & Speirs, P. (Eds.) (2002). *Contemporary issues in art education.* Upper Saddle River, NJ: Prentice Hall.

Golden, T. (2001). Place, considered. In *Art 21: Art in the 21st century.* New York: Harry N. Abrams, 20–65.

Gude, O. (2004, January). Postmodern principles: In search of a 21st century art education. *Art Education, 57*(1): 6–14.

Heath, S. B. (2001, October). Three's not a crowd: Plans, roles, and focus in the arts. *Educational Researcher, 30*(7): 10–17.

Hull, G., & Schultz, K. (Eds.) (2002). *School's out!: Bridging out-of-school literacies with classroom practice.* New York: Teachers College Press.

Mailer, N. (1974). *The faith of graffiti.* New York: Praeger Publishers.

Males, M. A. (1996). *The scapegoat generation: America's war on adolescents.* Monroe, ME: Common Courage Press.

Marshall, J. (2004). Metaphor in art, thought, and learning. In D. L. Smith-Shank (Ed.). *Semiotics and visual culture: Sights, signs, and significance.* Reston, VA: National Art Education Association.

Moje, E. B. (2000, June). To be part of the story: The literacy practices of gangsta adolescents. *Teachers College Record, 102*(3): 651–690.

Reisner, R. (1971). *Graffiti: Two thousand years of wall writing.* Chicago: Henry Regnery Company.

Robinson, D. (1990). *SoHo walls: Beyond graffiti.* New York: Thames and Hudson.

Romotsky, J., & Romotsky, S. (1975, September/October). Graffiti to learn by. *Children Today, 4*(5): 12–14.

Walmesley, J. E. (2005). In the beginning there was the word. In A. Rose & C. Strike (Eds.). *Beautiful losers: Contemporary art and street culture.* Cincinnati, OH: Iconoclast/D.A.P.

Walsh, M. (1996). *Graffito.* Berkeley, CA: North Atlantic Books.

Yokley, S. H. (1999, September). Embracing a critical pedagogy in art education. *Art Education, 52*(5) 18-24.

# Chapter 7

# What Color Was Joan of Arc's Hair?: Developing Critical Literacy through Historical Thinking Skills

*Jane Bolgatz and Kevin Colleary*

The cover of one children's book about Joan of Arc shows Joan as a demure maiden with a blond ponytail. Another book illustrates her as a fierce warrior in armor with closely cropped black hair. What color *was* Joan of Arc's hair?

How do we reconcile different depictions of Joan of Arc? Examining the various ways that Joan of Arc has been portrayed in images is the opening salvo Jane Bolgatz and Terry Kemme have used to teach high school students that there is no such thing as an unbiased portrayal of the past. In examining Joan of Arc, the teachers wanted students to learn how to examine sources critically, realizing that every author and artist is partial. Students were taught to "read" multiple genres (children's books, plays, historical accounts, movies) so that they could critique not just the texts given to them in schools, but the larger texts of the world around them, the texts of their everyday lives.

This chapter explores the teaching of a unit on Joan of Arc in a global studies class. We begin by describing the unit as it was taught. We then explore how we might have enhanced students' ability to carefully analyze multiple sources. We argue that good history teaching requires teaching critical historical thinking skills. We then explore how explicitly teaching historical thinking skills might dovetail with cultivating a more political and critical attitude. We posit that helping students enhance their critical literacy is vitally important in a social studies classroom and that it can be done even alongside the given pressures to conform to test-driven or "standards-based" curricula.

Why choose Joan of Arc? There are three reasons: the first is related to the teaching of history content, the second to the teaching of historical thinking skills, and the third to the teaching of critical literacy. First, the story of Joan of Arc serves as a lively vehicle to teach significant social, political, and military history required in most world history courses; second, because this story has been the source of so much art and writing, there is ample evidence to use to analyze the historical record, and such analysis is at the heart of learning historical thinking skills; third, Joan of Arc is a powerful symbol. It is important for students to understand how symbols are used, and not to be naively taken in by those who use them. A critical reading of the world demands that students can, for example, question the many people who have claimed Joan of Arc: How does one read *Transgender Warriors* (1996), in which Leslie Feinberg uses Joan of Arc as an example of a transgendered person, against *St. Joan of Arc: God's Soldier* (Wallace 2000), in which Sister Susan Helen Wallace holds her up as a warrior fighting for God? While not necessarily mutually exclusive, each of these different portrayals reflect the contemporary creator as much as, if not more than, the woman alive in the fifteenth century, and students should learn to be savvy about the ways that a historical figure—or any symbol—can be manipulated to support a particular message or cause. In a more overtly political context, for example, how does one read the current use of Joan of Arc as a symbol of traditional France used by the anti-immigrant, anti-Semitic, right wing National Front? In each case, certain people stand to gain—and others to lose—political and social power depending on how influential the message makers (spin doctors as they are sometimes called) are.

In teaching about Joan of Arc, the teachers asked students to question the author/creator of whatever media they were looking at. Who created the medium (monograph, historical fiction, play, movie, piece of art) and why? What is the agenda? What do the artistic representations of Joan of Arc tell us about the people who created them or the times in which they were created? While these questions were stated explicitly in the original unit, in hindsight, we realized that we did not give students clear guidelines for answering them. Moreover, although in the final assessment we asked students to consider the issue of power in society today, we did not clearly help students make the leap from addressing issues of power in the writing of history to tackling issues of power in society at large.

In this chapter, we model how students could examine primary sources from Joan of Arc's trials and secondary sources such as sculptures, paintings, plays, movies, and children's literature using the skills of a historian. Historical thinking skills, we will argue, will give students concrete ways to critically examine a variety of texts. They might then be asked to examine the impact of those texts and their uses at the societal level: Who benefits from these portrayals? Who is silenced in history? What is the social and political agenda of the writer? How has history been socially constructed to maintain the status quo?

## Critical Literacy

As many writers have suggested, it is important for students to be able to both, as Freire writes, read the word and the world. Nothing that we read is politically neutral. If, as teachers, we want students to be able to work for a more equitable society, then we need to teach them to be able to read the various texts in our schools and their out-of-school lives, to understand how these texts shape and are shaped by power relations in society. How, as Cynthia Lewis (2007) and others ask, do texts position readers and readers position texts? And how are texts positioned within sociopolitical contexts?

Critical literacy includes the skills we teach in order to foster political awareness and change in our students. Students who are critically literate challenge texts to discover and critique relationships of power in society. As other authors in this volume have written, critical literacy is a necessary component of any transformative education system. Our goal in this chapter is not so much to discuss critical literacy per se as to argue that using the skills of the historian would enhance critical literacy and hence are a necessary component of the process of growing into a critically literate citizen.

## The Joan of Arc Unit

To open a study of medieval Europe in our high school world history class, we introduced our focus project: putting Joan of Arc on trial. We wrote on the board:

> Joan of Arc was a 19-year-old French peasant girl who was put on trial in 1431 for more than 60 "crimes." After months of questioning, she was burned at the stake. What did she do? Why was she put on trial? What were the charges? Was she guilty of the charges? Of anything? What do *you* think of Joan of Arc?

After a brief discussion of their impressions, the class then created a list of "what we knew" about Joan of Arc. Some had a clear idea of who she was, gleaned from storybooks, movies, or other popular sources. We asked them to consider, as we studied the history, why we still talk about Joan of Arc. How has she been used as a symbol different from or similar to the history we will learn?

The first activity was to have the students examine a variety of children's books in order to try and answer the question "What color was Joan of Arc's hair?" What they found, of course, was a wide variety of images and descriptions of Joan, including her hair. In the children's books we examined, her hair was blond, red, black, and brown. This opened the discussion (connected to our year-long question "How do we know what we know?") about what was the "real" or "true" answer to the question about Joan's hair color. Students wondered about who did the illustrations in the books, what their purposes or directions were, and they also wondered where the illustrators got their information. This was an excellent segue into a discussion on multiple sources and the beginnings of our introduction to historical thinking skills.

We gave the students three charges for the week and a half ahead of us: (1) examine as much background as we could find on the historical period, (2) specifically study Joan and try to recreate her trial in order to better understand what happened to this young fifteenth-century French woman, and (3) answer the questions "Is she guilty? If so, of what? And why?" We began with readings, exposition, and class discussion from standard textbooks and articles the teachers had researched on standards-based topics including feudalism, medieval society, French society in the fifteenth century, the Hundred Years' War, the role of the church and the role of women. We then began to examine more closely the questions surrounding the story of Joan of Arc.

The next step was to begin an investigation of the charges that had been laid out against Joan. The charges included practicing witchcraft, dressing as a man, going against the authority of the church, and being a heretic and schismatic. We discussed these charges and their relationship to our previous study of the period ("dressing as a man" makes sense only in the context of the role of women in fifteenth-century France). The students were then divided into two large groups—one representing "the prosecution" and the other representing "the defense." These groups were then further broken down into threesomes who would concentrate on a particular person in history such as the Dauphin of France or the Earl of Warwick.

Each group was then given a variety of sources to gather evidence to prepare for their role in the trial. Giving students several sources served two purposes. First they provided differing versions and explanations of the historical people and events. A challenge was issued to each group. While researching and mining their data, they must also be responsible for answering the following questions: Is there a "true story"? Why do different historians and writers paint such different pictures? How do you decide which version to believe? We continually reminded students that while researching, they needed to question the author. By offering them a variety of sources, we were hopeful that they would come to discover that there are many versions of history.

In addition, we knew that our students had varying reading levels and that different students would be able to comprehend different sources. For some of the students who had difficulty with reading, the illustrated children's books were very helpful in preparing them to understand the story. Other students could handle more difficult texts such as Anderson and Zinsser's history of European women (2000/1988). For students who were more attuned to oral language, reading aloud from a section of George Bernard Shaw's *Saint Joan* and watching a movie version of the trial were useful ways to engage the information. These resources, in addition to the trial transcripts, gave them the data they needed to prepare for a mock trial of Joan of Arc. They were to prepare for their roles by gathering specific evidence supporting each charge against "the Maid."

After four class periods of research, note taking, and discussions, the trial was scheduled. Representatives from each group were assigned to make their arguments, and we invited other teachers to act as judges. Each judge had a rubric to use while listening to the arguments. As each charge was discussed, the students made their points about the charge. The judges marked how clearly the charge had been addressed, how much specific evidence had been used, and whether or not the students cited their sources.

## Assessing Students' Understanding

We created a leveled assessment that the students took at unit's end. This assessment not only checked their understanding about facts and information regarding medieval France and Joan of Arc's story but also included questions asking students to reflect on the process of studying history (how knowledge is constructed). Students were asked to describe their understandings of both the historical period and, as in the question below, how that historical period had been presented to them by various sources:

*When you were doing research for the trial, you saw how historians sometimes painted different and contradictory pictures of history.*

    *a.    Give an example of two different versions of the same event in the Joan story.*

    *b.    Why do you think the historians give different versions?*

    *c.    How do you decide which version of a story to believe?*

The assessment also tested student's abilities to apply critical literacy skills to new contexts and current historical realities, as seen in the following question:

*In our society today there are people or institutions that wield a great deal of power. Use specific evidence to back up your answers to the following questions:*

    *a.    In terms of having authority or power, what or whom could you compare from the present to the Catholic Church in the Middle Ages?*

    *b.    What beliefs do these people or institutions encourage the American public to have? How?*

    *c.    Who benefits and who suffers as a result of this belief system?*

    *d.    How is the use of power in society today similar to and different from Joan of Arc's time?*

Because students were able to demonstrate an understanding of the basic historical content as demanded by the global studies standards as well as to reflect on it critically, we considered the unit to be successful: students learned that there were several versions of history. Still, we wondered if we couldn't have been more helpful in teaching them specific skills for examining evidence. In the following sections, we describe what we have learned about teaching critical historical thinking skills and then explain how these might be incorporated in teaching the Joan of Arc unit.

## Historical Thinking Skills

According to the National Standards for Basic History Education, to think historically students need to consider multiple perspectives on events and to incorporate such skills as comprehension, analysis, and interpretation (1996). They must also grapple with the bias of the person behind the documents they read and the artifacts they view. Banks (1996) argues that students should examine how knowledge is constructed and that this understanding of knowledge construction is a critical dimension of multicultural education and critical pedagogy. Barton and Levstik (2004) have done extensive research on the ways that students approach history and how their historical thinking is developed and expanded through history education.

Historical thinking involves specific skills that can be taught to students. As Wineburg (2001) and Monte-Sano (2006) delineate, students can learn the skills of *sourcing* (figuring out who wrote a document or created an artifact and describing the possible impact the position of that person makes), *contextualizing* (situating a text in time and place), and *corroborating* (cross-reading and comparing often conflicting sources of information). After careful close reading of texts, students can come up with historical interpretations or arguments supported by evidence.

| Historical thinking skill | Questions to ask of each text |
|---|---|
| Sourcing | Who wrote/created the piece? What was the author's role in the events described? What purpose was behind the writing? For whom was the text intended? What agenda could the author have had? |
| Contextualizing | When and where was it written or created? What was happening at the time and place it was made? |
| Corroborating | How do the pieces compare to one another? Do they all agree? What do they not agree about? What details are included and left out of the various pieces? In particular, how do the secondary documents compare to the primary documents? |

In reflecting on the unit on Joan of Arc, we realized that we may be able to use the heuristics of sourcing, contextualizing, and corroborating to give students specific tools to analyze the texts they were reading and viewing. In the next section we describe how that may have happened.

## Examining the Evidence: Developing a Critical Historical Literacy

In preparing to put Joan of Arc on trial, students were already examining conflicting sources of information. Before they began researching in small groups, the teachers might model for students how they would use critical historical thinking skills in order to prepare their arguments about the evidence for the trial.

Below is an example we might use with students to explicitly teach the skills of sourcing, contextualizing, corroboration, and critical literacy. It uses a series of excerpts from three biographies on one very specific and important element of Joan's story: how she began to dress as a man.

> *One detail of her equipment might have been Jeanne's idea for her own safety, or it may have been first suggested by de Metz, in his fear of the ridicule that might fall upon him were he seen by his gay friends as the cavalier of the peasant maid in her shabby red frock. Jean (de Metz) certainly seems to have asked her if she would consent to ride in boy's dress, to which she readily agreed. Probably her own knowledge of the difficulties of the journey, and of her own ignorance of the art of riding, had already suggested the plan to her.* (Wilmot-Buxton 2004/1914, pp. 34–35)

> *Joan decided that it would be best if she dressed like a man. De Metz and de Poulengy agreed. In this way, looking like a court page, the 19 year-old wouldn't call any attention to herself and would be safer among the men. Joan cut her hair and slipped on the riding breeches, black cloak, woolen cap and soft leather boots the villagers had made for her.* (Wallace 2000, p. 39)

> *A practical man, the squire (de Metz) asked her if she expected to depart in the clothes she was wearing. She answered that she would prefer to wear men's clothes. He found among his servant's clothes something to dress her in: hose, jacket, and hat. Once she got back to the Le Royer house, Joan would find other apparel that the good folk of Vaucouleurs, now sympathetic to her cause, had made specifically for her: men's suits, hose, and all that was necessary, plus a horse worth about sixteen francs.* (Pernoud and Clin 1998, pp. 19–20)

> *"Is it God who commanded you to wear men's clothes?"*

> *"The clothes are a small matter, the least of things; and I did not take up men's clothes on the advice of this world. I neither put on these clothes nor did I do anything except by the commandment of God and his angels."* (Pernoud and Clin 1998, p. 114)

In order to help students learn the skill of corroboration, we could ask students to compare the four documents: What facts do the documents agree on? Where is there disagreement? Why might there be disagreement and how can we decide which version to consider most accurate? What further evidence would we like to be able to explore? If, as is often the case among historians, we do not have any more evidence, what other factors should we look at? What might be the author's agenda?

The last question leads us to examine the authors of the four accounts and to learn sourcing and contextualizing. Why might each author be interested in portraying Joan's wearing men's clothing in a particular way? This teaches students the skill of sourcing. We want students to interrogate the agenda of the historians and the purposes of even the recorder in the trial.

In addition, we could ask students to consider how the step of translation may have affected the documents they read. Both the trial transcript and the Pernoud book were originally written in French and then translated. In order for students to realize that subtle differences in meaning can get introduced when documents are translated, we might engage in a brief "translation" activity in which we ask pairs of students to take a section of a newspaper article about a current event and "translate" it for a variety of audiences. As we compare several of the translations, students can see how differently people in the same room can translate the exact same words. Translation, we want them to see, adds another layer of human involvement and text manipulation.

After modeling the historical thinking skills with the whole class, we could ask students to describe each of their sources, to describe the context of the document, to compare the document to others they encountered, and to note whether or not the document had been translated. Thus students would practice historical thinking skills and critical literacy throughout the research/preparation phase of the unit.

## End-of-Year Exercises: Joan through the Ages

Paintings and sculptures of Joan of Arc by artists over the past six centuries have portrayed Joan of Arc alternately as a delicate Renaissance maiden and a valiant woman warrior riding full tilt into battle. Throughout the history of film, stage, and television, she has been portrayed in a similar variety of ways by English, French, and American actresses. And there is even a recent incarnation of Joan of Arc as the heroine of a video game. Another way to extend the lessons attempted in the original unit would be a follow-up exercise asking students to examine several of the many visual representations of Joan that have been created down through the centuries. This exercise is a continuation of the historical thinking and is directed toward critical literacy goals of the unit. We might give students a wide variety of images (for an array of examples, see Warner 1981) and challenge them to explain the different "texts"—What do the various modes of presentation of Joan signify?

For each image presented, students would be asked to come up with theories explaining why Joan was presented or portrayed in the ways that she was and what purposes might have been served? We want students to look at the artistic representations as products of their times and creators. To do this, they would again look at the elements of sourcing and contexualizing that we had practiced earlier. For example, we might show students a postcard (e.g., "On the road to victory") depicting Joan of Arc as a mighty warrior in full armor on a white stallion. The picture was created in 1916. We can ask students to think about the context in which the portrait was made (in the middle of World War I when France was being devastated by war) and to conjecture how the source and the context impacted the making of the image.

Figure 1. A small sketch made by a recorder during her trial— the only extant visual of Joan.

The students' concern with Joan as a person had been greatly increased by their work on the mock trial. Having examined a variety of children's books, as well as the only extant visual of Joan (a small sketch made by a recorder during her trial, see Figure 1), they would likely be interested to see that so many artists, filmmakers, and others had treated Joan in so many different ways. Students might begin to understand that "reading the text" had a much broader definition than simply examining words on the page.

Finally, to explicitly link the new historical thinking skills with the habits of critical literacy, we might ask students to consider who benefits from each of the different portrayals of Joan of Arc. How do the representations position us as viewers, readers, and political beings? What is absent? And beyond corroborating, can we think about social action of some kind? As a final activity, for example, students might find ways to represent Joan of Arc or another popular symbol in order to challenge the positioning that has occurred thus far or to fill a void that has been left. In what ways can they as artists, authors, or filmmakers, or through other avenues of communication (graffiti, cartooning, rapping, and so on), disrupt an inequitable formulation of a current event or symbol? How might they "rewrite" a symbol in order to "rewrite the world"?

## Conclusion

There is much unknowable about the past, but a historian's job is to make arguments grounded in their reading of the available evidence, taking into account the particularities of that evidence. History teachers need to help students to be critical as good historians so that they can draw their own conclusions. Good teaching of social studies is, then, by definition, critical.

In schools, teachers are often so concerned with covering the required topics that students rarely construct historical interpretations of their own. Learning how historians actually construct accounts allows students to see that each writing of history is biased and, therefore, open to further debate. By examining various sources of evidence themselves, they can realize that the telling of history—and of current events—is always a construction (Bolgatz in press), which is an important part of the work of critical literacy.

This chapter describes a unit on Joan of Arc as an avenue through which social studies students can learn required content about medieval Europe as they question how historians come to conclusions and how we can make thoughtful decisions about sources. Teaching historical thinking skills, which are an integral part of social studies instruction, is a useful tool through which to teach critical literacy, particularly in school contexts where teachers are required to cover specific content. In this unit students "covered" the Middle Ages by addressing the specific charges leveled against Joan of Arc. They would not have been able to carry out their roles as prosecution and defense in the trial if they had not had a clear understanding of the social and economic structure of feudalism, the role of the Catholic Church, the Hundred Years War, and even the more abstract ideas such as rising nationalism. At the same time, they examined a variety of sources to see that history is written by people who have various ideas about the past and the present, and whose ideas can be critiqued.

There is abundant evidence about Joan of Arc's life from her trial in 1431 and retrial twenty-four years later, both of which are meticulously recorded.

Yet, as with any historical figure or event, there is nonetheless a great deal of ambiguity about who Joan of Arc was, what happened during her life, and what she might mean to us today. Because she is such a compelling figure (written about by everyone from Mark Twain to the makers of the television show *Joan of Arcadia*), her story provides rich material through which we can help students learn to critically read history and art. As Marina Warner writes:

> In the transformation of [Joan of Arc's] body, and in the different emphases of different times, we have a diviner's cup, which reflects on the surface of the water the image that the petitioner wishes to see, its limits and extensions drawn, as in all magic operations of this kind, according to the known quantities shared between diviner and petitioner.

Rather than be fooled by the magicians of spin in the texts all around them, students can learn specific historical thinking skills so that they can read texts critically. They can understand that all texts are constructed by particular creators who live in particular times and places, and that one way to come to one's own conclusion is to question the authors (sourcing), understand the circumstances of their creation (contextualizing), and compare texts against each other (corroborating).

As Allan Luke (http://wwwfp.education.tas.gov.au/English/critlit.htm) argued, just as "literacy ... is as much about ideologies, identities and values as it is about codes and skills," so too is history as much about historiography as it is about facts and dates. All students deserve to learn the valuable tools by which they can challenge, question, and critique what is offered to them as history. The skills of historical thinking offer an avenue through which they can become critically literate citizens.

# References

(1996). *National standards for history.* Los Angeles, National Center for History in the School

Anderson, B. and J. P. Zinsser (2000/1988). *A history of their own: Women in Europe from prehistory to the present.* New York: Oxford University Press.

Banks, J. A. (1996). Transformative knowledge, curriculum reform, and action. *Multicultural education, transformative knowledge, and action: Historical and contemporary perspectives.* New York: Teachers College Press: 335–348.

Barton, K. and L. Levstik (2004). *Teaching history for the common good.* Mahwah, NJ: Lawrence Erlbaum Associates.

Bolgatz, J. (in press). "Exploring complexity within a "best story" of U. S. history: Kernels of inquiry in a 5th grade class." *International Journal of Social Education.*

Feinberg, L. (1996). *Transgender warriors: Making history from Joan of Arc to Dennis Rodman.* Boston: Beacon Press.

Lewis, C. (2007). Talk at Fordham Literacy Institute. New York, Fordham University.

Monte-Sano, C. (2006). Conference paper. *American Educational Research Association.* San Francisco.

Pernoud, R. and M. V. Clin (1998). *Joan of Arc: Her story.* New York: St. Martin's Press. (Translated into English by Jeremy duQuesnay Adams. Originally published in French, 1986.)

Wallace, S. H. F. (2000). *Saint Joan of Arc: God's soldier.* Boston: Pauline Books & Media.

Warner, M. (1981). *Joan of Arc: The image of female heroism.* Berkeley: University of California Press.

Wilmot-Buxton, E. M. (2000/1914). *The story of Joan of Arc.* Mineola, NY: Dover Publications.

Wineburg, S. (2001). *Historical thinking and other unnatural acts: Charting the future of teaching the past.* Philadelphia, PA: Temple University Press.

# Chapter 8

# Critical Literacy and Human Rights Issues: The *Increase the Peace* Model in the Content Area Classroom

*Bruce Castellano*

We know from years of research and pedagogy that students and teachers are highly motivated when they are mutually involved in creating their curriculum as one functioning unit. The question then follows: How do we best accomplish this collaborative effort that is all inclusive as well as academically sound and rewarding? My own experience has produced a methodology that has served my students and me well for a number of years. It combines interactive, hands-on constructive curriculum with a partnership model that also uses works of literature to define, deconstruct, and redefine the text through the lens of human rights issues.

As a high school English teacher for thirty-four years, I have worked with the full spectrum of the academic student population and have used an equally wide range of techniques to establish a working continuum in and out of the classroom. However, it wasn't until I established the *Increase the Peace*™ (ITP) program that I truly taught and learned the value of critical literacy and its immediate connection to human rights issues.

Giving a brief and efficient description of ITP is a difficult task for me since it has been an important part of my life since 1990; but here I go—ITP is a human rights/peace education program that trains students to teach their peers to accept difference and to reject/reduce prejudice and bullying. Students are taught to construct, write, produce, and present workshops/lessons/performances to all grade levels. Some of these activities include formal presentations, interactive games, panel presentations, skits, student-made videos, art works, and discussion forums. ITP also establishes mentoring/teaching connections with local, national, and international human rights organizations where students have the opportunity to interact and learn directly from advocates, activists, and victims of human rights offenses.

ITP can be established as an elective course, a K–12 program, or in some cases as an after-school club. Regardless of the educational vehicle being used, ITP is constructed by students for students and functions as a student-based program that requires a teacher/advisor/mentor only to establish and oversee its operation. The word "oversee" is a crucial one since the teacher's role is less dominant and more partnership-based than it might be in the traditional classroom. This becomes clear when the ITP teacher/advisor requests that the classroom teacher be not present when ITP is being presented in her/his class. The ITP advisor has the added responsibility of being a nonparticipating "invisible presence" but can be stationed just outside the classroom door and is never introduced.

Generally, the presenting ITP students are older than the participating class and it is always best if they are not known to them. Sometimes too much familiarity between presenters and participants can impact the tone of the workshop and alter the participants' interpretation and involvement.

In addition, the ITP teacher/advisor needs to establish the "comfort zone" of individuals involved so as not to present material that is in any way inappropriate for the participants or the ITP students. The factors for establishing a comfort zone include the chronological age of all students involved, as well as their various emotional, social, and academic levels. Also, a major consideration must be the level of comfort regarding the issues being addressed and how the workshop will impact the school, the classroom teacher, and the community.

The content, nature, and kinds of activities that are used in any given workshop are established based on the above criteria as well as the issues that have been indicated as crucial focal points for the workshop. These issues can range from human rights issues or problems that the classroom teacher has cited, such as racism, sexism, and homophobia to topics related directly to a specific content area.

ITP students can construct a practical, human rights curriculum that is directly related to a work of literature, event, or time period. The English class then becomes the perfect setting for ITP students to create a critical literacy model that is inspired by these topics. The range of literary works that are related to human rights issues is infinite. Works of literature that focus on race, gender, religion, and socioeconomics are the obvious examples; in addition, there are works that contain more subtle themes that evoke a social justice response for a closer examination. Current literature contains themes of ageism, body image, subcultures within an institution, and many others. There is much to be learned from these themes and there are many avenues for students to explore by using a work of literature to reveal truths, beliefs, and misconceptions about human nature, human behavior, and human rights.

To take a closer look at the connections between literary content and thematic human rights activities, I have included in this chapter a unit that incorporates the two. Teaching human rights issues by using a historical model is a reliable and fundamental way to go, since it teaches the relevance of the historical event while it gives the students and the teacher an opportunity for practical expression of the issues raised by that event. Creating this connection requires a structured time frame on the part of the teacher as well as some creative energy in order to construct a unit that allows students to explore the many aspects of human rights issues and offenses, and the historical factors behind these.

Often when students are presented with the task of creating their own materials for total class involvement, they are highly motivated. The teacher, of course, is responsible for structuring the focus of the materials as well as their purpose, audience, and rubric for evaluation. Students who are familiar with creating and presenting activities for a workshop should be assigned the jobs of captains of the production and facilitators of the presentation. Sharing and rotating jobs are crucial elements of the ITP program.

This component gives all students a chance to explore various learning modalities while it teaches fundamental lessons of fairness and sharing. Therefore, in the course of the unit, the various functions within the project should be taught by the "master" learners in the class so that by the completion of the unit, all students would have had the opportunity to be a master of at least one of the skills required in the unit. For example, if a student is a good activity writer, that student should also be showing/teaching others how to construct a text-based activity that will be successful for that segment of the work of literature, time period, etc. If another student is a master presenter, that student works with those students who wish to present and shares with them her/his skills, ideas, and experience.

There are fourteen jobs in the ITP program. Students who have been in the program for one semester have usually mastered several and are familiar with others. Students who have been with the program for a number of years of high school can function as full time trainers and teachers. The ITP teacher determines who has mastered the skill and who is novice; however, every student should be encouraged to try her/his hand at as many jobs as is possible, given time constraints. It is very important to be honest with students about this point. They need to know up front that creating a program based on the contents of a specific literary work requires everyone's adhering to an organized structure, yet there should be plenty of room for creativity within that structure.

ITP is still possible in schools that do not offer electives. I have worked with teachers to create a modified, self-contained ITP model in their classes when an established ITP-trained group is not available. The first step is to teach those students who are interested in learning various ITP techniques and skills. This may require some after-school or free or lunch time for all concerned early in the school year, but the results are extremely rewarding. Teaching a small group in one class often grows to the request for all classes to get involved. This can sometimes be daunting, but the results are well worth it. Don't forget to have students instruct students under your supervision. In addition, as mentioned earlier, the ITP program, when taught in the content area class, can be done only in a modified form, given the required curriculum demands of any grade level in any school. A direct result of installing ITP techniques in a content area class is that students will often choose to take the ITP elective or join the after-school club to increase their skills and to exercise their newfound abilities.

Another way to duplicate the ITP model in a Language Arts class is for the teacher to facilitate and present the activities and for some of the students to construct an interactive model while they are participating in the class. That way, students can learn the presentation techniques and be the facilitators on the next go-round when there is another opportunity to integrate human rights issues into the curriculum.

## Integrating Human Rights Issues into the Content Areas

There are various methods available to integrate human rights issues into any content-based curriculum. The three basic methods are as follows:

1. **Begin with the curriculum**—This method starts with an element of your curriculum and then establishes the human rights issues that are linked to that element. One can use a work of literature, a topic or time period, a culture study related to the work of literature, etc. The issues should be well integrated in the unit, reflect the times being

studied, and be relevant to contemporary times. Realistically, this method is used most frequently since often curriculum is well established and teachers may not have the flexibility to choose their own.

**2. Begin with the human rights issue**—This method starts with a specific human rights issue and connects appropriate curriculum to the issue. It also assumes that the teacher has more freedom to choose her/his curriculum. Issues such as racism, gender, slavery, anti-Semitism, etc. can be connected to various works of literature from different time periods and genres. A human rights–based method will have the advantage of a broad range of curriculum choices, with the teacher controlling that curriculum.

**3. Build a follow-up**—As an ongoing thread, this method establishes various human rights issues for a unit or semester, and content curriculum is built around these issues. It also has a focus for its structure, such as journalism or creative writing, with the unit or course taught through the human rights lens. Elective classes work well with this method.

## Applying ITP to *Night* in a Ninth Grade Classroom

What follows is one of the literary works that incorporates ITP techniques and establishes a student-based, critical literacy model using *Night* by Elie Wiesel. The work is familiar to many Language Arts classrooms and also lends itself extremely well to interdisciplinary units and projects. The unit that I constructed involved a ninth grade class that had the same English and Social Studies teachers. Both of these teachers requested that an ITP project be created since the Social Studies class was studying the Holocaust, while the English class was reading and studying *Night*. The ITP students who volunteered for this project were juniors and seniors and had the task of reading, (or in most cases re-reading) *Night* and attending both of the ninth grade classes for a full understanding of the project.

I provided the outer structure for the unit: the possible activities that ITP students could recreate or revise; the structured time in our ITP class for discussion, reflection, and choosing of options for the course of study; maintaining the contemporary connection to the original time period studied; providing visual materials for all students and teachers to view and study, such as the film *Confessions of a Hitler Youth*, and the culminating experience, a trip to the Nassau County Holocaust Center where all students participated in the "Adopt a Survivor" program. This full-day field trip experience involved five Holocaust survivors who shared their personal experiences with the ninth grade and ITP students. All students were divided into groups so that the ratio of student to survivor was small, providing one-on-one Q and A sessions in an intimate setting. The survivors' personal stories of the Holocaust were intended to remain with these students for life as testimony to the veracity of the genocide that is the central focus of Wiesel's work.

The unit proved to be successful because of its content, immediate connection to the students' lives, interactive workshops, older peer instruction and guidance, and, of course, immediate and personal contact with the survivors themselves. Some of the materials and concepts that the ITP students created for this unit were based on excerpts from their school text. These excerpts were used in the English class in various ways and the ITP students chose them as springboards for discussion and workshop presentations. The assignment in the ITP class was to take the various themes of *Night* and give them contemporary and practical application for the ninth grade students. Some of the materials, concepts, and directed questions were teacher-created content, and some evolved from class discussion.

ITP students brought their notes from the English and Social Studies classes to ITP elective class and the work began with the construction of the small and large group discussion questions, the interactive activities, and presentations. What follows are the creations from the ITP class for the ninth graders. These lessons and activities were conducted in both the English and Social Studies classes, as was appropriate, and all the ITP students who were involved in the project participated in their presentation. The ITP activities were spread throughout the unit, but I will identify them as ITP Day 1, 2, and 3.

## ITP Day 1

The ITP students decided to begin their first presentation with a quote directly from the text which created the central focus of *Night*:

> *"Never shall I forget that night, the first night in camp, which has turned my life into one long night, seven times cursed and seven times sealed. Never shall I forget that smoke. Never shall I forget the little faces of the children, whose bodies I saw turned into wreaths of smoke beneath a silent blue sky. Never shall I forget those flames which consumed my faith forever. Never shall I forget that nocturnal silence which deprived me, for all eternity, of the desire to live. Never shall I forget those moments which murdered my God and my soul and turned my dreams to dust. Never shall I forget these things, even if I am condemned to live as long as God Himself. Never."*

Elie Wiesel's statement evoked the desired effect and the ninth graders' response was clear: they connected to the anger that Wiesel expressed and became motivated to discuss the concept and origins of hate. The discussion led to how hate starts and what it can lead to when it goes unchecked. The ITP students constructed the statement below and distributed it to the ninth graders. Following a brief discussion of the topic of hate, students formed groups—with the ITP students facilitating a group each. In their groups, students responded to the questions regarding hate as it is discussed in the text and how it affects society today and touches their own lives.

*Hate can spread everywhere. It has been compared to a disease. Any group, religion, nation can become the target of hatred. Often no one knows how the hate began. It can start with one word. One word can create the hate that can lead to death.*

After reading the above statement, the ITP students asked the ninth graders the following questions and a student-led discussion ensued:

- How is hate described in the passages you have read so far in *Night?*

- What are the effects of hate on the characters in *Night?*

- What are some effects of hate on our society today? Do you see hate in your life? Community? School? Explain and give examples without giving names or identifying individuals.

As a visual motivator, an ITP art student created a poster that showed the "Pyramid of Hate." This is a simple illustration that shows the accelerating effects of hate, starting at the base level with "a word":

Murder/Suicide/Genocide

Physical Violence (Fighting/Assault)

Constant Threats (Harassment)

Exchange of Threats

Exchange of Words

A Word

As discussed in *Night*, the Nazis started their campaign with small incidents of hate that built gradually but eventually very quickly led to mass discrimination and genocide. The visual presentation proved to be very effective since it evoked a whole class discussion that compared the hate expressed in Wiesel's text with the hate and hate crimes that students see everyday of their lives. The presenters asked that the students volunteer examples from the entertainment media and the news and to give anonymous instances from their own lives for each of the steps on the escalating pyramid of hate. Their responses were immediate and frighteningly detailed.

The presenter explained that starting from the bottom of the poster we see "A Word" and asked, "Can anyone give an example of a hate word and explain what effect it can have on a person or a group?" The presenter continued with all six steps in the pyramid, asking for examples and effects. It was also pointed out that a situation can and often does escalate very quickly and steps can be skipped, sometimes from the first level right to the top. Students were then asked how this Pyramid of Hate can be stopped. What can we do if we are involved in or witness to these levels of hate taking place? If we are participating, how do we stop ourselves? Will eliminating certain words from our vocabulary make a difference and help to break the pyramid?

## ITP Day 2

ITP students were motivated to respond to the ninth graders questioning of why the Holocaust happened. The ninth graders had a hard time understanding why the Jews were singled out and why they did not "fight back" and rebel early on in the pyramid of hate that the Nazis created. Their Social Studies teacher explained the carefully constructed plan that the Nazis had executed and how it was a gradual process that began with the removal of basic rights of some citizens and the establishment of stereotypes, prejudices, and discrimination that grew over time. The ITP students decided to take it from there and create a discussion and workshop based on these concepts.

They began by first reviewing the words on the classroom's display board—"stereotypes, prejudices, and discrimination"—and led a discussion about how these terms manifest themselves in our society. The facilitators asked the students for specific examples from their own experience.

The second phase of the discussion responded directly to the ninth graders questioning: How did the Holocaust happen? Why did it happen? ITP students created and distributed the following as a handout:

*There is much to learn on this subject, but one element remains true: hate and prejudice begin when people are isolated and are seen only as a member of a specific group. Have you heard people use the expression: "Those people...".? That's one example of group isolation. If that group becomes targeted and labeled with negative myths and misinformation, the hate and prejudice can grow to active discrimination.*

*Any group can become that target, any group can fall victim to discrimination, persecution, and genocide.*

- How does Elie Wiesel make these points clear in *Night*?

- What are some of the myths and misinformation about the Jews that we come across in our readings of *Night*?

- Do people today still use misinformation, opinion, or prejudice to judge groups of people? Explain.

The facilitators then distributed an activity they created entitled "Impressions, Opinions, or Facts?" When I read the draft of the activity I told the ITP students that they needed to exercise particular care in presenting this activity since it could easily become a bashing session and obviously have the opposite effect of the one desired. The ITP students constructed strict rules for participation. They strongly cautioned the students to take the exercise seriously and to respond to these statements with information that came to them spontaneously. Laughing, snickering, and any behavior making light of the exercise were to be stopped immediately. To carefully monitor the behavior of the students participating, an ITP student worked with each group of no more than five ninth graders. While the students were encouraged to respond honestly, they were also told that this wasn't a time for joking and that rather it was a mature discussion of the origins of hate. They were also reminded of the "Pyramid of Hate" that they witnessed earlier in the unit and that these statements were clearly placed at the bottom of the pyramid but had the potential of leading to murder or genocide.

IMPRESSIONS, OPINIONS, OR FACTS?

Finish the phrases below to make complete sentences.

As you do this task, ask yourself the following:

Is the statement I wrote based on feelings, impressions, or opinions?

Is the statement I wrote based on facts that are real and can be proven?

Where did I learn this information?

Gay men are

Jewish people

People in wheelchairs

Wealthy people sometimes

Why do people over 65

Black people think

Teachers are so

A White woman usually

Men from Middle-Eastern countries

People in their teens don't

I think people who don't speak English

Large people are

Upon completing these statements, you will remain in groups to share your impressions, opinions, and facts. Remember to include in your discussion, where you may have learned these ideas or beliefs. How can these statements be harmful?

This exercise became the basis for class discussions that continued in both the English and the Social Studies classes. Apparently students were intrigued and some of them were quite upset by the immediate connection they made between the horrific events of the Holocaust and the basic stereotypes that they heard and made every day of their lives. The discussions continued and the ITP students followed up by having whole class discussions on why we create these stereotypes and how they lead to prejudices and discrimination. Some students shared that they had become advocates in their own homes; one student called himself "the bias police" because he had become so sensitized to the power of language and its effects on society.

## ITP Day 3

I showed the ITP class a 1993 video interview of Elie Wiesel. The interview covered a broad spectrum of ideas pertaining to the Holocaust and to Wiesel's life, but the students were particularly interested in a segment that focused on human indifference. After all the work they had done with the concept of hate and its impact on society, one quote from the film caused them to reflect on a different issue, one they had witnessed in the ninth grade class they were teaching, and one that had been a sore point for them for some time. They decided to tackle the concept of human indifference. The ITP students commented that some of the ninth graders seemed unmoved and apathetic to some of the issues and activities that were discussed and presented. They decided to present real and current examples of hate that existed in their community and involve the students in the process.

The panel presentation was a workshop activity that ITP students had worked on and utilized in other class settings. This very personal and very real workshop seemed to be the right one to accomplish their goals. They wanted to express that apathy and indifference existed in our society and also in the class they were teaching and mentoring for weeks, and that one of the best ways to overcome this indifference was to examine real human rights violations with the victims who experienced them. They also noted that the activity would be most effective if the victims were in the same age group as the students and the violations were ones that they witness on a daily basis. As one student put it, "This activity needs to be 'in your face'; it has to make them think."

The panel presentation became a complex and large project; in fact, it took on a life of its own but proved to be worth the effort and time. I taught the ITP students the skills of interviewing and the basics of Q and A that were necessary to begin the process. Students then began to seek out other students (some of them ITP members, some not) who had experienced human rights violations or abuses and were willing to talk about them to the ninth graders. They also decided that including the ninth graders in the presentation was necessary to achieve their goals. A separate committee of ITP students was formed to find these individuals and work with them to create a presentation that would address the indifference that existed in some of the students in their charge.

My job, once again, was to create the external structure of this project. That is, I helped them create guidelines for the panel presentation, guided them in the construction of focused interview questions, and handled the logistics of the project, including specially written permission slips that were first approved by the school administration and then sent home with accompanying phone calls to the parents or guardians of the students who expressed an interest in presenting their brief stories of prejudice and victimization. These permission slips clearly stated the topic the student was to present and the presentation goals to the parents and asked their permission for their wards to make the presentation since some of the issues were sensitive and personal.

I also helped them construct guidelines for writing and presenting the presentation, paying particular attention to the role of each of the participants by first establishing the goals and objectives that each participant needed to establish prior to writing their stories. I constructed a template that has since been used as an excellent tool for a student-based presentation of true stories of prejudice or abuse. Here is the template. There are three groups who will work together as a team to present this workshop. The three groups are panel presenters, facilitators, and audience participants.

1.  Panel Presenters—There will be four to six panelists who will tell their true stories of victimization in a panel format before the class. Here are some guidelines you should follow: Keep your story brief and to the point. Your purpose is to convey the facts, so tell the story objectively, without trying to evoke sympathy from your audience. Tell it in an appropriate manner and with a serious tone. Be ready to answer any and all questions about your story, being prepared for possible criticism.

2.  Facilitators—There will be two facilitators who introduce the topics and the panelists, these facilitators should do the following: Remain objective throughout and let the audience express their views and opinions of the stories being told. Try to clarify a statement that an audience member has made that may not be clear, but don't interpret or change the meaning of the statement. Remember the "one voice" rule and keep the audience focused on the speaker by stopping private conversations that will distract, even though these discussions may be on the topic. Always enforce the discussion rule that the participants can criticize the issue but not the person. Have your summary prepared for each panelist and be sure to state it clearly at the end of the Q and A for each panelist.

3.  Audience Participants—There will be two or three audience participants. Sometimes a class needs to have guided questions from the audience to encourage other audience members to participate. If this is the case, the audience participants will ask questions that they have prepared to stimulate discussion or keep it on track. If the class is participating and involved with the presentation, please remain silent and let them interact. Remember this workshop is for them and they should be encouraged to express

their views and reactions to the panelists. Have your prepared questions ready for preview and be sure that all presenters and facilitators have copies of those questions.

At the start of day 3, the ITP members showed the brief video excerpt of Elie Wiesel's interview that illustrated his feelings about indifference and how it can be harmful. They also distributed a handout that quoted the video and listed some follow-up questions for discussion:

> *"I have devoted much time to exploring indifference. And, again, I came to a conclusion that the peril threatening humankind today is indifference, even more than hatred. There are more people who are indifferent than there are people who hate. Hate is an action. Hate takes time. Hate takes energy and even it demands sacrifices. Indifference is nothing, but indifference to hatred is encouraging hatred and is justifying hatred. So, what we must do—I mean your peers and mine—is fight indifference."*
> (Elie Wiesel, 1993. Video interview)

How would you define or describe indifference?

Do you agree with Wiesel's statement about indifference?

Why does he feel so strongly about indifference to hatred?

What are some examples of indifference that you remember from *Night?*

How did that indifference affect the characters' lives?

Where have you seen indifference to people in our own society?

Has this indifference had an impact on people involved in the situation? How? Describe the situation.

The panel presentation followed this discussion and students were required to write a journal entry in response to the presentation for their English class. The focus of the journal was to discuss (1) their own response to the situations that the panelists described, (2) the references to indifference or to the "silent bystanders" that the panelists made in their presentations, and (3) what their own reactions would be if they witnessed the incidents that were presented to them.

The coinciding follow-up lessons in the Social Studies class focused on the "Silent Nazis," people who were aware of the Holocaust and did nothing, and on "The Righteous," people who hid or in some way aided the Jews and other victims of the Holocaust.

Upon completing the reading of *Night* in their English class and the study of the Holocaust in Social Studies, the ninth grade students and the ITP students participated in the "Adopt a Survivor" program at the Holocaust

Center. Needless to say, the impact of this experience as a culminating activity to the unit was extremely powerful. Students were instructed by the survivors to take with them their personal life stories and gave each of them the specific charge to tell these stories so that the survivor and the events of the Holocaust will live on through these students. Everyone involved had a personal connection to history and to the memoir that Elie Wiesel carved from the horrific events that affected him and millions of others.

In the course of my years directing the *Increase the Peace* program, I have incorporated many human rights issues into the Language Arts curriculum. Teaching literacy through the human rights lens is a natural fit. Students are required to raise and think critically about sociopolitical issues addressed in texts in order to perform all the functions necessary to produce a successful project in the ITP program. When they are taught the essentials of the program, their approach to a work of literature, an event or time period in history, or any element of the curriculum becomes an automatic self-propelled, directed, and focused project addressing issues of inequity and social injustice.

We have approached issues such as sexism, racism, homophobia, slavery, ageism, socioeconomics, and others to bring to life the text and subtext of poetry, novels, short stories, and plays. But without question it is the memoirs, biographies, and autobiographies that produce the best results for the obvious reason: they are seen as "true" or "real" to the students and connect most easily to their own experiences with human rights issues and violations. I learned years ago that peer education and human rights education were meant for each other. When the elements of critical literacy are at the center of the mix, the results are truly dynamic.

## A Word of Caution

All of this comes with a word of caution. First, accept the fact that some adults are oblivious to human rights issues; some truly don't care to learn about them, and some become angry or defensive when the issues are brought up or discussed. When young adults are faced with these issues they are oftentimes reflecting what they have learned from their elders and, therefore, have not been previously educated in this area. I have found that this can bring extreme results. You will have students who are resistant at first, and others who are inspired and energized by their newly founded education. This latter group should be trained to be the peer leaders in your class in order to create a student-based program. Remember that many students are in unchartered waters when they are examining curriculum through the human rights lens.

Another piece of advice I give teachers is to not be discouraged when engaging students in this partnership model. After all, it is most likely new to them and is often a new experience for the teacher as well. Previously learned prejudices will emerge and students will often not recognize them as such. What I tell both teachers and students is that there is no magic wand for solving the human rights violations we encounter in life or literature. But students are often enlightened by their own discoveries.

Pre-service and new teachers will often be timid about attempting the hot-button issues that are a natural part of human rights education. This timidity is perfectly understandable, but not an excuse for avoiding the issues we encounter every day in our curriculum, our classrooms, and our daily lives. Establishing the correct comfort level, as previously discussed, is crucial, which often means helping students become comfortable with discomfort and disagreement. If a teacher places this methodology or these issues on the shelf until she/he is tenured or achieves a desired status in the school community, for sure they will remain on that shelf and never be employed by that teacher. The best advice is to gradually become comfortable with human rights issues, curriculum, methodology, and techniques to establish your own self-confidence and the confidence of your students.

Because of the *Increase the Peace* program, I have had the opportunity to work with a full spectrum of human rights organizations, agencies, and affiliations: advocates who work with various populations, law enforcement, social workers, activists who work with law makers, victims of rights abuses, reformed rights abusers, educators, and others. The consensus among these groups continues to be that education is the key element that creates the change that we are all working to achieve. As an educator, I learned early on that these issues should not be taught only in isolation. A Human Rights elective course is an excellent vehicle for high school students to learn about all the issues: local, national, and global, but the majority of the student population does not elect to take such a course. Teaching a Language Arts curriculum, or any curriculum for that matter, through the human rights lens creates a learning environment that redefines the curriculum and the issues being addressed but, most importantly, educates and empowers the teachers and the students involved.

# References

Wiesel, E. (2006). *Night.* New York: Hill and Wang.

# SECTION 3

# ENACTMENTS OF CRITICAL LITERACIES

# Chapter 9

# Resisting the White Gaze: Critical Literacy and Toni Morrison's *The Bluest Eye*

*Laraine Wallowitz*

### Background

In September 2006, I was hired by the Bard College Access and Preparedness Program to teach a literature course in a public high school in Harlem, New York. The program offers at-risk youth in New York City a four-credit college-level Humanities course taught by university faculty. The module includes six weeks in each of the following subjects: literature, writing, art history, history, philosophy, and math. Participants from my first school included high school seniors, juniors, and one sophomore, all of whom voluntarily applied to be part of the program for the intellectual stimulation and college experience. For six Fridays, I traveled to Harlem to be with the fifteen students, all of whom were African American, except for one Latino student.

We read Toni Morrison's novel *The Bluest Eye* (1994) and examined how literature is often crafted to challenge commonly held ideas about language, culture, and society. Her novel lends itself to critical inquiry due to its critique of racism, sexism, poverty, materialism, standards of beauty, and the cinema. Not only is the novel beautifully written, Morrison's prose is so vivid, she is able to implicate the reader in the destruction of one little girl and her dream to be "beautiful" as defined by white culture. It was Morrison's intent to involve the community in and outside the text in their own interrogation for the "smashing" of Pecola and for contributing "to her collapse" (p. 211). No reader can participate in the text without experiencing the devastating effects of racism on an innocent girl.

In preparing for the class, I was conscious of my positionality as a white woman and hoped that the students and I could have open and honest conversations about issues of race and gender; I was concerned that my race would silence the students. I was also worried that as the teacher—or in this case, as the visiting professor—students might assume I am the authority on the novel and the issues the book raises. How can a white teacher possibly understand the effects of the white media on identity to the same degree or in the same way as the black and Latino students? At the same time, as a critical pedagogue, I believe that educators should not avoid teaching texts by authors of different races, cultures, genders, religions, or sexualities; in essence, they should be willing to be *both* teacher and learner.

It is important to raise or confront sociopolitical issues in texts and not ignore controversial topics out of fear or discomfort. In fact, critical pedagogues argue that curriculum should be designed to move students out of their comfort zones; a pedagogy built on comfort and students' limited experiences privileges those already at home in the classroom and privileged in society. The same goes for teachers. In this case, I was the one moving out of my comfort zone. As the class progressed, the students began to feel secure enough to call me out on my whiteness. A couple of times I was asked, "I want to ask you something, but I don't want to offend you..." **On another occasion, in the beginning, when students expressed anger, others stried to assuage his anger and change the topic.** And on a couple of occasions, students stayed after class to talk how I personally felt about the racism pervasive in our culture. Instead of ignoring my race and theirs, we acknowledged our differences in a respectful way reminding ourselves that it is not "safer" to pretend we are all alike and that teachers should not "see" color.

Below I provide a small window into my attempt at applying the principles and practices of critical literacy using Toni Morrison's novel *The Bluest Eye* and other print and nonprint texts in order to problematize representations of "beauty" constructed by literature, advertising, music, and the media. What follows is by no means a faultless example. Upon reflection, there are many changes I would make; however, reflection and change are essential ingredients in any critical classroom and so is sharing our struggles and triumphs.

## The White Gaze

How can a fifty-two-year-old white immigrant storekeeper with the taste of potatoes and beer in his mouth, his mind honed on the doe-eyed Virgin Mary, his sensibilities blunted by a permanent awareness of loss, *see* a little black girl? (Morrison, 1994, p. 48) There is power in looking. (hooks, 1992, p. 115)

In order to understand the insidious effects of the white aesthetic on my students' self-image, I turned to the work of bell hooks and her critique of the "white gaze." hooks addresses the white gaze in her book *Black Looks: Race and Representation* (1992) showing how television and mainstream cinema have been used as a vehicle for white colonization and oppression. For black men, whose gaze was carefully controlled by white society, spectatorship in the white cinema was an act of rebellion. In the dark of the theater, black men "could 'look' at white womanhood without a structure of domination oversee- ing the gaze, interpreting, and punishing." Black women's experiences as spectators, however, were a practice in negation: "[B]lack female spectators have had to develop looking relations within a cinematic context that con- structs [their] presence as absence, that denies the 'body' of the black female so as to perpetuate white supremacy and with it a phallocentric spectatorship where the woman to be looked at and desired is 'white'" (p. 118). And although hooks maintains that today's films do not necessarily conform to this paradigm of black negation, I argue that many black entertainers today still embody the white aesthetic.

Despite the increasing presence of black celebrities, the white aesthetic still strongly defines beauty and worth in today's racist culture. Many of the contemporary black celebrities, such as Halle Berry, Mariah Carey, Beyonce, Vanessa Williams, are whitewashed to appeal to white audiences, thereby denying the black body. Famous black women are often anglicized on covers of magazines: their hair and skin lightened and curls straightened. A young girl's desire to attain whiter features resonates today. The novel is an appropri- ate springboard for examining whether the internalized surveyor in black youth is white as it was for Pecola Breedlove. If so, how does one resist the hegemonic white aesthetic ubiquitous in the media?

Morrison's novel, in which she investigates what happens to a young, black girl living under the white gaze of 1940s American society, was inspired by one of her black classmates who wished for blue eyes. Morrison wrote the novel to explore the roots and effects of racial self-loathing. She wondered, "Who told her [classmate]? Who made her feel that it was better to be a freak than what she was? Who looked at her and found her so wanting, so small a weight on the beauty scale?" Morrison's novel is an attempt to "peck away at the gaze that condemned her" (1994, p. 210). Like Morrison, I wondered how the white-controlled media affects the identity formation of adolescent black youth.

Similar to Mr. Yacobowski, the white storekeeper who cannot *see* Pecola, many of us cannot see what is directly in front of us, nor do we recognize the extent to which the white gaze affects our perceptions. Critical literacy helps make the invisible, visible, particularly the ways in which we are positioned by our gender, race, class, and sexuality. This kind of critical examination is never easy for anyone, especially students who have been schooled to passively receive knowledge and are not in the habit of questioning reality. Therefore, I find it helpful to begin any novel or discussion with the students' own experiences to make connections to whatever we will be examining by journaling at the beginning of each class. Journaling is an effective way to build writing stamina and fluency and to provide time for students to think through their ideas. In the first class, I asked students to free-write for five minutes about anything that they would want to change about their physical appearance. I was curious how a young group of African American youth would measure their own beauty against the white aesthetic of the media. Beginning a new class with such a personal writing assignment was risky, so I prefaced the task by explaining that they do not have to share if they are uncomfortable. This gave them permission to be honest with themselves without fear of embarrassment or judgment from classmates.

After about five minutes, I asked for volunteers. The first boy to participate wanted smaller lips; the second girl, "less nappy hair" (which she described as looking more "Hispanic"); the third, as did many others after her, wished for lighter skin. One black girl went as far as saying she plans to marry a Puerto Rican man so her children's skin will be lighter and hair straighter. A young Muslim girl confessed that she was planning on purchasing blue contacts to change the color of her brown eyes. Lighter or "better" skin dominated the discussion, as did smaller features (noses, behinds, lips, and feet). One student went as far as mumbling under her breath, "Sometimes I wish I was white." It is important in a critical literacy class to be honest in communicating one's observations. So, after the students shared their thoughts, I challenged them with a very controversial question, "So, you want to become whiter?"

There was silence. Then the room erupted with denials and justifications. They explained to me that they "just like straight hair" or they simply needed to "lose more weight" or have smaller feet to feel comfortable in their shoes. I was not surprised, as most students do not want to accept that they are influenced by cultural or societal forces. Resistance is often the first reaction from students when their worlds are called into question. It is important to continue the inquiry; I then asked students who they thought was beautiful. They listed Beyonce, Halle Berry, and Gabrielle Union. Seizing this opportunity to make a point, I pointed out how Beyonce's image in the media changed as she become more famous: Her hair became straighter, her skin lightened for magazine covers, and her body thinner, as it happens with many black stars under the white gaze of the media. How can they explain this phenomenon?

As students continued to debate, I introduced the questions "what is beauty?" and "Is beauty universal or culturally defined?" The class was split. Many students brought up in their arguments cultures in Africa that valorized larger women, while others thought that was "unhealthy." And still others quoted the adage, "beauty is in the eyes of the beholder." I then introduced pictures from various cultures around the world and throughout history of "beautiful" women. I included a picture of a bound foot in China, a Karen woman from Myanmar with her neck elongated by rings, and Renaissance women wearing grandiose wigs. I asked them, are these women beautiful? How has our concept of "beauty" changed over time and place? Is there a black aesthetic in American culture? How does it differ from a white aesthetic? And if beauty is a social and cultural construct, who defines what it means to be beautiful?

We spent a good remainder of our first class debating the answers to these questions before moving to the text of the novel. Our problematizing of beauty was an appropriate entry into discussion about Morrison's use of "Dick and Jane" to begin her story. After showing them an original primer, I introduced the concept of ideological indoctrination by comparing their responses to the journal prompt to the whitewashed world of Dick and Jane. I asked them to compare the world described in the primer to their lived realities in Harlem and the Bronx: Why would Morrison begin her novel with a children's primer? Why do you think primers were used to teach literacy at the beginning of the twentieth century? What effect might primers have on students of color, on urban students, on poor students? Why does Morrison play with the language of the primer? Can manipulating language be empowering, or perhaps an act of resistance? Here I took a moment to compare Morrison's choice with rap artists' stylistic preference for playing with language. I then quoted Adrienne Rich, "This is the oppressor's language, yet I need it to talk to you" (1971), and suggested that the language of rap is a form of resistance against the oppressor's language. Manipulating the English language was, in essence, a way of decolonizing the mind.

To end the first session, I read a familiar children's story, *Egyptian Cinderella,* so as to tie together our conversation about ideological indoctrination, hegemony, and the white aesthetic. Fairy tales act as primers for many American youth who grow up reading about beautiful, white princesses passively awaiting their prince charming. This supposedly multicultural text was particularly appropriate as all of the Egyptian characters have dark eyes and dark hair except for the blonde haired, green-eyed, "beautiful" Cinderella, sending the message that to be beautiful is to be blonde and white. I did not say anything to preface the reading; I was curious how the students would react. Angered by the blatant racism of the author and her obvious use of the "white gaze," the students (and I) were ready to understand and deconstruct Pecola's yearning for blue eyes.

## Internalizing the "White Gaze"

> Wherever it erupts, this Funk, they wipe it away; where it crusts, they dissolve it; wherever it drips, flowers, clings, they find it and fight it until it dies. They fight this battle all the way to the grave. The laugh that is a little too loud; the enunciation a little too round; the gesture a little too generous. They hold their behind in for fear of a sway too free; when they wear lipstick, they never cover the entire mouth for fear of lips too thick, and they worry, worry, worry about the edges of their hair. (Morrison, 1994, p. 83)

> We are not as white as we want to be. (hooks, 1991, p. 119)

Introduced in "Winter," the characters of Maureen Peale and Geraldine represent Morrison's critique of internalized racism. Both characters recognize the privileges that come with looking and acting "white" and, as a result, learned to hate all that was "black," all of the "Funk" that associated them with their culture: "That laugh that is a little too loud; the enunciation a little too round; the gesture a little too generous" (p. 83). Maureen Peale—with her yellow skin, her "[p]atent-leather shoes with buckles," "[f]luffy sweaters the color of lemon drops tucked into skirts with pleats so orderly," and "[b]rightly colored knee socks with white borders, a brown velvet coat trimmed in white rabbit fur, and a matching muff"—is granted the privileges that come with being white in a racist culture:

Black boys didn't trip her in the halls; white boys didn't stone her, white girls didn't suck their teeth when she was assigned to be their work partners; black girls stepped aside when she wanted to use the sink in the girls toilet, and their eyes genuflected under sliding lids. She never had to search for anybody to eat with in the cafeteria—they flocked to the table of her choice, where she opened fastidious lunches, shaming our jelly-stained bread with egg-salad sandwiches cut into four dainty squares, pink-frosted cupcakes, stocks of celery and carrots, proud, dark apples. She even bought and liked white milk. (pp. 62–63)

Like Maureen Peale, Geraldine learned self-contempt for her blackness and raised her son, Louis Junior, to distance himself from his culture and people. Allowed to play only with white children and not "niggers," Louis took out his anger and self-hate on those whom he perceived as weaker than himself—girls. He terrorized Pecola Breedlove and the dark, blue-eyed cat that received all of his mother's affections.

My students and I were intrigued by the difference between "colored" and "nigger" and understood Morrison when she wrote that the "line between colored and nigger was not always clear" (p. 87). The students felt pressure to "talk white" and "act white" in public to separate themselves from members of their community who identified with gang or "ghetto" culture. While many did not want to end up in a gang, they also did not want to be called out on "acting white." When I asked them what it meant to "act white," they defined it as talking "proper English" and doing well in school. "Niggers," they informed me, were loud on the subway and talked slang, making them look bad. One student aptly explained that he felt "damned if he did, and damned if he didn't" act like society expected him to. The students recognized the ways they were being positioned by the artificial constructs of race and class, feeling like their own oppressors, policing their behavior according to white standards. I brought up the current debate between Bill Cosby and other leaders in the black community who represented two sides of the assimilate or accommodate/separate debate. Is "acting white" (as they put it) the best way to succeed today or is it selling out to the "oppressor"? Is Cosby correct when he argues there is no place for black English in current society? Or should students recognize black vernacular as an organic outgrowth of American colonization of Africans, a resistant act of taking back the language that was once stolen from them?

Their opinions varied. Some felt that certain compromises had to be made in order to be successful as per the definitions of American society. Others felt they should not have to deny who they are, no matter what the cost. One student brought up "code switching," a phrase he had learned in his English class, and argued that there is a time and place for black vernacular English and all students should learn to switch their style of language depending on the situation. For example, in an interview for a job, the students should speak the language of those in power, but at home, they can speak how they wanted to. The students felt that they need to shift between identities and discourses in order to navigate their way through American society successfully. They recognized and identified with the tension within the African American community captured so powerfully by Morrison.

## Resisting the White Gaze

> She was never able, after her education in the movies, to look at a face and not assign it some category in the scale of absolute beauty, and the scale was one she had absorbed in full from the silver screen ... It was a really simple pleasure, but she learned all there was to love and all there was to hate. (Morrison, 1994, p. 122)

> Then there were those spectators whose gaze was that of desire and complicity. Assuming a posture of subordination, they submitted to cinema's capacity to seduce and betray. (hooks, 1991, p. 120)

In the third section of the novel, "Spring," the reader learns more about the life of Mrs. Breedlove, Pecola's mother, through the use of interior monologue. Altering between third person and first person narration, Morrison traces Mrs. Breedlove's life from the beginning in Mobile, Alabama; her courtship with Cholly Breedlove; and her relocation to Lorrain, Ohio, which led to loneliness and her escape to the movies. It is through Mrs. Breedlove's "education in the movies" that Morrison offers a critique of the media—a critique that is both profound and relevant today:

> Along with the idea of romantic love, she was introduced to another—physical beauty. Probably the most destructive ideas in the history of human thought. Both originated in envy, thrived in insecurity, and ended in disillusion. In equating physical beauty with virtue, she stripped her mind, bound it, and collected self-contempt by the heap. (p. 122)

It was there "in the dark" that Mrs. Breedlove learned to compare her reality to the sterilized, fictional world of Hollywood where "the flawed became whole, the blind sighted, and the lame and halt threw away their crutches" (p. 122). However, that "made coming home hard" (p. 123) for Mrs. Breedlove for, like her daughter Pecola, she learned to value white beauty and values. Thus, the movies create a false reality and her life becomes a constant disappointment.

Like Mrs. Breedlove, today's youth receive much of their "education in the movies" (p. 122). Therefore, I felt it was important to examine critically the effects of the media on our sense of reality. I began by asking students to journal about a time when they were disappointed. I needed to provide a few examples, as some students feel uncomfortable with such an open-ended assignment. The examples were meant to be generative and included the first day of high school; their first kiss; first boyfriend or girlfriend; first trip; or first party. After students shared their myriad disappointments, including first concert, first day of high school, first relationship, and first college visit, I asked them to what were they comparing their experiences? In other words, what was their initial expectation and from where did they get it. The students struggled at first, but soon we were swapping stories about a movie we saw, an episode of one of our favorite TV shows, or quoting from our favorite lyrics. We noticed the seminal role Hollywood plays in our conception of reality. We agreed that love is not like in the movies, and yet we expect it to be and are continually disappointed when a man does not send flowers or woo us with romantic gestures. High school was not one big party like it is on TV. With these unrealistic expectations in mind, how many more times will we be disappointed by life?

Inspired by a fascinating article by Thomas H. Fick (2000) entitled "Toni Morrison's 'Allegory of the Cave': Movies, Consumption, and Platonic Realism in *The Bluest Eye*," I introduced two pages from Plato's "Allegory of the Cave." The parable teaches how easily reality is manipulated and how quickly we are to accept that reality. I asked students to think about what connections they can make between the allegory and modern theatergoing. As Fick argues in this article, "Movies are the centrally destructive force in [*The Bluest Eye*] not only because of the values they present—but because of the way they present them: as flawless Archetypes above and outside the shadowy world of everyday life." The theater "reproduces the structure of Plato's allegory in terms appropriate of a technological and capitalist society" (p. 11); bound and shackled to a screen that is a reflection of a perfect world, reality is being manipulated by the media conglomerates that create an unrealistic ideal in the name of profit.

Using both Morrison and Plato as a springboard for reading the word and the world, I passed out advertisements and explained that it can be argued that the primary goal of advertising, like that of the movies, is to create a reality that objectifies women and promotes the white aesthetic. Advertisers are adept at exploiting the insecurities of women and men, thereby creating more uncertainty, anxiety, and disappointment. And since most products do not deliver on what they advertise, nor do they fill any emotional or psychological need, consumers continually search for new and improved ways to fill a void that was constructed by the advertising world in the first place. Mrs. Breedlove's initiation into the middle-class, consumer culture of the north led to increased insecurity and discomfort. Here she was introduced to high heels that only "aggravated her shuffle into a pronounced limp" and to a culture that told her that "her way of talking" (p. 118) was colloquial. To fit in, she tried to straighten her hair and make up her face. Instead of improving her quality of life, "her meanness got worse" (p. 123), she started to fight with Cholly over money and ultimately spent most of her days escaping into movies.

With this in mind, the students read their advertisements with a critical eye, looking for the ways in which the companies capitalized on the insecurities of men and women and employed the "white gaze." Students shared advertisements for antiwrinkle creams for the eyes, neck, arms, and legs; creams for the daytime with SPF; creams for nighttime without SPF; and creams that will create the look of having been in the sun all day without the damage. Others included teeth-whitening kits, diet programs, powders to help a woman look natural (natural defined in most cases as white), and even Botox (ironically), to express oneself. In order for a woman to look "naturally" beautiful, she must now buy six creams, toothpaste for killing germs, and a teeth-whitening kit. The students and I agreed that being "natural" meant looking white, something that is not only racist but also time consuming and expensive. More insidious, however, was the cycle of disappointment created by products that can never deliver on their promises, leaving consumers unsatisfied and ready to purchase the next miracle cream or diet guaranteeing "absolute" and "physical beauty" (Morrison, p. 122). In this sense, as Fick argued, we have become slaves to a consumer culture.

The students were outraged by the ways in which they were positioned and manipulated by the media. At the same time, they also felt confident that the media could be an avenue for social change, citing TV personalities such as Queen Latifah, Oprah, and Mo'Nique, all of whom resist the white aesthetic by publicly celebrating their curves. I mentioned the Dove commercials using "real" women as models in their advertisements. Together, we agreed that the media both reflected and fashioned a homogenized aesthetic, but we remained hopeful that resistant actors, singers, and producers (Beyond Beats and Rhymes; BET—Black Entertainment Television) can and will rewrite the cultural landscape.

## Disrupting the "White Gaze"

> I had only one desire: to dismember [white baby dolls]. To see of what it was made, to discover the dearness, to find the beauty, the desirability that had escaped me, but apparently only me...I fingered the face, wondering at the single-stroke eyebrows; picked at the pearly teeth stuck like two piano keys between red bowline lips. Traced the turned-up nose, poked the glassy blue eyeballs, twisted the yellow hair. I could not love it. But I could examine it to see what it was all the world said was lovable. (Morrison, 1994, pp. 20–21)

Near the end of our time together, we decided to "look among the garbage" and see "sunflowers" (Morrison, p. 206). Since students are not passive victims of racism, nor are they cultural dupes, we decided to challenge the ways in which we are all positioned by our cultures. I also discovered that my students were passionate about reading, writing, and performing poetry, so we decided to read poems by African Americans who resisted the white gaze through their craft. The students recommended Maya Angelou's "Phenomenal Woman," and then I searched the internet and found poems by African American poets. We devoted one class session to analyzing, reading, and performing the poems. First we used the poems as a lens though which to understand the novel, assigning the voices of the poems' speakers to empower characters in the novels. Then students got into groups and interpreted the poems through voice inflection and bodily movement, something at which they excelled as future performers and singers. Each student got up in front of the class and staged their own reading of the works, embodying the words of the strong black women who challenged society's attempts as circumscribing their power and beauty.

Next, we crafted our own pieces and I introduced poems with two voices (Romano, 2000). Poems with two voices are two stanzas of poetry written side by side, juxtaposing two voices or points of view written to highlight differences, tensions, or similarities between two ideas, peoples, books, etc. The poems are meant to be read aloud, as the voices are heard separately to emphasize differences and heard together at points of similarity. After providing my students examples from Tom Romano's book *Blending Genre, Altering Style*, the students went to work in pairs, using the novel as a vehicle for challenging society's construction of beauty. Their poems were powerful acts of resistance, talking back to the novel and society, often in Pecola's voice, rewriting the white aesthetic to include all people, all cultures. Even more moving was the performance of their pieces. As they stood in front of their classmates proud and empowered, the students' words transformed the class from one of passive transmission "to one of critical thinking, democratic resistance, and emancipation" (Kraver, 2007, p. 67).

Our act of resistance, subversion, and reconstruction was limited due to the nature of the course; however, in the six weeks' time we were together, we began to develop the "critical habits of mind" (Shor, 1992) that are necessary for resisting the word and the world. In the time we read the novel, we also discussed the craft of writing and Morrison's use of symbolism, character development, and setting as it arose from student observation and classroom discussion. On the very last day, I introduced the students, all of whom were singers, to ways in which *The Bluest Eye* celebrated blues music as a form of redemption for the characters in the novel and for the black community as a whole. The narrator, Claudia MacTeer, testified to the community's pain and complicity in the destruction of Pecola, lessons she learned from her mother who, herself, sang the blues to resist oppression. The students could relate to the ways in which music helps the singer transcend the pain of reality, "the hard times, and somebody-done-gone-and-left-me times," taking all of the "grief out of the words [leaving the singer] with a conviction that pain was not only endurable, it was sweet" (Morrison, 1994, p. 26). If I had had more time with the students, we would have written our own blues songs and performed them, using words as our weapon against oppression and rewriting our reality to celebrate all forms of beauty.

## Conclusion

As any teacher can attest, we never know how our teaching truly affects our students. We only hope that the conversations and habits of thinking transfer to their lives outside the classroom. On the last day of class, the young girl who, earlier in the semester, wanted blue eyes told me that she had decided against purchasing the blue contacts. Her small—or not so small—act of resistance illustrates the impact critical pedagogy can have on teachers' and students' lives. In my experience as a high school teacher, teaching critical literacy always led to the most fulfilling and enlightening teaching moments. Students stop their doodling and daydreaming, participate with passion and insight, stay after class to share thoughts unexpressed, and transfer their learning to their own lives outside the classroom in powerful ways.

The word most repeated by my students when I teach with critical literacy is "respect." The students feel "respected" when teachers do not "dumb-down" or decontextualize their teaching. Despite current thinking, today's students are not apathetic or indifferent—they are bored. The packaged curriculum does not challenge the students' thinking or prepare them for a successful life in the twenty-first century. And it is the students who benefit the most from critical literacy practices and hurt by "drill and kill," "chalk and talk," and "banking methods" so ubiquitous in poorer schools that do not receive high-quality instruction. It is not a teacher's job to use his/her class-room as a medium for maintaining traditional hierarchies and reifying stereo-types. However, when we mindlessly transmit standardized curriculum or teach to a state-mandated test that is exactly what we do.

# Note

Part of this chapter was published in *The England Association Reading Journal*, 43, (2), 36-42.

# References

Fick, T. H. (2000). Toni Morrison's "Allegory of the Cave": Movies, consumption, and platonic realism in *The bluest eye. Journal of the Midwest Modern Language Association, 22*(1), 11.

hooks, b.(1992). *Black looks: Race and representation.* Cambridge, MA: South End Press.

Kraver, J.R. (2007). Engendering gender equity: Using literature to teach and learn democracy. *English Journal, 96*(6), 67-73.

Morrison, T. (1994). *The bluest eye.* New York: Plume.

Plato. (1985). *The republic* (R.W. Sterling & W.C. Scott, Trans.). New York: W.W. Norton and Company (Original work publication date unknown).

Rich, A. (1971). *The will to change: Poems, 1968-1970.* New York: W. W. Norton and Company.

Romano, T. (2000). *Blending genre, altering style: Writing multigenre papers.* Portsmouth, NH: Boynton/Cook.

Shor, I. (1992). *Empowering education: Critical teaching for social change.* Chicago: University of Chicago Press.

# Chapter 10

# Beyond Tacos and Pizza: Critical Literacy in the World Language Classroom

*Rita Verma*

*While names, words, and language can be, and are, used to inspire us, to motivate us to humane acts, to liberate us, they can also be used to dehumanize human beings and to 'justify' their suppression and even their extermination.* —Haig Bosmajian

Educators of world languages have a unique opportunity to foster critical inquiry in their classrooms as they explore the intricacies of language. Critical literacy, however, is oftentimes absent in the world language classroom. While the assumption seems to be to place the burden of critical work of cultural understanding and competence on language educators, surprisingly many language educators do not engage in these dialogues with their students as they get caught up in memorizing and learning language as if it were a dead subject with no living, breathing history and culture. World language instructors tend to focus on the skill and drill of memorizing vocabulary and verb tenses, thus separating the life, history, and culture behind the words. Regrettably, educators miss valuable opportunities to engage in valuable critical discussions. For example, when asked, students oftentimes associate the canine mascot from Taco Bell with the Spanish language and culture. Deconstructing these notions and providing students with opportunities to critically understand their assumptions and ideas about cultural groups and language should be at the forefront of world language curriculum. Critical literacy should be integrated into the core curriculum and realized on a daily basis. When teachers make race, class, and gender explicit it becomes a critical intervention.

The cases that are presented in this chapter illustrate areas of critical inquiry that can be incorporated in the world language classroom. The main objectives of these critical inquiries are to encourage students to reflect on their individual biases and assumptions that may be racist, to analyze language as an oppressive force, and to humanize the language they are learning through putting a native voice to their daily readings and exercises.

## Why Critical Literacy in the World Language Classroom?

Language in all forms is central to human existence. Through language we are intimately connected and the words we speak echo our complex histories, personal identities, hopes and dreams. Knowledge of a language other than one's own is also an important element of liberal arts study. Currently, forty states in the United States mandate that second language study be offered in their core curriculum (Dutcher, 1995). Second language study can greatly enhance cultural understanding and awareness and is a necessary component in preparing students for a globally driven economy and society. The ability to communicate in a second language allows us to understand the hopes, dreams, and visions of others around the world. Joseph J. Rodgers, professor of Romance Languages, stated the following with regard to the importance of the change of attitude in the United States toward second language study:

> The study of foreign language by Americans, even if it stops short of functional mastery, can still be of great symbolic value, for it can represent a touch of humility, a touch of humanity, a reaching out towards other cultures in the hope of achieving some measure of understanding. Eventually, developing these attitudes may prove to be even more important than producing a few more specialists. (Rodgers & Hubbard, 1980, p. 12)

The purpose of this chapter, however, is not to engage in a debate about the value of second language study—but rather to argue for the ways the language classroom can become a site for empowerment and critical thought.

When embarking upon study of another culture and language, students need to be encouraged to recognize their own biases and assumptions about the world and engage in dialogues about social justice, and thus build bridges of understanding and empathy across different cultures and languages. Ira Shor (1999) states that:

> Critical literacy challenges the status quo in an effort to discover alternative paths for self and social development. This kind of literacy—words rethinking worlds, self dissenting in society—connects the political and the personal, the public and the private, the global and the local, the economic and the pedagogical, for rethinking our lives and for promoting justice in place of inequity. (p. 43)

Critical literacy, then, is an attitude toward history, as Kenneth Burke (1984) might have said, or a dream of a new society against the power now in power, as Paulo Freire proposed (Shor and Freire, 1987), or an insurrection of subjugated knowledges, in the ideas of Michel Foucault (1980), or a counter-hegemonic structure of feeling, as Raymond Williams (1977) theorized, or a multicultural resistance invented on the borders of crossing identities, as Gloria Anzaldua (1990) imagined, or language used against fitting unexceptionably into the status quo, as Adrienne Rich (1979) declared (Shor, 1999). Multiple discourses shape us in the neighborhood cultures we live in where the local and global come together. If language use is one social force constructing us, how can we teach oppositional discourses in the language classroom for the transformation of self and culture?

In this chapter, I will present case studies from secondary level Spanish classrooms in a public middle school in Long Island, New York. The student population is ethnically and socioeconomically diverse (46 percent Caucasian, 30 percent Latino, 14 percent African American, and 10 percent Asian). These case studies illustrate how prejudice and social justice, language and power, and critical analysis of the global political landscape become effectively integrated into the daily classroom curriculum and greatly enhance the students' lives in a positive way. These examples also demonstrate how the world language classroom can be used in powerful ways to foster serious discussions about the world that shapes us and how we can shape it.

## Unearthing Stereotypes and Assumptions

*Teacher: What comes to mind when you think about the Spanish language and culture?*

"*Spanish is tacos and taco bell, like yo quiero taco bell ... oh and tortilla chips too.*"

(7th grade student response)

"*Those illegals in our town that come from Mexico and won't learn English.*"

(8th grade student response)

The teacher posed the following question to her students at the beginning of every school year: "what comes to mind when you think about the Spanish language and culture?" The goal of this query was to unearth assumptions and stereotypes that students carried with them when entering the realm of second language learning and to invite students to situate what they were learning within their own lives and communities. Words (such as *illegals*) and ideas that they associated with certain imagery revealed many of their assumptions. Students tended to reiterate common negative beliefs about immigrants from Latin America—displaying the first world/third world binaries and with the immigrants clearly demarcated as "Other." Students expressed an unwarranted "fear" of "those immigrants" in their neighborhoods who they felt encroached upon their lives. In popular culture and images, the Spanish language and culture is grossly homogenized with little attempt to distinguish and to celebrate the rich diversity that exists in reality. Studies have shown that when Latinos are discussed in the media, they are often portrayed as being social deviants and/or criminals (Rodriguez, 1997). Another major stereotype of Latinos that the media perpetuates is that of "illegal" immigrants (Rodriguez, 1997). Latino journalist Rodriguez (1997) describes the portrayal in the following quote: "The preoccupation with immigration has contributed to the misperception that most—or at least many—Latinos are unauthorized immigrants" (p. 16). In fact, the irony of this portrayal is that undocumented immigrants make up less than 10 percent of the total Latino population.

The response the teacher received from her students revealed many derogatory and negative biases and assumptions about the Latino community. An introductory exercise such as this brought out the stereotypes, biases, and assumptions that the students held and set the platform for further discussion. The follow-up exercise then welcomed students to develop awareness about the messages that were received about other groups and how it is that groups become targeted and misrepresented by media and hegemonic forces. The teacher shared visual imagery of various groups that were loaded with stereotypes and assumptions about them. The reflection exercise required students to think about what messages existed behind these images, how they misrepresented groups, and further how someone might feel marginalized by them.

Students were given the following images to discern stereotypes and misconceptions.

Advertisement for Taco Bell

Advertisement for Frito Lay*

Advocacy for
misuse of mascots

Advertisement for
Aunt Jemima Pancakes

Abercrombie and Fitch t-shirt design
"Two Wongs Can Make It White"

Initial responses by students were as follows:

*I see the Indian sign for many school teams. It looks cool with the feather and the long hair—it seems to be something that people like a lot.*

(8th grade student response)

*We all eat pancakes and have seen Aunt Jemima. It is just a lady with an apron—why is that so bad? Maybe she really like pancakes.*

(6th grade student response)

*It is not offensive*

(8th grade student response)

*The dog in Taco Bell commercials is cute—He is funny. He shows up in different commercials and wears a cute hat and scarf. I don't think it is so bad to have him speak Spanish.*

(7th grade student response)

*I think these are really ... well ... funny. I don't think people really get upset*

(7th grade student response)

*I thought all Spanish people wore sombreros. They are big hats that shade you from the sun when you work in the gardens.*

(6th grade student response)

Student responses were initially celebratory and noncritical of the images and mimicked the generalized attitude in popular culture of accepting these as the norm. Statements such as "the dog is cute" and "all Spanish people wear sombreros" reiterated such feelings. The obvious assumption was that we all come from a common perspective and laughing at these images is acceptable. Prior to this activity, students were never asked to think about why they associated these ideas with the Spanish language and culture. So, students were invited to look once again and try to discern how people were objectified and turned into dehumanizing caricatures with the following queries.

- Do you think someone might find these images to be hurtful or to be misrepresentations of their cultures?

- Would you like for your culture or family to be represented with these images?

Students wrestled with this question for some time and struggled to come up with answers. Some of the responses were as follows:

*Well I don't want to be represented by something—I would like to choose how I would be represented in a TV or commercial. I personally would not pick a dog to represent me.*

(8th grade student response)

*I guess the frito lay bandit stealing chips is telling a message that is not fair.*

(7th grade student response)

*I know if you want to really hurt someone's feelings you can call them Aunt Jemima and that is really a mean thing to say.*

(8th grade student response)

*I think we need to ask different groups how they want to be represented.*

(7th grade student response)

*Why do we still have these types of commercials to sell products?*

(6th grade student response)

The practice of being critical about the media and discerning where racist stereotypes exist sparked a meaningful debate in the class. As students began to think critically about media representations and the words that they associated with immigrant groups, such as *illegals*, they started to think about how these assumptions were based on information that was coming from the media or others around them.

The teacher continued this lesson on dispelling myths and stereotypes throughout the school year in order to prompt students to engage in self-reflective practice. Linking the languages students speak with Arabic roots, for example, can be enlightening and powerfully pedagogic for youth in today's political climate. Throughout the school year, this particular class continued to engage in rich dialogue on issues of oppression and justice. Several students took the initiative to develop school-wide programs that would address issues of racism within the school community and further promote conflict resolution. Students put on assemblies on dispelling stereotypes and prejudice before the school and initiated peer mediation programs in various classrooms to resolve conflict creatively. The teacher felt that she had awakened awareness within her students that led them to become activists within the classroom and school.

What is taught in the language classroom can have a positive effect in interrupting stereotypes and assumptions about ethnic groups. Painting a more accurate picture of what is happening in the world and understanding the complexity of issues such as terrorism, immigration, and cultural difference are integral to achieving this goal. Yet the limited resources and prescriptive curriculum of most schools require educators to be creative in engaging students in such discussions. Values, cultural forms, and traditional knowledge that originate from Eurocentric perspective form "core knowledge" and create limitations in curriculum. The celebration of core knowledge also excludes the voices and experiences of many immigrant communities. For example, Cameron McCarthy states that the production and negative arrangements of the third world in textbooks draws on the media language, which is powerful and saturates popular culture both within the school and outside (McCarthy,

1997). Readings and lessons on Latin America are often excluded or form a minimal part of the curriculum. Moreover, there is a significant failure to disrupt emerging stereotypes. With the absence of an informative curriculum about the factual histories of peoples of the Middle East, Latin America, and South Asia, students in many ways become forced to "teach" fellow students about their ethnic backgrounds. For example, with regard to images of Native Americans in the media, Dr. Cornel Pewewardy (1998), a Comanche/Kiowa educator and activist, states:

> I believe that the hidden agenda behind Indian mascots and logos is about cultural, spiritual, and intellectual exploitation. It's an issue of power and control. These negative ethnic images are driven by those that want to define other ethnic groups and control their images. To me, power and control is the ability to make you believe that someone's truth is the absolute truth. Furthermore, it's the ability to define a reality and to get other people to affirm that reality as if it were their own. As long as such negative mascots and logos remain within the arena of school activities, both Indigenous and non-Indigenous children are learning to tolerate racism in schools. (p. 4)

Through thoughtful discussions, students can learn to deconstruct their own false assumptions and resist the stereotypical images they are bombarded with from the media.

## Language as an Oppressive Force: The Oppressor and the Oppressed

Does the language we speak oppress others? How? How can a language take away your identity or your way of communicating with the world? We speak about endangered species—but what about endangered languages? When Spanish was brought over from Spain, what were the languages that it took over? The topic of endangered languages and language as an oppressive force is frequently a novel concept for young language learners. When diminishing languages are likened to endangered species students seem to approach the question with a sense of curiosity and empathy. Students may not realize that the words that they attach to meanings and the expressions they use have deep international, historical, and political roots.

In the second case study, the instructor engaged students in a discussion on the colonization and oppression of the English language in the United States and of the Spanish language in Mexico and in Central and South America. The world language classroom also became a space to discuss issues such as language, power, and oppression.

Through experiential learning, students in an eighth grade Spanish class engaged in an activity on language as an oppressive force. Students were not formally introduced to the idea of language oppression prior to this activity in order to preserve the possibility of important realizations and frustrations that students would feel through the role playing that the activity involved. The teacher divided the class into two separate groups: The Oppressors and The Oppressed. As students entered the classroom, they were each handed a note card designating a role, either the Oppressor or the Oppressed. The tasks for the Oppressor group were as follows: Through speaking the English language backward—students were asked to alter the speaking habits of the Oppressed group. For example, in order to say "hello, how are you?" the Oppressor group would say *"olleh woh era uoy?"* The Oppressor group would send students out to the Oppressed group with information on the new language and instructions on how to speak it. The group was to prompt the Oppressed group to speak in a certain way in order to gain access to the classroom. The Oppressed group would not be allowed access to many things in the classroom unless they spoke the language of the Oppressor. The Oppressed group was told that they would be asked to speak the language of the other group. If students chose to do so, they could have access to certain things in class such as a desk, pencils, paper, and a snack. If they refused to speak the new language, students would be fined and remain on the other side of the room and would not be able to participate in class.

This activity was a very dynamic and powerful learning experience. By the end of the class period, there were two students who refused to learn the new language. The rest of the class, using the language of the Oppressor group, was seated in class with materials and a snack. The entire class wrote a reflection paper about how they felt about the roles they played in their respective groups. Some of the student responses included:

> *I did not feel comfortable speaking in a strange way and I don't think it is important for me to try to learn another language since I am happy the way I am.*

> *I could not pronounce the words and it didn't seem like a real language—so why should I waste my time to learn it. I know I was asked to stay out of class—but it is not fair.*

> *It was fun trying to get the other group to speak the new language. It was funny how they were struggling to pronounce the words.*

Students were then asked to ponder these questions the following day: Why do you think people are forced to speak the same language? What if the English language was replaced again and you were asked to learn something new? What does language say about you as a person? Is it your identity? Students reiterated the common public belief that the class would be better off if they all spoke the same language and that such linguistic homogeneity would mean that we could all understand each other and, consequently, all get along. A few students argued that having multiple languages would lead to a lack of communication and, therefore, lack of cultural understanding. The teacher then prompted the class into a discussion on the practical problems of getting everyone in any given community of speakers with more than one language to speak the same language. Students were invited to debate whether forcing a language would promote mutual understanding and respect, or have the opposite effect. Nest, students were introduced to the term *lingua franca* (a language adopted as a common language by speakers who do not share a common native language) and discussed the role of English as a global language. As students agreed that a lingua franca was useful, the teacher encouraged students to see the value of multiple languages as also useful as most people in the world speak more than one language.

The discussion also turned to the Spanish language. The teacher drew parallels between what the Oppressor group did in class with language assimilation to the Spanish colonialists with the indigenous peoples in Latin America and the French colonialists in African nations. The instructor spoke of the more than 6,900 languages in the world and that many may be in danger of disappearing in the next several decades. Students were presented with case studies of language communities that have been so ravaged by warfare or disease that the people and their language risk extinction.[1] Other languages are dying because parents are teaching their children English or French or Spanish for economic reasons. Ethnologues (lists of endangered languages in the world near extinct languages only spoken by elders[2]) were presented for students to research as were Indigenous languages and the bicultural identities of immigrant groups. Presenting students with readings by indigenous writers and recognizing indigenous languages such as Maya, Toltec and Quechua lead to an important realization for young learners. The students were now able to understand such important and sophisticated concepts as cultural denigration, place and displacement, and postcolonial identity.

## Linking Languages Globally

*"Arabs are all terrorists"*

*"I would never learn their language—why would I?"*

With the presence of Islamophobia in our schools and curriculum today, the world language educator can also play an important role in linking the words we speak to the Arabic language. Islamophobia is an unfounded fear of Islam and its followers (Van Driel, 2004), and this fear has extended to all things (regardless of any factual resemblance) that have to do with them. The following lesson provides a powerful learning opportunity for students in terms of their understanding of the intimate connections we all share and invites them to evaluate their biases and fears of the Islamic "Other." When students come to realize that many words they speak have their origins in Arabic, a language they associate with fear, it can become quite the "teachable moment."

Students explored the origin of words in the Spanish and French language that could be traced back to Arabic. Students were told that if they spoke either Spanish or English, they were probably speaking more Arabic than they thought. After Latin and English, Arabic is one of the major contributors of words to the Spanish language, and a large portion of English-Spanish cognates (words that the two language share) that don't come from Latin come from Arabic. For instance, The English word *magazine*, and the French word *magasin* come from the Spanish *almacén* and the Arabic *al-makhzan*, for "storehouse." Our sofa, and the Spanish *sofa* come from *suffa*, Turkish and Arabic for rug or divan. *Algebra* is Arabic for "the reduction" and came into European languages as part of the title of an Arab mathematical treatise. This opened up discussions on the ways languages are intimately tied to one another. Students were surprised to realize that the language and words they spoke had roots in Arabic. That the Arabic language contributed to many world languages gave students the opportunity to relate to the language and culture in a positive way, contrary to the very negative treatment of it in the media. During the school year, students also met with native speakers and worked with them collaboratively on international service learning projects.

This direct communication led to friendships and allowed the students to see and relate to the world through the words and ideas of another

## Conclusion

Possibilities for critical inquiry in the world language classrooms are endless. Media in the classroom can greatly enhance the learning experience and provide students with opportunities to open their mind to global dialogue. Through videoconferencing with international sites, students in the language classroom can engage in thoughtful dialogue with students from various nations. The United Nations provides many valuable programs for youth to open their minds to the world around them. A vibrant student-led conference is held every year at the UN Headquarters where students from around the globe gather to work on developing a plan of action to solve global problems such as poverty and the AIDS epidemic. Teachers from the school mentioned in this chapter used the UN forum to take their lessons one step further. The connections that students made with peers from around the world also led to the critical realization that there exists a rich and fascinating world outside of the United States. The yearly conference is held at the UN and is sponsored by the organization called Global Education Motivators http://www.gem-ngo.org/.

The value of engaging in discussions on controversial issues, according to Diana Hess (2002), is correlated with powerful educational outcomes and the encouragement of effective participation of secondary students in democratic processes. Hess notes that many teachers may not engage in such discussions due to a fear of reprisal. In these experiences, speaking about stereotypes and the growing animosity toward targeted groups did spark an emotional discussion in the classroom, but the educators felt compelled and responsible to engage their students in such dialogues despite the discomfort levels. Teaching is political and interventions that take place to deconstruct and demystify emerging stereotypes and prejudice seen in students can no doubt prepare them to be better informed and participatory citizens. In Michael Apple's words,

> Those committed to a more participatory curriculum understand that knowledge is socially constructed, that it is produced and disseminated by people who have particular values, interests and biases. This is simply a fact of life, since all of us are formed by our cultures, genders, geographies and so on. In a democratic curriculum, however, young people learn to be 'critical readers' of their society. When confronted

with some knowledge or viewpoint, they are encouraged to ask questions like: Who said this? Why did they say it? Why should we believe this? Who benefits if we believe this and act upon it? (Apple & Beane, 2007, p. 151)

Simply learning verb tenses and expressions makes language learning mechanical and devoid of key lessons of language learning—communication and understanding. Living in a vacuum and believing that the world starts and ends within the United States greatly limits students. As their minds open up to the unique world around them, attitudes and beliefs can change.

To begin, world language teachers can discourage stereotypical celebrations such as "taco day" or "make your own pizza day." The exemplary world language educators mentioned went a step further, putting critical literacy into practice and encouraging students to understand the many aspects of spoken and written languages that both oppress and liberate individuals. These case study examples advocate for the importance and integral value of critical literacy in the world language classroom. Educators need to believe that their classrooms can have a powerful impact on the transformation of societal norms and hegemonic culture and then actualize it in their classrooms.

# Notes

1. In the 1970s, Latinos rallied to protest the use of the image of a sleepy bandit in a large sombrero as an advertising symbol in a commercial for Frito's corn chips. The so-called Frito Bandito was eventually taken off the air.
2. See Spoken Here: Travels Among Threatened Languages by Mark Abley.
3. For example in the following areas numbers are indicated for endangered languages Africa (46 total) The Americas (170 total) Asia (78 total) Europe (12 total) The Pacific (210 total). http://www.ethnologue.com/nearly_extinct.asp

# References

Anzaldua, G. (1990). *Bordelands/La frontera: The new mestiza.* San Francisco: Spinsters/Aunt Lute.

Apple, M. & Beane J. (2007). *Democratic schools.* Portsmouth, NH: Heinemann.

Bosmajian, H. (1983). *The language of oppression.* Lanham, MD: University Press of America.

Burke, K. (1984). *Attitudes toward history.* Berkeley: University of California Press.

Dutcher, N. (1995). *Overview of foreign language education in the United States.* Center for Applied Linguistics: Washington, D.C.

Hess, D. (2002). Controversial public issues in secondary social studies classrooms: Learning from skilled teachers in theory and research. *Social Education, 30*(1).

McCarthy C. (1997). *The uses of culture: Education and the limits of ethnic affiliation.* New York: Routledge.

Pewewardy, C. (1998). Why educators can't ignore Indian mascots. *Educators resources.* Retrieved October, 2007, from www.aistm.org.

Rich, A. (1979). *On lies, secrets, and silences.* New York: Norton.

Rodgers, J. & Hubbard, L. (Spring, 1980). The minority student in foreign languages. *The Modern Language Journal, 64*(1), 75–80.

Rodriguez, C. (1997). *Latin Looks. Images of latinas and latinos in the U.S. media.* Boulder, CO: Westview Press.

Shor, I. (Fall, 1999). What is critical literacy? *Journal of Pedagogy, Pluralism and Practice, 1*(4).

Shor, I., & Freire, P. (1987). *A pedagogy for liberation.* Westport, CT: Greenwood.

Van Driel, B. (2004). Confronting *Islamophobia in educational practice.* London: Trentham Books.[Query: Please list Van Driel, 2004 here]

Williams, R. (1977). *Marxism and literature.* New York: Oxford University Press.

# Chapter 11

# "It just seems to be more intelligent": Critical Literacy in the English Classroom

*Robert Petrone and Carlin Borsheim*

Adolescents in the United States today are steeped—whether by choice or not—in a daily bombardment of print and nonprint texts, all of which, implicitly or explicitly, present perspectives on race, gender, class, sexual orientation, as well as many other political, social, and economic issues. According to the 1997 documentary *Advertising and the End of the World,* during the mid 1980s the average American was exposed to about 500 advertisements a day; in 1997, that number had increased to about 3600 advertisements a day. With the increased use of the Internet and the seemingly daily advents in technology, that number is certainly much higher today.

As the quantity of texts in society continues to increase and diversify, so does the nature of these texts. Proponents of the New Literacy Studies (NLS) posit that the changing nature of the world—economically, technologically, and socially—is changing the nature of texts and textual activities (Alvermann, 2002; Cope & Kalantis, 2000; Kist, 2004; Kress, 2002; Lankshear and Knobel, 2003; New London Group, 1996). For example, Lankshear and Knobel (2003) argue that the rise of an attention economy gives way to a range of new forms of literacy such as "Meme-ing," "Contact Displaying," "Attention Transacting," "Scenariating," and "Culture Jamming," all of which radically shift traditional perceptions of what counts as literacy and texts. In essence, these scholars argue for an expanded notion of text, suggesting that texts today are more multimodal and multimedia than in previous times.

Given the textual demands placed on today's adolescents—in terms of volume, diversification, and complexity—and the changing nature of our social and technological world, secondary literacy education needs to be reassessed by calling into question what is being studied, how it is being studied, and for what purposes it is being studied. This chapter, by examining how a 10th grade English class operates as a space for critical textual inquiry, analysis, and production for its students, seeks to understand how the secondary English classroom might work to help adolescents manage the multiplicity of texts in their lives, both within the schools and outside, through the explicit teaching of critical literacy.

## Literacy: A Critical Perspective

Critical literacy educators, theorists, and researchers recognize that literacy is not simply a neutral, ahistorical, and/or universal set of cognitive skills or processes one engages in when reading and/or writing, or, as Freire (1970) writes, "an inconsequential matter of *ba, be, bi, bo, bu,* of memorizing an alienated word" (p. 339). Instead, and without negating cognition as an aspect of literacy, a critical perspective of literacy focuses on the ways that texts and the consumption and production of them function to maintain and perpetuate the contexts in which they are embedded and/or function to name, examine, and potentially transform these contexts, paying particular attention to issues of power, representation, normativity, and ideology (Freire & Macedo, 1987; Luke, 1997, pp. 1–18). By extending the scope of understanding literacy to include ideological and political dimensions, critical literacy researchers and educators call into question any perspective of literacy that does not explicitly address these facets of literacy learning, namely, strictly cognitive or "technical" perspectives that dominate current public policy for literacy learning and that, according to Freire, actually promote passivity, decrease critical consciousness, and indoctrinate its recipients into the existing structures of their world.

That is why, for Freire, literacy is nothing short of revolution; he sees its development as a humanizing, liberating practice, where in the process of becoming critically literate, people move from being an object *of* to a subject *in* their historical realities, as interveners in and transformers of their own oppressive conditions. From this perspective, a person is literate "to the extent that he or she is able to use language for social and political reconstruction" (Freire & Macedo, 1987, p. 159).

Drawing upon and extending Freire's work, critical literacy researchers focus their attention on the ways in which texts and people's textual activities work to promote their critical consciousness, their "naming of the world," or indoctrinate them into oppressive conditions, usually along the lines of race, gender, and/or class. For example, Martino (2001) explains how dominant ideologies of masculinity frame the ways that adolescent boys engage with texts. He notes that his study "examines the extent to which boys' acquisition of literacy is implicated in a network of wider social, cultural, and political practices through which boys enact their masculinity" (p. 172) and that any attempts to address the literacy practices of boys "must be situated within an alternative to a restrictive gender system in which masculinity and femininity are structured as oppositional categories" (pp. 172–173). Critical literacy educators attempt to facilitate their students' critical consciousness and reading of the world. For example, Wallowitz (2004) explains a unit of instruction in which she worked with her students to understand various ways they were being positioned as gendered subjects by media texts. Additionally, critical educators call into question the ideological and political nature of curricula and the institutions in which they teach, all along encouraging and helping their students to do the same (Bigelow, 2001; Loewen, 1996; Petrone & Gibney, 2005). In other words, the curriculum itself becomes the object of critique. For example, Loewen suggests that American history teachers actually teach their students how to read against their textbooks.

Then, for purposes of this chapter, bringing together this critical perspective of literacy and the aforementioned New Literacy Studies, we define critical literacy as the acquisition and/or utilization of skills, dispositions, and habits of mind to understand (i.e., "name"), question (particularly along race, class, and gender lines), and potentially challenge and transform the status quo (i.e., the various "contexts" that seem commonsensical and/or natural) through the consumption, production, and distribution of print and nonprint texts. What follows is a description of a long-term collaboration in which we—a high school English teacher and part-time MA student (Carlin Borsheim) and a full-time English Education PhD student (Robert Petrone)—codesigned, conducted, and assessed the implementation of a secondary English curriculum designed to facilitate high school students' development of critical literacy. This particular curriculum is an example of how one classroom and one curriculum has been transformed by a commitment to critical literacy. We hope to inspire teachers to look at their own teaching contexts and existing curricula to think about how a critical approach could change the way they think about what it is that they are already doing.

## Context

Located thirty miles from the nearest city, Finely High School in Finley, Michigan—a hamlet of approximately 8,500 people, 97 percent of whom are White—is where our work takes place. With 54 churches serving its community, Finley is the county seat to a predominately rural and Republican constituency, and yet the town and community members defy a single taxonomic label, such as suburban or rural. Some of its members describe Finley as a "bedroom community" serving as a residence for university and government employees; others consider it a "blue collar town" serving as a hub for small manufacturing companies; and still others call it "a small hick town," meant to signify Finley as a rural, agricultural community. Given these three perspectives of the town, Finley's population, although very limited in its racial diversity, consists of a broad range of socioeconomic and ideological backgrounds and beliefs, many of which are currently being challenged by the changing economic scenario of Michigan.

Deeply imbedded for generations in the traditions of local agriculture and Michigan's automobile industry, many families in and around Finley are confronted with realities different from those that previous generations faced. In the past, for example, many students' parents and grandparents made good livings in the auto industry and agriculture, without needing to pursue formal education beyond the high school level, and many students at Finley High School have intentions of following in their families' footsteps. However, as Michigan faces major changes with the decline of the auto industry and the local family-run farms as well as with an increased economic need for a highly skilled and schooled workforce, many of these students and families are realizing that academic achievement (and quite possibly schooling beyond high school) will be necessary in their lives in ways that it may not have been twenty or thirty years ago.

These demographics and current economic and ideological issues prove significant since, in many regards, this community represents and adheres to the status quo—a concept that becomes the focal point of critique throughout the curriculum. However, even as we describe the student population as one that represents the status quo, we want to be careful not to generalize the entire student body. Although Finley High School lacks racial and ethnic diversity, its students come from a wide variety of socioeconomic backgrounds. For the portion of the population of students who benefit from positions of socioeconomic privilege, our greatest concern is not oppression, but apathy. To overcome this apathy, which is a result of being part of a constructed and invisible mainstream, they must be pushed to question that which seems normal, comfortable, even beneficial to them. In many cases, ignorance is bliss; they have no self-interest in doing this work because it doesn't serve their immediate concerns. They have not often been asked to recognize their own privilege, nor do they understand or readily accept the ways they are shaped and constructed. Students who *are* in marginalized positions due to socioeconomic status are unlikely to acknowledge or label themselves as such. Many of these students either do not recognize themselves as being in a position of marginalization or do not want to openly and publicly draw attention to it and discuss it. Our challenge as educators in this context has been to make these conversations meaningful to students no matter what their demographic status. Our goal is to help students see themselves in their contexts, to see the ways in which we are *all* constructed, to see the role that texts play in shaping beliefs, and to see the role they play in the creation and consumption of texts.

## The Class

Our inquiry into how the secondary English classroom might work as a space for critique focuses on a nontracked 10th grade English class, which meets daily for 90 minutes over the course of an eighteen-week semester and is typically comprised of approximately 30 students, almost all of whom are White and monolingual. The curriculum for this class is divided into five units—Personal Narrative Writing, "Voices of the Great Depression," *The Giver* and Satire, the Research Paper, and "Courage and Integrity"[ii]—and in many regards conforms to the standards and assessments of traditional high school English curricula. While each of the units we present here was supplemented and reconceptualized to reflect the overarching goals of critical literacy, our work did not require—and could not have required—a complete overhaul of the existing curriculum. Traditional academic literacy skills as outlined by the district curriculum, as well as state standards, remained a priority. For the most part, we did not replace existing and traditional texts or assessments; instead, we approached them from another angle, using a different framework to achieve a balance between critical and traditional literacy skills.

It is also important to note that we discovered early on in the process that critical literacy cannot be "achieved" in isolation or implemented in one unit. Instead, critical literacy develops as a result of a consistent approach to texts, a way of asking questions, an explicit commitment to critical values in a class-room. Therefore, each unit is designed to scaffold the skills of the next, explicitly and intentionally layering skills and habits of mind we want students to begin to develop over the course of the eighteen-week semester. Our commitment to critical literacy has influenced us to think differently about every aspect of the semester curriculum, as well as about English Education in general.

## The Personal Narrative

One purpose of this first unit was to nurture a classroom atmosphere and student dispositions that are conducive for critical literacy. Becoming critical requires students to participate in very honest conversations about issues of race, class, gender, privilege, and the status quo. It requires them to examine their beliefs, values, and assumptions about themselves and other people. To encourage students to open their minds and hearts—in order for them to feel comfortable examining themselves in ways that can leave them feeling very vulnerable—we begin the course by building a foundation of comfort, trust, and community in anticipation of the important work to come.

In the first weeks of the class, we ask students to write personal narrative essays about subjects meaningful to them. Early in the writing process, students share personal artifacts from their lives that represent them, draw pictures of their neighborhoods, and tell each other stories about growing up. Sandra Cisneros's *The House on Mango Street*, the central text of the unit, works well to launch reader response-style discussions about how individuals are shaped by their contexts. While reading the vignettes in this collection, we address topics including family, friends, gender, religion, school, writing, social class and race. Discussions related to Esperanza, the main character, open up possibilities for students to discuss these same issues in relation to their own lives. In this context, students are free to explore experiences that have shaped them. Students wrote about divorce, abusive relationships, friendships, deaths, influential people, substance abuse, eating disorders, athletic feats, and academic accomplishments. Finally, we asked all students—in a show of their willingness to contribute to the sense of community—to take a leap of faith and share their essays.

While students are not engaged in overtly critical activities in this first unit, these discussions about beliefs, identities, and contexts helped to cultivate the dispositions necessary for critical literacy. Students began to recognize and accept that they are positioned in a context that shapes aspects of their identity.

## Voices of the Great Depression

This unit asks students to examine people and texts from the past that could be described as critical in and of their historical contexts. The unit is organized around John Steinbeck's *Of Mice and Men,* a text commonly used in high school English classrooms but not often associated with the goals of critical literacy. We introduce John Steinbeck as someone who was critical of his context, someone who understood, questioned, challenged, and transformed conditions of the 1930s and the Great Depression through his writing. Using fiction, poetry, and other genres, we discussed the ways and reasons others were critical of 1930s American society. For example, we supplemented Steinbeck's novel with Langston Hughes's poem "Let America Be America Again" and Woody Guthrie's song "This Land Is Your Land." In these works, Hughes and Guthrie question the notion that the "American Dream" is equally accessible to all Americans. In his poem, Hughes speaks for those marginalized populations that were denied access to the freedom and prosperity so often associated with America: "O, let America be America again/The land that never has been yet/And yet must be/the land where *every* man is free./The land that's mine/the poor man's, Indian's, Negro's, ME." And in "This Land is Your Land," Guthrie uses lyrics to protest poverty and injustice during the Great Depression: "In the squares of the city, / In the shadow of a steeple; / By the relief office, I'd seen my people. / As they stood there hungry, I stood there asking, / Is this land made for you and me?" These pieces pushed students to reexamine ideas about equality and equal opportunity in America during the 1930s and today.

In discussions about the "American Dream," students often reveal limited understanding of issues of race, class, and gender by oversimplifying or undervaluing factors that contribute to poverty and oppression. To complicate their ideas about equality and access, we began, in one of the classes, a discussion by asking them to respond with "true" or "false" to the following statements:

- Every American has equal opportunity to pursue the "American Dream."
- Education is a key to success in achieving the "American Dream."
- Every American is guaranteed quality education.

- The Civil Rights movement resulted in equality for people of all races.
- Social class doesn't matter in the United States.

Clearly, these questions are designed to generate conversation about race, class, and gender. They are also designed to encourage students to consider difficult questions for which there are no simple answers, to push past "black and white" thinking to consider issues that they do not normally have to consider, and to hopefully build empathy in the process. Undoubtedly, discussions can be heated and complicated as insensitive comments about race, class, or gender are a reality. Teachers can control the questions they pose, but they cannot control students' responses to those questions; when students reveal prejudice in class discussion, it can leave teachers (as it did us) wondering, "Did I do more harm than good today?" In many cases the discomfort is enough to steer teachers clear of these contentious conversations, but critical literacy demands that we ask difficult questions about difficult topics, topics that some people prefer not be addressed. These encounters can cause anxiety, but we continue to be motivated by the belief that these important questions are necessary for students to consider in the process of becoming critical.

Another way that a focus on critical literacy shifted our approach to the teaching of *Of Mice and Men* was through the idea of critical lenses. In *Critical Encounters in High School English*, Appleman (2000) suggests using a variety of literary theories to encourage students to look at texts from multiple perspectives. While we did not delve into the depths of literary analysis that she describes in her book, we did use her metaphor of "lenses" to help students look at *Of Mice and Men* from different perspectives. Looking specifically through race, class, and gender lenses helped students consider perspectives other than their own, thereby building empathy and respect for multiple perspectives. For example, when we turned a gender lens on the novel, it pushed students to consider, "Who are the female characters in this novel? How are they portrayed? What seems to be John Steinbeck's purpose for portraying female characters the way he did?" These questions led students to the conclusion that *Of Mice and Men* includes very few female characters; in fact, only one plays a significant role in the story and she remains nameless. The other periphery female characters are Lennie's aunt Clara and two prostitutes. The race and class lenses encouraged students to ask similar questions and come to similar conclusions about other marginalized populations represented in the book. Then we asked, "So what? What might John

Steinbeck's purpose have been? What happens when we read the story this way? What happens when we turn these lenses on other texts?" The lenses led to a richer, more critical interpretation of the novel. From that point on, we described the process of looking from multiple perspectives as looking through a "critical lens."

To practice with the concept of the critical lens, we watched clips from several Disney movies—*Peter Pan, Oliver, The Little Mermaid, Dumbo,* and *The Lion King*—from the critical lenses that highlighted the racial and gender stereotypes found in these cartoons. This activity, inspired by a conference presentation given by Linda Christensen (2002), helped to make the point that no text is neutral. Even seemingly innocent cartoons have the potential to shape our perceptions, sometimes dangerously so. While students are incensed by the prospect of "ruining" cartoons this way, they did not deny the stereotypes they uncovered by looking from this perspective. For example, female students were particularly disturbed by the lyrics of "Poor Unfortunate Souls" in *The Little Mermaid,* in which Ursula, the sinister octopus, advises Arial, the beautiful mermaid, to "keep her trap shut" in order to "get her man." Students went on to evaluate the messages sent to children when they realize that Arial sacrifices her voice and relies on her physical beauty to successfully attract her prince. This process prepared students for similar conversations as they turned the lenses to *Of Mice and Men* and other "texts," including their schools and community, later in the semester.

## Learning to "See Beyond"

Lois Lowry's popular young adult novel *The Giver* provided the inspiration for our four-week satire unit, in which students also read a variety of popular culture texts, including political cartoons, a newspaper article titled "The Bikini and the Burka," the film *The Truman Show,* and an episode of *The Simpsons.* While *The Giver* was part of the official English 10 curriculum, the other texts were not; we chose them to supplement *The Giver* to highlight the ways writers use different genres to challenge and transform important issues in contemporary society. These satirical and pop culture texts were used to generate discussions that encourage students to turn the critical lens away from fiction and toward their own world—to help them read "the word and the world."

In the beginning of the novel, Jonas, Lowry's main character, accepts the controlling and contrived circumstances of his life as normal. Likewise,

Truman, the main character of *The Truman Show*, is blind to the ways he is being constructed by his society. He is no different than anyone else, because "people accept the reality with which they are presented," as another character, Cristof, explains. Throughout the course of the stories, Jonas and Truman each go through a metamorphosis that results in their more critical perspectives on their worlds. They each begin to understand, question, challenge, and ultimately transform their circumstances and themselves. To push students thinking about what this transformation is like and why it is important, we asked them to visually represent Jonas and Truman's journeys using a metaphor. These "metaphor maps" encouraged students to describe the process the characters—and the students themselves—go through as they become more critical. Students sometimes struggled to articulate this concept, so describing what it looks like in fiction scaffolds the process of describing it as it relates to their own lives. Using giant pieces of colored paper that plastered our classroom walls, students compared the process to climbing to the peak of a mountain, blossoming into a flower, and walking toward a bright light. In the end, we reflected on these metaphors as a large group and generated an official definition of "critical." Ultimately, these metaphor maps helped students understand their own experience of developing critical literacy.

In our quest to turn the critical lens on our society, we read "The Bikini and the Burka," an editorial by Joan Jacobs Brumberg and Jacquelyn Jackson, which critiques the symbols of the bikini and the burka, drawing a parallel between societal pressure on American women to conform to an unrealistic physical ideal and the Taliban's oppression of Afghani women. The article sparked heated debate in class discussion, as it forced students to begin to question something as seemingly All-American and innocent as the bikini. The article, once again, reinforced the practice of looking at a text—in this case the bikini—from a critical perspective to uncover values and perspectives it represents.

During this unit, students also watched "Lisa the Vegetarian," an episode of *The Simpsons* satirizing American institutions—from the meat industry to the public education system. During their viewing of the episode, students identified elements of satire—exaggeration, understatement, parody, incongruity, absurdity, and reversal—and articulated what exactly the creators are trying to say about particular American institutions through this text. This exercise inevitably pushed students to watch a familiar show from a different perspective. It opened their eyes to a way of thinking and "reading" TV that began to translate into their lives. Once students felt more comfortable with the concept of satire, we asked them to bring in and share examples of satire they identified in their daily lives.

In many regards, this unit is representative of our attempts to achieve the dual aim of critical engagement and academic access. For us, the work of critical literacy does not happen in lieu of academic literacy but alongside it; in fact, the goal of critical literacy creates for us a directive and unified goal toward which the entire curriculum points as it works to subsume the required and more traditional aspects of the curriculum. For example, in this unit, while teaching about the literary genre satire, complete with its conventions, we pushed the students to more critically examine various aspects of their own lived experiences, be it their beach apparel or the shows they watch on television, or, as will be discussed below in the section on student reactions, their experiences in school and their community.

## The Research Paper

Critical literacy, which asks students to "understand and question" the realities with which they are presented, can leave students to deal with feelings of helplessness or cynicism if they are not also empowered to "challenge and transform." We find these elements to be crucial for developing critical literacy, because in these phases students are no longer merely consumers but also producers—and even distributors—of texts. With our goals of "challenging and transforming" in mind, we revised the traditional research paper of the existing curriculum into a Critical Research Project for Social Action—the most important critical literacy project of the semester. This "new" approach to the "old" research paper unit was an important part of helping our students to see how texts are created.

In the process of the Critical Research Paper for Social Action, students accomplished the following:

- Developed research topics rooted in school/community and society-based topics they want to learn more about and/or change;

- Conducted primary as well as secondary research, including interviews, observations, and surveys;

- Wrote a "traditional" research paper;

- Produced a "real" research text (e.g., documentary, newspaper article, Web site, brochures, or editorial);

- Distributed their texts to real audiences to help raise awareness about or change some aspect of their school or community.

From the beginning of the unit, we nurtured commitment, sincere curiosity, and intrinsic motivation, believing that it is important for students to see themselves as researchers who have the ability and opportunity to make real differences in their school and community contexts and not just as students doing a required research assignment, yet another hoop through which to jump. For example, on the unit's first day, we gave a "pep talk" about the project and distributed research notebooks, deputizing the students as "official critical researchers." The remainder of the first day of the unit was spent practicing the research skill of observation by turning the school into a text to be observed and interrogated. After a brief introduction to becoming observers of their school outside of the classroom, the students roamed the school, noting in their new notebooks what they, as critical researchers, observed. As they explored the building, examining their school as researchers for the first time, they began to see things differently. In the cafeteria and hallways that had seemed familiar and ordinary, they detected areas of curiosity, points of unease, and ultimately potential research questions. For example, a small group passing through the hallway outside the guidance office commented on and jotted down a note about the number and nature of military posters targeted at young men and women. They later wondered about the military's methods of recruitment and the school's policies regarding that issue. Students who visited a rather dank area of the lower level of the school—an area few students have a reason to visit—were bothered that this was the area that housed many of the special-education classrooms. They saw possibilities for exploring issues related to that often-hidden population of the school. Two girls in the cafeteria began to generate questions about nutrition, health, obesity, and school lunches. Connections between the students' observations and their emerging research questions did not always come easily for all of them; at this point, it was our job to help those students who were struggling to identify topics worthy of research meaningful enough to engage them.

As students worked to generate topics, we studied contemporary examples of others who are critical in their lives and who are using research to affect change. For example, we watched the documentary *Super Size Me* and discussed the impetus for Morgan Spurlock's research—how he identified an issue affecting people in the United States and set out to find answers through research. We also read excerpts from Eric Schlosser's 1999 exposé *Fast Food*

*Nation: The Dark Side of the All-American Meal* to examine critical research in another genre. Some students chose topics that affected the community as a whole, including the effects of large corporations on our small-town economy or the legacy of racism and the history of the KKK in our area. Other students focused on issues facing the school, such as the controversy of advertising through Channel One or the quality of the district's sex education curriculum. And some students chose topics as a result of personal experience and curiosity, including healthy versus unhealthy relationships among teen couples, cosmetic surgery, or genocide in Darfur. In all cases, students identified audiences they wanted to reach with their message.

As the students focused on their research topics and questions, they began to collect data, which consisted of interviewing students, teachers, and community experts (e.g., mayor, members of Alcoholics Anonymous, physicians, business owners); surveying students and community members; conducting archival, primary-source research at the local historical society; reading print-based research (book and Internet); observing naturalistic settings; and analyzing various institutional or mass media texts (e.g., teen magazines, brochures, Web pages, advertisements). Once the data collection was completed, the students moved on to organizing and analyzing their data and then writing up their methods and findings. To maintain consistency with the English department's requirements and our interest in preparing students for subsequent engagement in academic discourse, we asked each student to write a traditional research paper in addition to his or her "real research texts." This exercise proved to be useful in helping the students not only to understand and develop traditional expectations of and skills to write an "academically oriented" research paper but also to analyze and synthesize their data prior to creating a distributable text. Subsequently, students produced "real" research texts and distributed them to an audience outside the classroom. In the weeks leading up to the production of these "real" texts, we discussed rhetorical elements and examined examples of other research and the ways researchers have published their findings to communicate to wider audiences. For example, we examined the documentary *Tough Guise* to discuss the following rhetorical strategies: What point is the author making? How might this person have gone about accumulating sources? Is the argument effective? Why? How? What is the tone? How is the genre or method of distribution effective? How does the genre enhance the argument or make it more accessible? Is the research credible? This reading and analysis of other research texts helped students better understand their production and distribution processes.

Early on, students were asked to identify an audience that would benefit from their research. From there we discussed which "forms" or genres of writing would most effectively reach this identified audience. We used the equation "Form = Audience + Purpose" (just as we did in previous units) as a way of facilitating their thinking. Their research products took various forms, including letters to the editor of the local newspaper, articles for the school and local newspaper, PowerPoint presentations for school and community organizations or high school classes, documentary films for school news programs, letters to organizations such as MTV and Channel One, brochures or pamphlets for health or counseling offices. One group wrote to a newspaper editor a letter encouraging citizens of the community to support local businesses by shopping locally. Another group worked on a short documentary film to be shown on television with the morning announcements to educate other teens about making choices related to healthy dating and relationships. The group researching racism and the KKK wrote a letter to the editor of a local newspaper inspiring citizens to be good representatives of the community; a group that explored teen smoking distributed information through pamphlets in the school guidance office and a local doctor's office; the group that focused on advertising and Channel One sent an email to the organization encouraging it to change the nature of its advertisements; and one student studied media influence on teen girls and wrote a persuasive and articulate article for our school newspaper. In all cases, students were expected to look for opportunities to publish; although not every product made it through the distribution phase, some students did, in fact, distribute impressive products to make a difference in our community.

## Media Literacy

The first four units of the semester adhered to the curriculum as outlined by the school district. The fifth and final unit, a thematic unit titled "Courage and Integrity," originally incorporated a variety of short stories and culminated with a traditional book report. The unit lacked depth and presented our biggest challenge in terms of relating to our ultimate goals of critical literacy. With the permission of the department, we opted to finish the semester with a "Media Literacy" unit inspired by the Center for Media Literacy and their publication, *Five Key Questions that Can Change the World* (2005). These five questions provided a framework for working with a wide variety of multimedia texts throughout the unit: Who created this message? What creative techniques are used to attract my attention? How might different people understand this message differently than me? What values, lifestyles, and points of view are represented in, or omitted from, this message? And, why is this message being sent? We began the unit with excerpts of the PBS Frontline program *Merchants of Cool* (2001), which explores creators and marketers of popular culture and their influence on teens. Students were inevitably shocked by new insights into the ways media strive to gain access into their lives. In addition, we explored the construction of newspapers, photos, advertisements, commercials, news broadcasts, and videos. In an effort to reveal rhetorical strategies behind these texts, we asked students to construct and deconstruct a variety of texts by editing a news broadcast, deconstructing photographs found in newspapers, dissecting maps, analyzing magazine covers, and designing collages illustrating persuasive techniques. We also drew on our knowledge about the elements of satire we had learned earlier in the semester to analyze Adbuster ads found on www.Adbusters.org; students then designed original parodies to critique other popular ads or issues they identify on their own. The unit culminated in a writing assignment designed to solicit a definition of "media literacy" and address the five key questions.

This unit was a natural fit and an appropriate finale for a semester dedicated to critical literacy. After using literature, video, music, nonfiction, poetry, and visual texts throughout the unit, students were prepared and receptive to an examination of how texts work to construct us all in our own lives, as well as the importance of awareness for making informed decisions as readers, writers, consumers, and citizens.

## Students' Reactions

Over the last three years of implementing this curriculum, we have noticed certain trends across the different groups of students. In essence, we discovered that in response to this curriculum, students demonstrate preexisting critical literacy, develop emergent critical literacy, and/or resist the enactment of critical literacy.

### "And then they try and get you to stop it": Demonstrating Preexisting Critical Literacy

For many students, this curriculum offered a space for them to air their preexisting critical sensibilities and skills. One of the key discoveries of our work was the fact that so many of our students even before they came into our classes already had critical stances toward institutions, knowledge, and power, many of which get silenced, dismissed, or even overtly denigrated in schools. For many of these students, the curriculum served as an affirmative place in which their otherwise "taboo" ideas are given official sanction.

Throughout the curriculum, texts were used as springboards for students to "name" and better understand, interrogate, and potentially transform their world. Their reading of the world during the curriculum included understanding and inquiring into the following institutions: schools, family, government, religion, and media and popular culture (i.e., TV, music, film, news, video games, advertising, and celebrities), and it was during this inquiry that many of the students articulated many of their preexisting critical sensibilities and abilities. In one class section, for example, after a whole-class discussion on the relationship between the film *The Truman Show* and the ways the mass media potentially influences Americans, the students gradually shifted their critical inquiry and "naming" to the institution of schooling, explaining how it operated as a normalizing force in the world and in their lives. The following excerpt comes from this whole-class discussion based on their understanding of *The Truman Show* as a satire; the discussion led to another discussion on how they saw people's thoughts being shaped in society:

> Carlin [CB]: Now [questions] 7 and 8 [questions from their discussion sheet], I wanted us to take *The Truman Show* as one example and then connect it with our world and kinda look at the bigger picture. Can you think of examples of how people's thoughts are constructed or shaped today? Like, how, how are our beliefs or thoughts, like if we put ourselves, if Truman is like an exaggerated example, is the real example us, and if so, how are our thoughts constructed?
>
> Peter: Through the media and school
>
> CB: Ok, um. [CB begins to write the words Media and School on the board.]
>
> The class talks about the media for 18 seconds in which they rehash some of the key ideas from their previous day's discussion on this topic.
>
> CB [to Peter]: "So, what do you want to say about school?"
>
> Peter: We...we are made by what we're taught.
>
> CB: Say more.
>
> Peter: And you decide what we're taught. So [he pauses for 2 seconds.] you shape our lives [CB sighs as if in of appreciation and giggles.] and our thinking.

Derrick: Not really you.

Rebecca: That's kinda scary.

Derrick: Not you but the school.

Andy: The hippie organization. [Andy's comment refers to an ongoing discussion the class has been having about how English teachers are all former hippies and that CB, they have joked with her, is among that group.]

The class continues to discuss schooling for 3 minutes, talking specifically about what gets taught in a way that their thinking gets shaped, using the creationism-evolution debate as an example. Kate then moves the conversation to what they learned in elementary school.

CB: In elementary school or middle school whatever, what do you learn to *be*?

Peter: Good study habits, and a good student, like...paying attention, raising your hand.

CB: Yea.

Rebecca: And not getting your name on the board.

This excerpt reveals the use of classroom texts, in this case *The Truman Show*, as facilitating the students' naming of the world, in this case schools. In this conversation, the students brought into the classroom discourse an examination of the very institution they are physically a part of at the time of the conversation. In addition, their comments revealed an awareness of deeper levels of influence on the relegation of sanctioned knowledge in the classroom. For example, Drew's comment "Not you but the school" and Andy's allusion to the "hippie organization," demonstrated an awareness of how teachers and classroom instruction and space is part of a larger web of institutional forces.

They revealed a great deal of awareness and naming not only of institutions and people but also of the ways the students' description of and investigation into the ways certain ideas are made and maintained as invisible, natural, and/or commonsensical. And in many ways, this shift from an awareness of the "what" (institutions and people) to the "how" (the means of perpetuation) is more telling of developing critical literacy in students as it necessitates a deeper degree of making the invisible visible, of unpacking the status quo. Throughout their move toward this facet of critical inquiry and denaturalization, the students articulated at least the following means by which certain ideas are made and maintained as normal or commonsensical and in many instances applied these ideas to their everyday lived experiences: emotional pressure, fear, regulation of discourse by authority figures, access to and/or control of knowledge. The following examples and analyses come from one class's work on *The Giver*.

During one conversation, the class moved from discussions of the circumstances of the novel into the novel's investigation of contemporary society by applying the same set of questions to the society depicted in *The Giver* and to contemporary American society; to prepare for the conversation, the students individually answered in writing on the previous day the following questions: What do people accept without questioning? What is considered "normal"? What is the "invisible" to people in society? How do people accept what is invisible? How are these aspects of their society made and maintained invisible? How are the people made to accept these things? Should these things be accepted? Questioned? Why? As the conversation moved into questioning that which is accepted as normal in contemporary American society and how those things are perpetuated as normal, the students generated and discussed issues such as laws, violence, stereotypes, schooling, social norms (i.e., knowing which way to stand in an elevator without ever having to be told), and certain professions (i.e., prostitution), and how these things are perpetuated by fear, pressure, and regulation of knowledge and discourse by authority figures. For example, in responding to some of her classmates' observations, Carolyn made the following comment about how some of these processes work at Finley high school:

> I think it's hard for, like, kids to do it [question what is accepted as normal] sometimes just because, not really in this class and all that, but in some of our other classes, like we'll like talk about stuff and teachers don't think it's stuff we should talk about in school or whatever. And then they're like, "No, no, don't talk about that." It doesn't even have to be bad, just something that, it's a topic that people don't normally discuss. And they try to get you to stop it. And then that way makes everyone stop because then people don't think about it if it's looked down on."

Carolyn's comment moved beyond the awareness of institutional ideologies or sanctioned discourses (as discussed above) to an awareness of a process or means by which students' discourse and access to knowledge is mediated by authority figures, in this case teachers; she also articulated a process of how once an idea is deemed negative in some way by an authority figure, it becomes off limits, so to speak, and, in some way, "invisible." In my (Robert) follow-up interview two days later, she expanded on her understanding of these regulating processes:

> Oh, yea. Like, well, I think that sometimes like when you approach like, um, like, this sounds really dumb, like a "taboo" subject or whatever, I think that like aren't normally discussed, I think that teachers kind of like, like students will just be talking amongst themselves like during class discussions and somehow, like we do, and we'll get on different subjects and if we start getting on a topic that the teacher doesn't think, like that is something hard for them to talk about or something like, like a topic like, sometimes like race or something like that, they'll be like, "oh, no" and try to redirect the topic even though they don't want it to seem like they are but you can tell that it's happening because it's too hard. If you start talking about something about race or like people being treated a different way. Do you know what I mean? I think they're afraid to offend people. That's why I like this classroom, because we can talk about it, and people, like don't get offended.

Of particular interest in this excerpt is the fact that Carolyn specifically mentioned "taboo" topics that relate to race or "people being treated in a different way," thus linking the regulatory processes by teachers to particular ideas and concepts; in this case, those dealing with people who are or are treated "different." Additionally, she mentioned the subtle nature of many processes that attempt to normalize behavior or thinking, saying that teachers "try to redirect the topic even though they don't want it to seem like they are." She also offered a reason why this process might occur, noting that "it's too hard" and that teachers might be "afraid to offend people." Finally, this example is theoretically significant in that she mentions how this classroom "space" is somehow different than others, that it is a space wherein it is safe to talk about otherwise unsanctioned issues, a point that will be addressed in the next major section on these findings.

Carolyn's comments, although perhaps more substantive, are representative of many other students' awareness of similar and other means and processes by which various institutions and people work to legitimate and perpetuate certain ideas and beliefs. For example, within the same conversation as the one in which Carolyn's comments came, many students discussed issues of fear, "emotional pressure," and control by authority as means by which certain notions of race, ethnicity, language, body image, and other ideas are made and maintained. For example, during the section of the conversation when the class was talking about stereotypes and assumptions they had about people who were of "different ethnic or racial backgrounds," several students began talking about having suspicions of people who appear to be from the

Middle East as carrying bombs. One student, Jared, said, "I was just going to say that our country's in a pretty sad state when you see someone of a different ethnic background and you think they're a terrorist. It's pretty sick how the media frightens us so much that we see a person walking around and we think they have a bomb. That's a pretty sad state of America." Jared's comment explicitly pointed toward an awareness of the use of fear by the media to shape thinking and attitudes toward people of particular ethnicities.

A bit later in the conversation, Liz, suggesting the class go back to the "media thing," explained how the media creates a "standard of 'thinner is better'" and how it is "becoming invisible" because that standard is being expected of "younger and younger girls." Liz's comment revealed an awareness of a connection between the processes (i.e., setting a standard through the media) of making an aspect of society invisible and age—that one of the means by which ideas are made invisible is through the introduction of them to "younger and younger" people so as to make them seem commonsensical sooner and more easily. Toward the end of the class conversation, Andy, referencing a workshop he attended at the latest Lansing-area youth diversity festival, mentioned how we accept certain words such as "redneck, redskin, and gypped," explaining that "Not a lot of people know about these," which suggests an awareness of how access or lack of access to knowledge works as a means to regulate attitudes and ideas. These examples offer a representation of the types of critical textual study the class underwent during the entire curriculum whereby the curriculum and the nature of textual study created a space for students to articulate and discuss their preexisting critical sensibilities.

## "I never would have thought this in-depth about a bikini": Emergent Critical Literacy

In addition to creating a space for preexisting awareness and/or for critiques that students had about various institutions, ideas, and normalizing processes, this curriculum also facilitated the development of emergent or new critical awareness and understandings of the world, oftentimes eliciting a surprised response from the student as what was once invisible became more visible.

During group discussion among a focal group of students, I (Robert) asked them to tell me what they were learning in the class. After several minutes of discussion in which the students mentioned how they liked the class, the teacher, and how they were learning to "look at things more in depth," Audrey, one of the students, mentioned the idea of "lenses," and the group spent most of the rest of the session discussing the concept. The idea of the lenses resonated strongly with the students and became a part of the lexicon of the class thereafter. Below is a representative example of the students' emerging critical literacies related to the idea of critically examining texts through various lenses:

Derrick: Like, we watch a movie. All those different childhood movies...we've all seen those. We never really look at it the way she [Carlin] wanted us to look at. Now that you notice that stuff is there, you see it more often and realize it's there.

The group talks for a few minutes about watching movies more than once in order to better understand them. I notice Gloria hasn't spoken yet, and when the discussion dies down, I encourage her to share.

RP: Gloria, what are you thinking?

Gloria: I don't know, I guess... [She pauses for 3 seconds.] Now, since, umm, with the movies and stuff, I can't just kinda like watch movies and kinda sit there now. I sorta subconsciously scan all of it and find myself sitting there saying all this kinda crap.

The group chuckles with Gloria's "crap" comment. I wait until it dies down and then I ask my next question.

RP: Ok, so tell me what "all that kind of crap" means. Does somebody else know what that means?

Peter: You start to analyze every thing.

Alicia: Yea, you think about it.

Peter: You've taken away the fun of watching it. [The group breaks out in laughter]

Alan mentions how it hasn't taken away the fun for him since he already analyzes everything already, and then Peter talks about how he already thinks about these things and how Ms. Cassidy has them write it down and so they have to put "thought process into it." I asked him if the process they are undergoing in class is helping him do it better. Although I asked Peter the question, Derrick answered.

Derrick: It makes more sense.

RP: What do you mean?

Derrick: Umm, you're starting to realize it more. You're starting to get a better grasp of it and stuff. You know it's there. I never really knew it was there until we watched

the movie like that. Now I do, and I see it all the time. More stereotypes and discrimination.

This short excerpt reveals how the critical textual study in which the students
engaged in the class helped them see aspects of texts and their world that they
weren't previously aware of, at least not consciously. Derrick, for example,
"see[s] it all the time" now, "it" referring to racial and ethnic stereotypes
depicted in films. The fact that "the fun of watching it" has been "taken away"
or that "you think about it" demonstrates the process of the invisible becoming
visible to the students. Of particular significance is Derrick's comment about
how they've all seen these films before and never thought of them or saw them
in this way until now, which indicates a sense of making what was once natural,
normal, or commonsensical strange and problematic; it pushes the students to
reexamine that which was invisible. In addition, Derrick's "I never really knew
it was there until we watched the movie like that," supports not only the idea of
students' emerging awareness about particular issues, in this case racial and
ethnic stereotypes in films, but also the recognition of another or a new way to
consume texts, in this case watch films, a way that necessitates different
dispositions and skills, much as Gloria described how she now "subconsciously scan[s] all of it."

This sense of an emerging awareness and/or a changed perception of
some facet of society as depicted in this discussion is consistent with other
moments in the curriculum. For example, during one class session, the
students viewed and discussed an episode of *The Simpsons*, focusing on how
it, as a satire, critiques aspects of American society, namely schools and
cartoons. During the conversation, Alicia, one of the students, said to her
classmate Andy, "I never thought of cartoons like this before." Peter, who also
overheard the conversation, said to both of them, "It kinda ruins cartoons in a
way." In the class session when the students read and discussed "The Bikini
and the Burka," Heather, discussing the article with a small group of students
as part of an assignment, expressed her surprise in thinking of the bikini as a
potentially harmful aspect of American culture, saying, "I would never [prior
to reading this article] think this in-depth about wearing a bikini." Each of
these examples capture the phenomenon of emerging critical literacies as the
students—through their engagement in critical textual practices—articulate a
sense of being able to "see" anew/differently something previously familiar to
them.

### "Whoa. Whoa. Whoa. Now you're crossing a whooole new level": Resisting Critical Literacy

In addition to our aforementioned discoveries, the nature of critical inquiry cultivated by this curriculum proved to be a source of difficulty for many students. Questioning the status quo can feel very empowering for students who recognize the ways in which they are being oppressed or constructed. For students who benefit from the status quo—or who do not immediately recognize or accept the ways they are constructed or oppressed—the process of questioning can leave them feeling very vulnerable, and even resistant. In some cases, students have become very emotional. In the beginning we were unprepared for some of the personal and emotional reactions of students, but as we reflected on the process, we came to understand their feelings of vulnerability. As the students participated in textual practices designed to facilitate critical literacy, moments of confusion, contradiction, seeming resistance, and overall conflict became salient features of their experiences. The nature of the students' conflicts manifested most prominently through their dismissal of the object or act of critique as irrelevant or insignificant, and through their countering or arguing against critique through their reliance, trust, faith, and/or renewed commitment and devotion in previously held ideas, beliefs, and attitudes.

On the day when the class studied the newspaper article "The Bikini and the Burka," a group of five students spent 9 minutes discussing female body images, the "pressures" many of the girls feel, the influences of the media, celebrities, and the comparison between the bikini and the burka. Sitting off to the side, observing and taking scratch notes, I (Robert) was surprised throughout the conversation by the insightful nature of the students' comments, particularly as they talked about how the writer uses the bikini as an example to show the larger problems of social pressures on women. Seven minutes into the discussion, Bobby interjected saying, "I think she's [the author] jealous" and several of the girls laughed. He continued, explaining, "Since she doesn't fit the image, she's mad. She's like, 'Oh I can't fit this, so....'" at which point another student interjected and said, "She'll complain about it?" Bobby says, "Yea, complain about it." Bobby's comment about the author being jealous shifted the entire focus of inquiry from the content of the article, and to what American society is, to the character of the author, thus diffusing the nature of the conversation. This maneuver—that is, this shifting from a topic or issue related to something relevant in American society today to the agenda or personality of the writer, such as a hysterical or "jealous" woman—works to subvert the critical nature of the work by simply dismissing the argument as an expression of the writer's "jealousy" and anger "since she doesn't fit the image."

Another example of the students' dismissive nature toward critiquing American society is evident in the conclusion of Melanie's final essay for the unit. She wrote about how *The Giver* and *The Truman Show* are satires "created to criticize the modern world and our ways of living." After explaining how the two texts operate as satires, she offers the following conclusion for the entire essay:

> Both of these satires show how important our freedoms are, but on a deeper level they also show that we do not take advantage of our freedoms. We allow ourselves to be controlled. Once Jonas and Truman discovered that they were living a 'fake' life, they had to get out. They could not stand the fact that everyday they would miss out on making their own decisions. People in America accept the way things are everyday. We do not question standards or everyday things. We simply abide by the rules. But, if someone was to question America, point out how much we were controlled everyday, how many people would really want to live here then?

Of significance is Melanie's final sentence where she dismisses the claims she had made throughout her essay by suggesting that questioning America might reveal its unfavorable aspects. Like Bobby, Melanie shifts the focus of her argument from what needs to be critiqued about America to suggesting that it should possibly not be critiqued for fear of the consequences, thus dismissing the importance of being critical.

Another way students distanced or dismissed critiquing aspects of American society was revealed in their contradictions of themselves. An examination of a class discussion about the film *The Truman Show* revealed several fissures or potential spaces of resistance, distancing, or contradiction on the part of the students. For example, as Doug brought up the idea that video games might be influential on people's thinking, Derrick, albeit seeming lighthearted, shows a sense of disapproval, saying, "Whoa, whoa, whoa. Now you're crossing over a whooole new line," which we interpret as his way of saying that the nature of the critique is problematic for him, hitting too close to something that is important to him. What made Derrick's comment especially interesting is the fact that he was in many regards one of the most "critical" students in the class. For example, earlier in that same discussion, commenting on the nature of media influences, Gloria said, "Lots of people are not going to like me for saying this ... but" and then she talks about the *Lizzy Maguire show,* it's not part of the title and how girls watching that show might get the message that "16 lbs of makeup is what teenagers are supposed to wear"; to which Derrick, immediately after Gloria spoke, said that he "totally agrees with Gloria. TV shows us what we really are." On the one hand, Derrick "totally agrees" that TV influences people and yet, when it comes to video games, he is resistant to "crossing over" that "line." While there is a difference between video games and TV, the disparate remarks—one the one hand, "totally agreeing" that TV influences people and then, on the other, resisting to talk about video games in the same way—seem inconsistent, suggesting in a sense that the students have topics sanctioned for critique and topics not sanctioned for critique.

In addition to these moments of resistance, there were times when many students often articulated their ideas about the curriculum and the manner in which it was taught by explaining that the teacher was "making this up" in order to act out of an agenda (in this case a "Feminist," "liberal," and/or "hippie" agenda), and some even said, "Oh, here we go," with a roll of their eyes or a head to the desk for a nap. At times students exhibited downright hostility for being pushed toward critical literacy, while others claimed that the teacher or writer or filmmaker was "pulling that out of nowhere" or that "it's just an ad," "Nobody thinks about it that much," or "I'm not affected by advertisements. Not me." Some students respond with a sense of "Who cares?" or "What can I do about it?" saying things such as "I can't do anything about it. We're still going to buy stuff" or "This is an overreaction. Americans have the right to buy whatever they want." The nature of the students' resistance to or subversion/dismissal of critique suggests that once critique moves from articulation to action, lines get drawn; it seems to be acceptable for many of the students to "be critical" in words but much less so in action, particularly when it involves something (e.g., video games, constructions of gender) in which their sense of identity is heavily invested.

## Discussion

Critical literacy, or "being critical," is linked to a sense of identity, performance, and context more strongly than cognitive abilities or skills are. In other words, critical literacy is less the property of an individual (something someone "has" or does not have) and more an *enactment* of a certain someone at a particular time in a particular context for particular purposes. For instance, Bobby, in the above example, is discussing gender body image issues in a small group of female peers, and his statement "I think she's jealous" must be understood in that context. Is his comment an attempt to get a rise out of his peers? A laugh? An attempt at preserving his masculinity? Therefore, when discussing the enactment of critical literacy, it is crucial to keep in mind the fact that all literacy activities serve social roles and functions within particular contexts. As Yancey (2004) states, "What we ask students to do is who we ask them to be" (p. 738). To return to Freire's definition of literacy, it might be more apt to say that critical literacy is determined by "the extent that he or she is able [*and willing*] to use language for social and political reconstruction" (Freire & Macedo, 1987, p. 159). Or, to borrow from sociocultural conceptions of literacy, it might be more suitable to think of critical literacy as *sociocritical literacy*. Pedagogically, this insight pushes us to review our curriculum and ask ourselves, who is it we are asking our students to be? And, how do the roles and performances we ask them to enact facilitate and/or delimit their learning?

Regardless, though, of their resistance to, development of, or demonstration of critical literacy, the vast majority of students overwhelmingly felt that what was happening in their English 10 classroom was important and significant to their lives; in fact, several students from one section dubbed the class "real life English." We deliberately set out to create a humanizing and highly intellectual classroom space that encouraged discussion of issues and ideas that are oftentimes, in the words of one student, "taboo" for students to talk about in school, and there was a feeling among the students that, especially in comparison to their friends in other teachers' sections of English 10, what they did in this class was more relevant to their lives and "smarter" in some ways, or as one student said in an interview, "It [the class and the approach to it] just seems to be more intelligent."

## Considerations for Teachers

Although committed to the goals of critical literacy, there are times when we questioned our decision to prioritize a critical approach to the English curriculum. In the context of No Child Left Behind and increased assessment and accountability, curricular, collegial, and administrative pressures are as real as they've ever been, forcing us to constantly justify—to others and to ourselves—our placement of critical literacy at the center of the curriculum. In a climate of accountability and assessment, it is sometimes difficult to make a case, because when educators choose to include something in the curriculum, they must also necessarily choose to leave out something else. There are times when we were concerned about whether or not our students could write complete and coherent sentences, or whether or not they were to comprehend the complex texts they were asked to read. In light of these concerns, we have been thoughtful in designing a curriculum that balances traditional literacy skills with critical literacy skills in a way that we feel serves the needs of our students in the most responsible way.

To accomplish this balance, it was crucial for us to clearly articulate our objectives. We asked ourselves, "What is it that we want students to know, do, and feel as a result of their experience in this class?" Like many English teachers, we wanted our students to be able to read and write for a variety of purposes and in a variety of styles, to use writing as a tool for communication and self-expression and to use literature as a way of thinking critically about themselves and their worlds. We wanted our students to use the tools of rhetorical analysis to uncover authors' purposes and strategies for creating texts, thereby becoming savvy creators of authentic texts themselves. We wanted students to develop habits of mind that prepare them to approach all texts—the word and the world—from a critical perspective. We wanted to empower students to be active citizens, equipped not only to consume texts but also to produce texts of their own for their own purposes. We designed this curriculum around these goals. Ultimately, we feel that pedagogy that addresses critical literacy results in an experience that is more meaningful and relevant to students' lives in the twenty-first century.

# Notes

1.   Names of all students and locations have been changed.
2.   Eventually, we replaced the Courage and Integrity thematic unit with a Media Literacy unit. The rationale for the change and details of the unit are described in a later section of the article.
3.   This text is free and available to download on their Web site: http://www.medialit.org/.

# References

Alvermann, D. (Ed.) (2002). *Adolescents and literacies in a digital world.* New York: Peter Lang.

Appleman, D. (2000). *Critical encounters in high school English: Teaching literary theory to adolescents.* New York: Teachers College Press.

Bigelow, B. (2001). On the road to cultural bias: A critique of the Oregon trail CD-ROM. In Comber, B., & Simpson, A. (Eds.). *Negotiating critical literacies in classrooms.* Mahwah, NJ: Lawrence Earlbaum, 101–118.

Christensen, L. (2002).Reading, writing, rising Up: Unlearning the language stereotypes that bind us. Paper presented at the National Council for Teachers of English Annual Convention.

Cope, B., & Kalantis, M. (2000). *Multiliteracies: Literacy learning and the design of social futures.* New York: Routledge. Freire, P. (1970). The adult literacy process as cultural action for freedom. In Beck, S., & Olah, L. (Eds.) (2001). *Perspectives on language & literacy: Beyond the here and now.* Cambridge, MA: Harvard Educational Review, 335–352.

Freire, P., & Macedo, D. (1987). *Reading the word and the world.* Westport, CT: Bergin & Garvey.

Kist, W. (2004). *New Literacies in action: Teaching and learning in multiple media.* New York: Teachers College Press.

Kress, G. (2002). *Literacy in the new media age.* Routledge: London.

Lankshear, C., & Knobel, M. (2003). *New literacies: Changing knowledge and classroom learning.* Philadelphia, PA: Open University Press.

Loewen, J. (1996). *Lies my teacher told me: Everything your American history textbook got wrong.* New York: Touchstone Press.

Luke, A. (1997). Critical literacy and the question of normativity: An introduction. In Maspratt, S., Luke, A., & Freebody, P. *Constructing critical literacies: Teaching and learning textual practice.* Hampton Press, 1–18.

Martino W. (2001). "Dickheads, wuses, and faggots": Addressing issues of masculinity and homophobia in the critical literacy classroom. In Comber, B., & Simpson, A. (Eds.). *Negotiating critical literacies in classrooms.* Mahwah, NJ: Lawrence Earlbaum.

New London Group (1996). A pedagogy of multiliteracies: Designing social futures. *Harvard Educational Review, 61*: 60–92.

Petrone, R., & Gibney, R. (2005). The power to speak, the power to listen: Democratic pedagogies for the American literature classroom. *English Journal, 94*(5): 35–39.

Public Broadcasting Service (Producer) (2001). Frontline: Merchants of cool: A report on the creators and marketers of popular culture for teenagers [Online video]. Boston, MA: Public Broadcasting Service.

Wallowitz, L. (2004). Reading as resistance: Gendered messages in literature and the media. *English Journal, 93*(1): 26–31.

Yancey, K.B. (2004). Postmodernism, palimpsest, and portfolios: Theoretical issues in the representation of student work. *CCC, 55*(4): 738–761.

# Chapter 12

# Visual Critical Literacy: Resistance, Activism, and Agency in Collaborative Art Making

*Alice Pennisi*

*I used to have a dream about a 2-year-old girl sitting on a couch next to a middle-aged man. The little girl's feet hung over the edge of the couch, far from the floor. She wears a nightgown that touches the top of her knees. The middle-aged man that she's sitting next to holds a glass in his left hand. His face is like a shadow. He puts his glass down on the coffee table and reaches into his pocket. He pulls out a cylinder-shaped candy in a blue wrapper. He motions to the girl to take it. She looks for an O.K. from her mother before taking it. It is the only memory that I have of him. He died 17 years ago.*

## Talking Back through Artwork

The above story is part of *Fathers*, an art installation created by a young women's art collective called Voices of Women Arts or VOW. The powerful piece, which incorporates members' hidden stories and reflections of fathers and father figures, is both revealing and disruptive; it challenges the viewer's concept of father-daughter relationships as well as expectations of artwork by young women.

VOW was a group comprised mainly of high school girls that met after school and created collaborative artwork based on personal experiences and concerns with society's treatment of women and girls. Karen,[i] an English teacher in their urban vocational arts school, had been concerned with the high incidence of sexual harassment she encountered at the school, where only one in four students was female. When administration resisted dealing with the problem, Karen founded VOW as a discussion group where girls could feel safe to meet and talk about issues that concerned them.

When the group realized that they wanted to share their discussions with a larger audience, members quickly shifted to making art about their concerns. Since many students were disappointed with the school's formalist and technical-skill centered curriculum, they were eager to have the opportunity to make art centered on ideas. As an artist and art educator, I became involved with VOW to understand their art-making process and how making artwork together helped members consider their art a form of activism.

VOW's first artwork, *Listen* (figure 1), appropriately focuses on sexual harassment. It is a large (3' X 5') wall installation incorporating beckoning and grabbing plaster hands protruding from a background of text consisting of cat calls and reflections of unwanted touching and bullying, all part of members' lived experience. The power of the piece is the ambivalence it evokes; at the same time as I am made to feel uncomfortable by the text and familiar gestures, as a woman I also feel empowered by the boldness of the subtext. Several girls joined the group after viewing the piece. One member later explained her reaction to me:

> Maya: It was just amazing! It was just so beautiful! The hands would call your attention, so I would go to them. The writing, well, I got choked up.
>
> Alice: Do you remember any writing that sticks in your head?
>
> Maya: "I told him not to touch me."

Maya was interested in a group that would find that comment important enough to emblazon on an artwork. *Listen* was also what caused my interest in VOW. When I was invited in as a temporary adult member, I learned that in conjunction with the exhibiting of *Listen*, sexual harassment and abuse counselors were invited to VOW meetings to discuss their work. Counselors trained VOW members to conduct sexual harassment workshops, which they provided at their school. Thus began VOW's seeing their artwork as a catalyst for interaction with the public.

Art critic Suzi Gablik (1991) has called for artists to consider their relationship with the public and think of their work as a "social practice" (p. 181). Educator Ira Shor (1999) uses the same phrase in reference to critical literacy, as it "involves questioning received knowledge and immediate experience with goals of challenging inequality and developing an activist citizenry" (p. 11). How young artists engage in such practice is the focus of this chapter, which deals with the creation of *Fathers* (the artwork VOW made while I was a member). I will discuss how the process of and reason for making the work, along with the work's exhibition, combined are an example of visual critical literacy. As we worked in an after-school setting, I will also discuss implications for the traditional classroom.

## Visual Critical Literacy

> Veronica: "The art isn't just for us, but to tell others what's going on—that things are not what they seem."

Henry Giroux (1993) highlights an understanding of literacy as "the practice of representation as a means of organizing, inscribing, and containing meaning" (p. 367). In describing *critical* literacy, Ira Shor (1999) emphasizes its ability to "help develop students as critically thinking citizens who use language to question knowledge, experience, and power in society" (p. 8). As an educator steeped in democratic practice, he also sees its connection to challenging power relations through teacher-student "cogovernance" of classroom practice. What brings criticality to the concept of literacy is whether it encourages reflection on and problematizing of dominant cultural discourses.

Peggy Albers (2004), finding that many literacy researchers tend to narrowly define the field as limited to print-based texts, advocates for a broader understanding of what constitutes literacy, pointing out that it also involves human experiences with the visual arts and visual communication modes. As art educator Kevin Tavin (2001) explains, "visual images are ideological texts—representations that help to construct a view of the world" (p. 130). Albers also notes that opportunities to work with the visual arts encourage the development of a "richer literacy," which allows students to deal critically with the images of popular culture, "images that reveal only partial truths about social markers like gender, race, class, and sexual orientation" (p. 32).

Tavin, as well as many art educators (Duncum, 2002; Freedman 2000; 2003), advocate for the analysis of visual culture as central to the art classroom so as to encourage, as Tavin explains, "an active, engaging, and questioning relationship with visual texts in order to understand how meanings are produced in various historical, political, and cultural contexts" (p. 130). What seems to be deemphasized is a critical theorizing of visual culture through students making art. Though they discuss the importance of student art production, not enough of the work described and illustrated seems to, as Carol Becker (1997) emphasizes, help students "learn to ask themselves the difficult questions" (p. 24) about their world, let alone challenge the viewer. The point of critical visual literacy is not simply to be able to verbally and visually critique the media for its simplistic use of the female body to sell everything from beer to bathroom tiles. Many young people are quite savvy at these types of critique and it is easy for these activities to become intellectual puzzles rather than experiences in agency. For students to engage with the critical, they first need to find their learning personally meaningful. What is needed is for art to be a means of understanding and reflecting on how people act in the world and then for young people to use their own work to engage others. It becomes essential then to study literacy processes involved in artistic idea development and production, as well as to examine the cultural and personal experiences that influence the artworks that young people *choose* to make, not simply those assigned by teachers.

In Jane Martin's (1992) discussion of critical thinking, she puts great emphasis on the difference between teaching *about* the world, and teaching to take part *in* it. She critiques the concept of critical thinking as equated with analytical or rhetorical argument, explaining the flaw in this kind of education as a separation of "mind from body and thought from action" (p.171), seeing it as promoting a type of critical spectatorship. Martin finds this to be inappropriate for a democratic society, as it does not encourage participation, nor care or concern for, or connection with, others; nor does it encourage people "to bring intelligence to bear on living" (p.175). She explains that, "the best thinking in the world is of little avail if a person has not acquired the will, the ability, the skill, the sensitivity, and the courage to act on it" (p.178). As young people adapting to the transition from childhood to maturity, adolescents need to be allowed opportunities to express their opinions and views on issues that affect their lives (and not simply to be "expressive"). The way to decide where one stands on an issue is to discuss it, learn about it, and try out ways to communicate ones ideas, perspectives, and possible solutions (Tappan, 1991). In this way, by making choices and actively responding, creating art about social issues can be a form of action.

Many adolescents tune out to education in high school because they feel it is no longer relevant to their lives. Schools often do not allow for the space to grapple with the ethical and social dilemmas that adolescents face (Fehr, 2000; Weis & Fine, 2000) and then go out of their way to avoid and suppress talk about the social issues that affect students. Michelle Fine (1991), in her study of inner city high school dropouts, found that "with important exceptions, school-based silencing precluded official conversation about controversy, inequity, and critique" (p. 33). These topics that are deemed "dangerous, controversial, and chaotic" (Check, 2000, p.138) are precisely what make up many of adolescents' lived experiences. The result is that when students insist on bringing up these topics, they are seen as "insubordinate" and punished, if not pushed out of the school, or they become disengaged from their learning (Fehr, 2000; Fine, 1991).

Sometimes teachers do encourage students' critical thinking and creating based on timely social issues, only to have the work censored by a skittish school administration (Karp, 1997/1998; O'Connor, 2007; Ryzik, 2007). Contrary to perceptions, art teachers do censor topics outright (Bowman, 1999) or ignore their existence by focusing curricula solely on technical skills, avoiding content (Gude, 2004). Unfortunately, this avoidance is not only dishonest but also neutralizes one of art's highest purposes—to illuminate and to confront enduring facets of human experience (Desai & Chalmers, 2007; Gablik, 1991; Greene, 1995).

## Dialogue as Resistance

Shari: "We need to talk truthfully about ourselves and what we think, even if it hurts us. It'll be better than not talking at all about stuff."

VOW members met Wednesday afternoons in a classroom in their school. When I became a member, I immediately understood how dialogue was central to the group's existence, and to their art making. All meetings began with a "go-around," in which members sat in a circle and discussed topics that came to mind, usually what had happened in the previous week. They talked about issues that many young as well as older women often keep to themselves, incidents that irritated them, frightened them, and excited them. They discussed racism, sexism, family celebration and turmoil, conflicts among members, accomplishments in and outside school, anxieties over the future, even stories of death, abandonment, and abuse. Members were not all close friends or even from the same clique; some had not known one another before joining the group. Yet, many members agreed with Shari when she explained, "in the circle, we listen, we condone."

This is not to say that these sessions of honest talk were easy. As Natalia admitted, "sometimes our process is very stressful—it's hard to *really* tell the truth," a comment that brings into focus not only the difficulties of disturbing the status quo, but also VOW's understanding of truth telling as central to their work (Pennisi, 2007). Because the discussions centered on their own lives in relation to topics that are so often avoided, silenced, or left impersonal, I would characterize them as acts of resistance, in line with Lyn Mikel Brown's (1991) claim that for adolescent girls to authorize their own experiences, "in the face of pressure not to know—would be to engage in an act of resistance—an act of moral courage" (p. 84). Just by discussing such issues with one another, they were beginning the process of critically reflecting on and questioning the received knowledge and power relations that helped shape their world (Shor, 1996; 1999).

VOW did not see their discussions as separate from art making; such talk was understood as the beginning of artistic idea development. Their experiences were given elevated meaning by discussing them together. What made them critical was bringing them out in the world as art. Many members agreed with Natalia's comment that "the go-around is so connected to who we are, it's part of the art. They're like two sides of us; they go together." Also, as Lisa explained, the accepting atmosphere of the group encouraged participation: "Everyone's ideas are listened to. Period. That's why we get such good ones, because nobody's afraid to contribute." Maya was even more enthusiastic about the process, "When we're in that room, it's like electricity. Ideas are just jumping all over!" VOW's entire brainstorming process of developing ideas and making artistic decisions stemmed from dialogue. Everything they did in the creation of their art always came back to the go-around, in which everyone was given her time to talk as well as the group's absolute attention, a truly empowering experience for many members, who often felt silenced in other situations.

## Art Making as Activism

> Veronica: "We don't give speeches, we give artwork. People tend to listen more to the artwork than to people talking."

The installation *Fathers* (figure 2) began as a response to an art piece exhibited at a local gallery. In my second week with VOW, we went to see Fred Tomaselli's *Gravity's Rainbow*, an 8X20-foot wall installation that appears from afar as colorful beaded strands or necklaces draped in patterns along the entire length of a smooth black surface. Up close the viewer realizes that the "jewels" in the necklaces are actually different pharmaceutical pills and colorful magazine cutouts of body parts, birds, insects, and plants, including marijuana leaves, all suspended within a glossy resin. We found the piece beautiful and arresting, and many of the girls were excited about the possibilities the work suggested.

Eschewing the gallery educator's suggestion to mimic Tomaselli's piece by visually responding with a collage in unconventional materials, we focused on the immense size of the work and the duality of meaning the piece took on from different distances. The idea for a path-like floor installation made up of individual stories was developed during this time.

When we returned to our classroom, we also returned to our discursive ways of idea development. Barbara, the gallery's teaching artist who came to assist, quickly adapted her more traditional teacher-led Q&A mode to VOW's more consensus-based one. Instead of moving right into planning, our go-around dealt with members' immediate lives: college essays, paying bills, and finding funds for school. Then came a discussion of the story path and the theme of the superficiality of surfaces versus the "depth" of reality. We decided that everyone would come the following week with her own visual interpretation of the theme.

Again, before discussing our sketches, the next week's meeting began with a go-around centered on family situations that members found unfair. Thanksgiving had just passed, and Cynthia had been waiting for a call: "I didn't hear from my father. Go figure. I wasn't expecting to. Like always, he disappoints me." As I contemplated the impossibility of talking with my father on Thanksgiving Day as long as we were both alive, I also noticed the number of members who nodded in agreement or support. Others spoke of being expected to take care of and clean up after brothers who were teenagers themselves. This led to a discussion of whether it was necessary for a person of Latino descent to speak Spanish; members had differing and heated opinions on this topic.

Members understood that these discussions not only enabled them to talk about concerns often ignored or avoided in other arenas but would also lead to ideas for artwork. Something would surface that ignited interest in the group and would also connect to nonmembers. As Veronica asserted, "the art isn't just for us, it's to tell others what's going on." This dialogic process is reminiscent of Gablik's (1995) concept of "connective aesthetics," an idea of art that is "not the product of a single individual but is the result of a collaborative and interdependent process" (p. 76) that also assumes the involvement of an active audience.

During several weeks of go-arounds and brainstorming, ideas were discussed, combined, and transformed. Eventually, the work would become an organically shaped oval path ("circular, cuz memories are nonstop," Jessica explained) in which would be written stories of members' lives. Having seen the power of a large artwork, we decided on a four-foot wide path made up of seven interlocking pieces of plywood, taking up a space approximately 20 feet by 10 feet, the largest size our room could accommodate. Like Tomaselli's piece, the background would be shiny black, while the stories would be in bright colors. We printed dark gray impressions of our bodies onto the surface of the path to represent the concept that memories are, as Lucinda said, "always there but also not there." Cynthia also thought that they might be considered "shadows of scars that are left behind." Lucinda suggested that the stories be in decorative shapes, so that, "it can be all flowery and decorative far away, but we can tell them what really goes on when they read it." When Natalia later wondered why we didn't just use flowers as the shapes, we realized that she had hit upon the perfect idea, since, as Jessica pointed out, "everybody thinks flowers are sweet, girlie, and decorative—things people think have no deep meaning." The "flowers" would engage in a type of "contested discourse" (Anstey & Bull, 2006, p. 84) with that of the stories that formed their shape. VOW understood the ideological history and ironic meanings of visual imagery and would be incorporating it as a means of critique.

In terms of the types of stories, we agreed that they would be members' own narratives, not composites or creative writing pieces. Lucinda was the first to point out that "since we want our own words, why don't we use what we say at these meetings?" As I was documenting the group's process, I provided tapes and notes on several meetings that helped members with their stories.

During one go-around, the subject of abuse was discussed. Several members talked about being sexually abused, while others shared experiences of physical abuse. Still others discussed the pain of abandonment. In response to this meeting, the following week Barbara presented her own artwork and explained how her collaged photographs were "appropriating family pictures to make them more real," as she had been sexually abused at the age of five. She transforms photographs of herself at that time to create a world for the one whom she called "the five-year-old woman" as a means to reclaim her story. She described this work as empowering her, explaining that "making art about yourself is a feminist statement," something that helped members situate VOW's work more clearly. Explaining her work also helped members see possible ways to bring to their own work narratives hidden and forbidden.

As we discussed Barbara's work, we decided to find a way to incorporate the stories from the previous week's meeting. This is how the theme of fathers came about; it seemed that many of the untold stories in members' lives centered on fathers or father figures, whether they were dreams, nightmares, wishes, or dim memories. In order to keep it a group work and ensure more privacy, the stories would not identify their authors, making it easier to present such narratives publicly. Members also hoped this would ensure that the work had "a personal voice and a group voice at the same time" (Lisa), something VOW found important to its goal of using its artwork to engage with the public. It could then, as Veronica often stressed, "represent girls who don't have a way of speaking out." Natalia also pointed out that anyone could put herself or himself in the position of the narrator, explaining that, "when your father leaves, we are all affected." Their sense of seeing their art as a form of witnessing was quite strong, as was their understanding that they had a solid platform from which to voice their concerns.

As Freedman (2000) maintains, such artwork from young people "is not therapeutic—it is social. It is not about individual emotions, it is about personalizing of social issues" (pp. 323–324). For VOW, the meetings might have been therapeutic, but the making and exhibiting of *Fathers* was a form of action. As Maya explained, "it's about us taking a stand and helping others, talking about issues that are important to us as a whole, and saying through the work: This is wrong." VOW understood their artwork as "speaking to important social, political, and cultural issues from a deep sense of the politics of their own location" (Giroux, 1993, p. 369), that of young women who personally experienced that which they critiqued.

Just as "room-sized installations only become art through audience interaction," (Freedman, 2000, p. 320), *Fathers* was not "finished" until it was exhibited, and members, easily identifiable by the flowers we carried, talked with visitors, who then "became an active component of the work" (Gablik, 1995, p. 37). The opening was noticeable in that visitors tended to quietly and slowly walk along the path, reading the flowers and taking in the stories. When women talked with members, it was often to convey stories of their own. As Donna related to me later, "I thought we might be speaking for other girls. I hadn't realized that we'd be speaking for grown up women, too." By creating *Fathers* and engaging with its viewing public, VOW members were able to experience art making as "transformative praxis" (Lankshear & McLaren, 1993, p. 26). Their critical response to how young women experience a particular family relationship not only contradicts our society's unproblematic daddy/daughter narrative, it also forces the adult world to shift its understanding of young girls' social realities. Also, through this work, it is not just understanding that is transformed, but members' own realities. As Maya tried to explain, "Through this art, you put a certain emotion about a certain situation in the work. You no longer have it but you still own it. It's no longer there soaking you up; it's not there taking up space. It's out *there* now. It has another purpose."

## Agency through Cogovernance

Maya: "I don't think the artwork I do in classes expresses me as a person. It doesn't explain me. But with VOW, I can do that work. I actually get to accomplish the ideas that I have—the stories: ours, everybody's, society's stories."

As a participant in the go-arounds and art making, I understood VOW's process as a mutual inquiry that was based on democratic principles of responsibility and consensus. The group took ideas as they developed, digested them, and finally came to something that best represented all of their ideas. As Maya explained, "If I do something with other people, I can't just do it cuz I want to. I have to tell everyone. If they approve, then O.K. I can't do everything I want to!" This was true creation through negotiation, an example of young people and adults making decisions together on both the content and structure of what they were doing, reminiscent of Freire's (1970/1997) problem-posing concept of education. Ira Shor (1989; 1996) has written about how such an educational experience works in the classroom, where power and responsibility are negotiated as part of the learning experience. As he explains, "the materials of study and the process of study are mutually developed by the students and the teachers," and curriculum materials came not only from "the life, language, culture and themes of the students" (Shor, 1989, p. 35) but also from a process developed by teachers and students throughout the course. This is surprisingly close to how VOW worked. It was this sharing of decision making that brought about VOW members' engagement and sense of agency.

When asked to compare VOW's art-making process with members' art classroom experience, many had quick and like-minded responses. They felt that with VOW they were making artwork, while in class they were completing assignments. The lack of autonomy over decision making caused them to see the work they did in class as not entirely their own:

Shari: "In class, it's like, 'You have to make a table. It has to be this size by this size.' They'll give you all the dimensions because there's only one way the table can look. With Karen, it's like, we have an opportunity to make a table for someone, and we go from there. It's better, cuz you feel like an artist. You are an artist because it's *your* table."

Veronica "It's not someone telling me, 'Draw this.' cuz that's what *they* do in class. That's what *they* want, what *they* think. That's not what *I* think. I just do it cuz I have to get a grade. It's just a class. It's not really *art.*"

They did not mind having classes that taught art skills but found that too much of class was about those skills and not enough about using them for their own ideas. This tension between skills and content is well documented, but Olivia Gude (2004) has provided concrete ways to update art curricula that not only place skills in support of content but also encourage students' lived experience and treat the contemporary world as central to that content. To do this, art educators must understand and appreciate contemporary art-making processes and see their students' perspectives as valid art content.

The adolescent members of VOW also discussed how the "adult" members—Karen, Barbara, and I—did not act like the classroom art teachers with whom they were familiar. They felt comfortable talking with us about personal and artistic issues, asking us questions about art and for guidance on making artwork. Some perceived us as simply older members who had more experience but had not relied on the adult/child hierarchy to establish our relationships. That seemed to be the strongest reason for their respecting us:

Lisa: "I think that VOW is one of the very limited environments where the adults and the kids are at the same level, where we're all seen as individuals. It's not 'I'm the adult, and I'm here and this is my art project, so we're gonna do it the way that I'm *suggesting* you to do it.' We're all together trying to come up with an idea. That's what it's all about."

Donna: "The adults involved in VOW do not impose the hierarchy that most do. I don't view them as adults but more as other people with whom I can relate. That's why I have great respect and appreciation for them."

Most of these young women were between seventeen and eighteen years of age, and it was easy to see what they meant by the difference between how VOW works and how they work in school. Karen did the administrative and fundraising work but made no decisions without the group's consent. At times, Karen was a leader, but usually she was simply an adult member. The group understood the value of experience and expertise; when they needed to learn a technique or get information, they knew that adults were often whom they could go to. When I introduced them to feminist artists who used text in their work, they were not simply polite or passive; they asked important questions that helped with the project.

VOW's process, as compared to the average classroom's, was open-ended. The final work was not known in the brainstorming stages; it developed through reflection with the group. When Barbara began, she quickly realized that she was perceived as a member and a resource, but not as the leader who ran the show. She explained,

> I felt from the beginning that I couldn't come in and put a structure on top of this group. The creative process is about having the courage to let go, going out into an unknown place where you have absolutely no clue where you are going and what you're going to do...They let things happen as they discover ideas between them. I think that the creative process—whatever that is—is exactly like this.

In the traditional classroom, members felt that they were not given enough opportunity to create from their own ideas, that if art was about creating something either from within or in response to the world, then they needed to be allowed to do that. Shari's comment vividly describes how a lack of autonomy helped shape her disengagement: "Basically, they drain all your energy and all your love for the art out. You don't get to put yourself into it. It's just about getting the job done." What they seemed to desire was to be treated more like artists and less like students.

Even though the girls often mentioned how the adults in the group were working with them as equal members, the adults still had certain responsibilities. No matter how informal the situation, adults working with adolescents understand that their experience, maturity, and position ensure that they are not equal. As Shor (1999) explains, knowing "how and when a teacher should use authority and expertise to promote rather than to silence student agency" (p. 13) can be incredibly difficult to determine. Barbara and I discussed how the back and forth of moving in to give guidance or to teach and then pulling back to give space was sort of like playing an accordion, a wonderful metaphor for working with adolescents, as both movements are needed for the instrument or cogovernance to work.

An example of an adult/teacher using authority to control rather than encourage occurred during our initial meeting at the art gallery to view the Tomaselli piece. The gallery educator walked VOW through a traditional art history lesson as he extracted answers about the artwork that seemed to conform to already decided upon "responses." I watched as members went into "classroom mode," becoming quiet and passive as they listened, raised hands, and gave short answers that he guided them to. He even had the habit of taking their answers and rewording them the way he wanted them ("So you're saying that ..."). In contrast, Karen was always careful not to speak for the group. When members had trouble articulating a central theme, she suggested that everyone write their ideas out to reflect on and clarify them ("O.K., let's take a minute and write in longhand what we want to say"). They were then able to present them without her mediation.

A couple of members, including Karen, commented how the gallery educator's way of working felt "unintentionally condescending," and that he did not seem to understand the group he was dealing with. As Shari told me, "I don't mean to sound ungrateful, but it seemed like he was telling us what to do ... It was too much like the classroom stuff we're assigned, and that's not what VOW is about." She was referring to the fact that he gave them a time limit (six weeks) and that he several times suggested that they create a collage and begin brainstorming in the gallery. Whereas he might have been viewing what they would do as a "school art project," they were thinking about making art. Understanding, respecting, and incorporating students' perspectives helps encourage engagement.

This experience also raises the point that in order for adolescents to make work about issues that are personal or that have personal perspectives, they must feel comfortable and safe to express ideas and opinions. Being a contributing artist in *Fathers* and creating my own father stories helped me understand the difficulties of making such narratives public. Teachers should do the assignments they expect of their students that deal with personal issues so that they understand what is involved. I do not mean that they should make teacher exemplars for students to emulate; I mean that they should make actual artwork based on the same issues that students are expected to make.

The realization that dialogue was what kept the group together as well as where ideas for art making came from should give rise to the understanding of the importance of classroom dialogue, particularly in terms of idea development. Also, discussions during VOW meetings almost entirely involved talk of members' lived experiences and their wish to make sense of and respond to them through art. This connection of creation to lived experience is essential to help students to see art as a means to "critique the way things are, imagine alternatives, hypothesize ways to get there, and act from those plans" (Shor, 1999, p. 16).

## The Art Classroom as a Center of Inquiry

Shari: "We make art about life, not about art."

Shari's comment refers to the skills and technique-laden assignments she and other VOW members were so familiar with. Many art teachers state how important it is for students to be able to "express themselves" by making work from their experiences, understand cultural meanings, and value process as much as product—this also is perennially echoed by art education students as they craft their teaching philosophies. Still, there is a dissonance because many teachers, both in classrooms and in those same philosophies, also insist that before students can make art, they first must learn (even master!) what turn out to be exactly the lessons that VOW members described—exercises to practice skills and techniques based on the elements and principles of design. In this way, those previous ideas of process, experiential art making, multicultural inquiry, and imaginative response are pushed to the side.

It is important to recognize the power of the common "presumption that a skills approach to studio art is not a teaching of theory" (McKenna, 1990, p. 75), but simply the way to teach art, as well as the erroneous perception that a knowledge of and familiarity with the elements and principles of design are necessary in order to make or understand art (Gude, 2004). Assuming that formalism is a universal lens through which to create, experience, and critique, art enables the artwork discussed to be decontextualized; analysis then focuses on appearance and art as a solitary and one-way act of expression. This lens also is inadequate for the understanding of contemporary work, as "postmodern artists often reject formalistic uses of elements and principles of design in favor of symbolic uses that suggest multiple and extended social meanings" (Freedman, 2000, p. 316). The irony is that many young people are familiar with such meanings from the visual culture that surrounds them—they just do not have opportunities to connect it with what is going on in art class.

In his discussion of the problems in language arts curriculum design, Applebee (1996) could be also describing traditional art curricula in secondary schools. He points out that teachers often "begin with an inventory of important skills and concepts and then move on to arrange them in logical ... order" (pp. 51-52), rather than "considering the conversations that matter" (p. 52). For art educators, such conversations might include: What does it mean to make art now? How do different artists come to their ideas and make work? What kind of art is important to make? These are not questions that can be answered by a curriculum focused on skills and techniques; rather, they require reflection, discussion of nascent ideas, and focusing on the many ways to visually represent those ideas. What might it be like to ask students to consider beginning their work with a question, and to see the process of making the work as the means of answering or investigating it? Such an inquiry-centered process, which is how filmmaker Francis Ford Coppola describes the way he works (Bahr & Hickenlooper, 1991), might bring students closer to understanding art as a means of naming and engaging with the world.

Art teachers who wish their students to "make art about life, not about art" can find inspiration from VOW's process, which developed out of members' desire to make artwork about what they considered conversations that matter. Though VOW met after school and was comprised only of female members, what made the group noteworthy was their dialogic idea development, their shared understanding of art as a communicative means to visually represent ideas, and their strong sense of autonomy. Decisions on both content and procedure were made as a group, and skills were learned as needed (often taught by me) to help get the group's ideas across. Input and ideas were valued, and uncertainty was considered part of the process as the concept of the finished piece was not known at the start. This might not fit with some teachers' usual assignments, but it is closer to how practicing artists make their work. These aspects align with Gude's (2004) three criteria for a solid postmodern art curriculum: student art is based on diverse practices of contemporary art making, art is understood as a form of investigation or inquiry, and curriculum is based on generative themes relating to students' lives and communities.

VOW's work provides an example of adolescents who become involved in critical inquiry through their discussions, their choice of issues from which to work, and through the active process of their art making. A transformative educational experience took place that encouraged young women to use their all too often unheard voices to interact with society. Their collaborative art making enabled adolescents to construct a visual social world that placed and held youth activism at its center.

Figure 1. *Listen*

Figure 2. *Fathers*

# Note

1. All proper names except the name of the group have been changed. Quotes from VOW members were recorded during meetings and interviews while I was a member of VOW.

# References

Albers, P. (2004). Literacy in art: Questions of responsibility. *Democracy & Education*, 15(3-4): 32-41.

Anstey, M., & Bull, G. (2006). *Teaching and learning multiliteracies: Changing times, changing literacies*. Newark, DE: International Reading Association.

Applebee, A. (1996). *Curriculum as Conversation: Transforming traditions of teaching and learning*. Chicago: University of Chicago Press.

Bahr, F., & Hickenhooper, G. (dir.) (1991). *Hearts of darkness: A filmmaker's apocalypse*. Paramount.

Bowman, B. (1999). Art teacher censorship of student produced art in Georgia's public high schools. *Culture Work*, 3(3) (retrieved July 20, 2007).

Brown, L.M. (1991). Telling a girl's life: Self-authorization as a form of resistance. *Women and Therapy*, 11(3/4): 71-87.

Check, E. (2000). Caught between control and creativity: Boredom strikes the art room. In Fehr, D., Fehr, K., & Keifer-Boyd, K. (Eds.). *Real-World Readings in Art Education: Things Your Professor Never Told You*. New York: Falmer Press, 137-145.

Desai, D., & Chalmers, G. (2007). Notes for a dialogue on art education in critical times. *Art Education*, 60(5): 6-12.

Duncum, P. (2002). Clarifying visual culture art education. *Art Education*, 55(3): 6-11.

Fehr, D. (2000). Gender politics in the back seat of a lowrider. In D. E. Fehr, K. Fehr, & K. Keifer-Boyd (Eds.), *Real world readings in art history: Things your professor never told you*. New York: Falmer Press, 37-45.

Fine, M. L. (1991). *Framing dropouts: Notes on the politics of an urban public high school*. Albany, NY: SUNY Press.

Freedman, K. (2000). Social perspectives on art education in the U. S.: Teaching visual culture in a democracy. *Studies in Art Education*, 1(4): 314-329.

Freedman, K. (2003). *Teaching visual culture*. New York: Teachers College Press.

Freire, P. (1970/1997). *Pedagogy of the oppressed*. New York: Continuum.

Gablik, S. (1991). *The reenchantment of art*. New York: Thames and Hudson.

Gablik, S. (1995). Connective aesthetics: Art after individualism. In S. Lacy, S. (Ed.). *Mapping the terrain: New genre public art*. Seattle: Bay Press, 74-87.

Giroux, H. (1993). Literacy and the politicals of difference. In. C. Lankshear & P. L. McLaren (Eds.). *Critical literacy: Politics, praxis, and the postmodern*. Albany, NY: SUNY Press, 367-377.

Greene, M. (1995). *Releasing the imagination: Essays on education, the arts, and social change*. San Francisco: Jossey-Bass.

Gude, O. (2004). Postmodern principles: In search of a 21st century art education, *Art Education*, 57(1): 6-14.

Karp, S. L. (1997/1998). Banned in Jersey, welcome on Broadway. *Rethinking Schools*, 12(2): 14-15.

Lankshear, C., & McLaren P.L. (1993). Introduction. In C. Lankshear & P.L. McLaren (Eds.). *Critical literacy: Politics, praxis, and the postmodern*. Albany, NY: SUNY Press, 1-56.

Martin, J. R. (1992). Critical thinking in a humane world. In S. R. Norris (Ed.), *Generalizability of critical thinking.* New York: Teachers College Press, 163-180.

McKenna, S. E. (1999). Theory and practice: Revisiting critical pedagogy in studio art education, *Art Journal* (Spring): 75-99. :

O'Connor, A. (2007). "Monologues" spurs dialogue on taste and speech. *New York Times,* March 8, B1.

Pennisi, A.C. (2007). Voices of women: Telling the truth through art making. *Journal of Social Theory in Art Education,* (26): 85-104.

Ryzik, M. (2007). Unwelcome at home, student play is a hit in New York, *New York Times,* June 14, B1.

Shor, I. (1989). Developing student autonomy in the classroom. *Equity & Excellence,* 24(3): 35-37.

Shor, I. (1996). *When students have power: Negotiating authority in a critical pedagogy.* Chicago: University of Chicago Press.

Shor, I. (1999).What is critical literacy? In I. Shor & C. Pari (Eds.). *Critical literacy in action: Writing words, changing worlds.* Portsmouth, NH: Boynton/Cook/Heinemann, 1-30.

Tappan, M.B. (1991). Narrative, authorship, and the development of moral authority, In M.B. Tappan & M.J. Packer (Eds.), *Narrative and storytelling: Implications for understanding moral development, 54.* San Francisco: Jossey-Bass, 5-25.

Tavin, K. (2001). Swimming upstream in the jean pool: Developing a pedagogy towards critical citizenship in visual culture. *Journal of Social Theory in Art Education,* 21: 129-158.

Weis, L., & Fine, M. L. (Eds.) (2000). *Construction sites: Excavating race, class, and gender among urban youth.* New York: Teachers College Press.

# Conclusion

*Laraine Wallowitz*

As the contributors of this book have demonstrated, we feel it is important to make the distinction between *critical thinking* and *critical literacy*. To ask students to think critically means that they should be able to apply, analyze, synthesize, and evaluate information, all valuable skills. But to stop there leaves a student vulnerable to lessons taught by the informal curriculum. Armed with only the critical thinking skills, they learn about themselves and their world from advertising, music, media, and other texts constructed by corporate culture. As we see it, we are irresponsible as educators if we stop short of equipping students with the means to recognize how they are being positioned—or manipulated—by homogenizing texts and the written and spoken word as students negotiate it in all aspects of their academic and nonacademic lives.

Literacy across the curriculum programs focus primarily on teaching skills and strategies for comprehending texts. Content area teachers understand that efficient readers are able to do several things: activate prior knowledge, visualize the text, ask questions for clarification, and use context clues to decipher difficult vocabulary. But creating independent readers does not necessarily produce independent thinkers. Teachers must use content-specific texts to help students problematize the familiar, recognize the contextual nature of all knowledge, and inspire social activism. To create critical readers, the contributors of this text have provided many exemplars of how to begin applying the principles and practices of critical literacy to the curriculum. What follows are more examples to begin thinking about the possibilities of critical literacy pedagogy in your secondary content area classroom.

## Develop Critical Habits of Mind

Before students can engage in the deconstruction and reconstruction of their worlds, they must develop "critical habits of mind" (Shor, 1992, p. 4) or a way of thinking about reality as socially constructed and mediated by language, and the production, consumption, and distribution of texts and other artifacts both reflecting and shaping our lived experiences. Once students understand that their way of life is not "natural," but literally "man-made," they can begin to problematize taken-for-granted assumptions about race, class, gender, and sexuality, as well as other linguistic constructs designed to maintain the status quo. There are a number of ways to achieve "critical habits of mind" and it is up to teachers to choose texts that connect to the lives of the students and then move them beyond the familiar to investigate larger societal concerns as they relate to everyone. Teachers should ask themselves (and the students) the following exploratory questions: What real world issues does this text challenge or problematize? How does this text uphold or disrupt traditional power relationships and hierarchies? In what ways does this text problematize or reify race, gender, class, sexuality, power, and privilege?

It is, therefore, important to raise or confront sociopolitical issues in texts, particularly race, gender, class, and sexuality, and not ignore controversial topics out of fear or discomfort. The contributors in this book have provided numerous examples of thinking about the social and political nature of texts, curriculum, and pedagogy. For example, de Freitas, in chapter 3, showed how teachers can use word problems as a text to show how math is—in fact—value laden. Students engaging in critical mathematics learn the ethical dilemmas in problem solving when math is placed in a sociopolitical context. As Kurt Love outlined in chapter 2, scientific knowledge must be understood as "situated," having its own history, culture, and values. How, then, is the information presented in texts a product of cultural values, beliefs, and agendas? Whose agenda? To what extent is corporate and government funding affecting science and the kinds of information we are delivered? Here are a few ways to raise sociopolitical issues in other content areas:

- Art: How have artists used their craft as a vehicle for social justice? Barbara Kruger, for example, employs collage to challenge her audience's attitudes about feminism, consumerism, and desire. How can students use art to raise awareness about the sociopolitical issues in their own lives /neighborhoods/ communities?

- Art: Historically, male artists have objectified and marginalized women. How have women used art to liberate themselves from the male gaze and create a uniquely female aesthetic?

- English: "Good" literature raises questions and problematizes the familiar. Canonical and noncanonical texts lend themselves to social and political conversations about race, class, and gender and sexuality. How are women constructed in texts written by men? Minorities? Whose voices are privileged and whose voices are missing in the texts most often taught in secondary schools?

- Language Arts/World Language: Teachers can use language as a tool for inquiry, asking the following queries: How does language mediate our reality? How have languages evolved and how does the change reflect and shape the society in which they were spoken/created? To what extent does language control thinking? How has language been used to colonize, oppress, and control? What is the intended effect of political correctness? How does the current debate over Standard English reflect racial tensions in the United States? How might the English-only debate in the United States lead to language genocide?

To further a dialectical relationship with the word and the world, it is also important for students to examine and deconstruct various viewpoints.

## Examine Multiple Perspectives

Interrogating multiple perspectives (Lewis et al., 2002) is another way in which to help students gain a critical perspective on literacy. As Finders asks in her book *Just girls: Hidden literacies and life in junior high* (1997), "How can one expect a critical stance when there is no suggestion of any alternative readings?" (p. 127). Instead of asking students, "What is the correct reading of this text," critical pedagogues ask, "What are possible readings of this text?" Reading from different stances or "lenses" allows new understandings to emerge and creates a democratic space for various voices to be heard and examined. Deborah Appleman, in her book *Critical encounters in high school English: Teaching literary theory to adolescents* (2000), suggests that English teachers introduce literary theory in order to "recontextualize the familiar and comfortable, making us reappraise it" (p. 2). "Critical lenses," she maintains, "provide students with a way of reading their world; the lenses provide a way of 'seeing' differently and analytically that can help them read the culture of the school as well as popular culture" (p. 3). Any text, whether it is a music video, an advertisement, a Shakespearian play, or a poem, can be used to help students "see what factors have shaped their own world view and what assumptions they make as they evaluate the perspectives of others" (p. 3). Here are a few ways to include various perspectives in your classroom:

- Science: In order to problematize scientific knowledge as "objective" and "value-free," students should read their texts from feminist, eco-feminist, or eco-justice perspectives. How has science been used in the past to justify gender and racial discrimination? How has the medical industry been used as a tool for social control throughout history?

- English: Introducing critical lenses or literary theory as a way of changing our understanding of texts allows for a multitude of perspectives and voices to be heard

(Appleman, 2000; Wallowitz, 2004). What might be revealed by a feminist reading of Steinbeck or a Marxist reading of *Native Son* by Richard Wright? How can these lenses help us read our world from a critical literacy perspective?

• Art: Art teachers can introduce lesbian artists to their students to show how art can be used to disrupt the traditional male gaze. Catherine Opie, for example, uses her work to decolonize the female body and challenge the male gaze by using her back as a canvass for her art. How does using a queer lens change the way we view and understand art as it has been defined and dominated by the heterosexual, male perspective?

• Social Studies: Problematizing the ways in which history is written, presented, and sold to the public shows students the artificially constructed nature of American traditions and folklore. Whose story is being told? From whose perspective? Whose voices are missing? What do the writers of the textbook value? What knowledge is of most worth?

Inquiries such at these remind students of the highly contextualized nature of all knowledge, the inherent bias in all disciplines, and our responsibility to continually question what we read, hear, and think.

## Recognition, Resistance, and Revision

Finally, a critical perspective on literacy demands that students not only engage in deconstruction, but reconstruction. That is, students should be producers of knowledge, not just passive receivers. Freire reminds teachers that students learn to read the word in order to rewrite a more inclusive, just world. Therefore, a crucial component for developing critical perspective on literacy is social action. What are the possible ways of resisting labels that marginalize? What are the alternative ways of being in the world? How does change happen? Can one person make a difference? Students can apply their understanding of critical literacy to their lives via small and large acts of resistance. They learn the importance of being informed and participating in a democratic society. For example:

• Social Studies: Textbooks are a logical place to start since too often teachers rely on them as their primary source of information. Once students have read like historians, asking who is missing and whose perspective is privileged, students can re-draft a more inclusive history by rewriting the chapters—individually or in groups—to include the voices and perspectives that were originally omitted. Then, students can present their revisions to younger students, other classes, or send in the revisions to the publishing company with a letter asking them to justify their choices.

- Science: Creating and maintaining a community garden or other commons-based projects teaches students not only about food preparation, plant life, and ecology, but also about the importance of community and environmentalism.

- World Language: With access to the Internet, students can communicate with other students all around the world. As our world gets "flatter" (Friedman, 2005), students need to become more comfortable with other cultures, languages, belief systems, etc. Students can find out how they are perceived by the world and, perhaps, alter or amend their perception of others. How has globalization affected their communities both positively and negatively? What are the common stereotypes of Americans, of others? What can we learn from other belief systems and cultures?

- World Language: As part of a unit on clothing/shopping in a Spanish class, have students research sweatshops and associated human rights violations on the National Labor Committee Web site (www.nlcnet.org). Students can then raise money to donate to GlobalGiving (www.globalgiving.com) or engage in micro-lending through Kiva (www.kiva.org), which allows students to direct the funds to entrepreneurs of their choice in the developing world.

Once students recognize that culture is a dynamic construct, they are empowered to intervene and work for a more inclusive society by fighting what they perceive to be injustices. As Kraver (2007) aptly put it, "The result is a pedagogy that transforms the school from a site of ritual performance to one of critical thinking, democratic resistance, and emancipation" (p. 67).

The contributors of the book invite educators to engage in critical thinking, democratic resistance, and emancipatory teaching and to amend, enhance, and continue the critical literacy work described here and in the works of those who inspired us. What is possible in today's secondary classroom is yet to be discovered.

# References

Appleman, D. (2000). *Critical encounters in high school English: Teaching literary theory to adolescents.* New York: Teachers College Press.

Finders, M.J. (1997). *Just girls: Hidden literacies and life in junior high.* New York: Teachers College Press.

Freire, P., & Macedo, D. (1987). *Literacy: Reading the word and the world.* South Hadley, MA: Bergin and Harvey.

Friedman, T.L. (2005). *The world is flat: A brief history of the twenty-first century.* New York: Picador.

Kraver, J.R. (2007). Engendering gender equity: Using literature to teach and learn democracy. *English Journal, 96*(6), 67–73.

Lewison, M., Flint, A. S., & Van Sluys, K. (2002). Taking on Critical Literacy: The journey of newcomers and novices. *Language Arts, 79*(5), 382–392.

Shor, I. (1992). *Empowering education: Critical teaching for social change.* Chicago:University of Chicago Press.

Wallowitz, L. (2004). Reading as resistance: Gendered messages in literature and media, *English Journal, 93* (3), 26–31.

# Contributors

**Jane Bolgatz** is an associate professor of social studies education in the Division of Curriculum and Teaching at Fordham University Graduate School of Education in New York City. She is the author of Talking Race in the Classroom (Teachers College Press, 2005) and she facilitates the website www.talkingrace.org. Her research interests include anti-racist education, helping elementary and secondary students develop historical thinking skills, and preparing students for standardized tests.

**Carlin Borsheim** is a PhD student in Curriculum, Teaching, and Educational Policy at Michigan State University where her interests include English teacher education, critical literacy and pedagogy, critical multiculturalism, and multiliteracies. Before entering the doctoral program, Carlin taught English, Drama and Creative Writing in high schools in Michigan and Ohio for seven years. While teaching, she earned an MA in Critical Studies in the Teaching of English, also from MSU. She continues to work as a teacher consultant affiliated with the Red Cedar Writing Project in East Lansing. Carlin has published several articles in national journals, including English Journal.

**Bruce Castellano** teaches peace education and human rights issues in the Ruth S. Ammon School of Education at Adelphi University and co-chairs their Peace Studies Committee. He was a high school English teacher in the Mineola School District for thirty-four years, where he won the Teacher of the Year award. He also created a human rights program called Increase the Peace™ (ITP). ITP is a student-based program that trains students to create, produce, and present workshops and forums that teach their peers acceptance of difference and prejudice reduction. ITP also establishes mentoring/teaching connections with local, national and international human rights organizations where students have the opportunity to learn and become activists.

**Kevin P. Colleary, Ed.D.** Kevin's experience includes: classroom teaching in public and private schools in Harlem and Brooklyn, New York; writing and developing new curriculum materials; and working with teachers, administrators and parents nationwide discussing issues of multiculturalism, citizenship education and the K-12 social studies curriculum. Kevin has presented at many state and national educational meetings such as the National Council for the Social Studies, the American Educational Research Association and the National Catholic Education Association. Kevin currently teaches both graduate and undergraduate courses in the Curriculum and Teaching Department at Fordham University in New York City. He is also involved in a variety of pre- and in-service teacher development programs in New York City's public and parochial schools. He received his BA in History and Education at Siena College in Albany, New York. He earned his masters in education and his doctorate in education, focusing on elementary social studies and diversity in curriculum issues, from the Graduate School of Education at Harvard University in Cambridge, Massachusetts.

**John A. Craven, III** is associate professor in the Division of Curriculum and Teaching at Fordham University Graduate School of Education in New York City. His research interests include science teacher education, non-formal learning environments, the nature of science, and science literacy. He teaches courses in science-, environmental-, and technology education.

**Elizabeth de Freitas** teaches in the Ruth S. Ammon School of Education at Adelphi University. She has published papers in Educational Studies in Mathematics, Teaching Education, The International Journal of Education and the Arts, Language and Literacy: A Canadian Educational e-Journal, The Journal of the Canadian Association of Curriculum Students, and Interchange: A Quarterly Review of Education. Her current research interests include critical mathematics education and theories of identity.

**Lisa Hochtritt, Ed.D.** is the Chair of Art Education at The Rocky Mountain College of Art + Design (RMCAD) in Denver, CO. Previous to this position, she was the Director of the Master of Arts in Teaching program and an Assistant Professor of Art Education at The School of the Art Institute of Chicago (SAIC). In 2005 she was awarded the honor of SAIC Faculty of the Year for Excellence in Teaching. She holds a Doctor of Education degree in Art and Art Education from Teachers College, Columbia University in New York City, a Masters of Arts degree in Creativity and Arts Education and Teaching Certification (K-12) in Art and Drama from San Francisco State University, a Bachelor of Science degree in Communications: Radio/TV/Film from the University of Wisconsin Oshkosh.

Lisa's current research focuses student teaching as action research and on urban adolescents and the artwork they create outside of schools. Her dissertation is entitled, "Creating Meaning and Constructing Identity through Collaborative Art Practices Among Urban Adolescents." Before coming to RMCAD and SAIC, Lisa was an instructor at Teachers College in the Art and Art Education program; a faculty member at Bank Street College of Education in New York City; a consultant for The Heritage School, a public high school in East Harlem; a program assessor for arts partnerships in NYC and CT; and a high school and middle school teacher. She is also an exhibiting visual and performance artist who practices under the name of Dr. June D. Cleavage.

**Tracy Hogan** is currently an assistant professor at Adelphi University, Garden City, New York where she teaches courses in adolescent development and science education. Her research interests include cognition and learning, educational media and science literacy. She has published works in the fields of educational psychology and science education.

**Kurt Love** is an assistant professor of education at Central Connecticut State University. He taught science for five years in public middle schools. He taught in Hartford, West Hartford, and Cheshire, Connecticut. He is interested in reforming science education by using critical, feminist, and eco-justice pedagogies. He is also focusing on providing analysis that includes democratic participation in order to revitalize the public commons, resist neo-liberalism and corporate globalization, and working towards a sustainable and diverse environment.

**Rachel Mattson** is a historian, a teacher educator, and an Assistant Professor at SUNY New Paltz. She earned a PhD in U.S. History from New York University in 2004, and then served for several years as the Historian-in-Residence in the Department of Teaching and Learning at NYU's Steinhardt School of Culture, Education, and Human Development. Her scholarly writing has been has appeared in the *Radical History Review* and in a forthcoming issue of the journal *Rethinking History*. She also has two collaboratively-written books forthcoming from Routledge in 2009—one that offers strategies for using visual knowledge and contemporary art in the history classroom, and another that brings historians together with high school teachers to develop methods for teaching complicated historical ideas to young people. An active public historian, Mattson has been involved in local anti-racist, immigrant justice, and queer organizing for over 14 years. She has also written, co-written, and consulted on a range of historical and educational performance work with groups such as Circus Amok, Great Small Works, the Workman's Circle, and Domestic Workers United.

Critical Literacy as Resistance

Cara Mulcahy is currently an Assistant Professor in the Department of Reading and Language Arts at Central Connecticut State University. She teaches courses on content area reading, literacy in the elementary and secondary grades and critical literacy. Formerly a middle school Language Arts and Social Studies teacher, Cara's areas of interest include adolescent literature, adolescent literacy, critical literacy, critical pedagogy, social justice, and diversity.

Alice Pennisi is an Assistant Professor of Art Education at Buffalo State College. She received her doctorate at Teachers College, Columbia University. Current research interests include interdisciplinary teaching at the college level, as well as working from a negotiating curricular model as a means to re/engage adolescents, including first-year college students.

Robert Petrone is an Assistant Professor of English Education, Literacy, and Youth Cultures in the College of Education at the University of Nebraska-Lincoln. His most recent work focuses on the learning and literacy practices found within skateboarding culture and the ways that conceptions of youth enable and/or constrain life opportunities for young people. Robert has had several articles published in state and national journals such as "English Journal."

Rita Verma is currently an Assistant Professor in the department of Curriculum and Instruction at Adelphi University. She received her Ph.D. from the University of Wisconsin. Rita has been involved in developing innovative teacher-centered initiatives related to peace and global studies with local and international organizations. Her research interests are in the areas of immigration education, the South Asian diaspora, and multicultural education and she is currently completing her first book title *Backlash: South Asian Immigrant Voices on the Margins.*

Laraine Wallowitz holds a Ph.D. in English education from the University of Virginia. A former high school English, American Studies, and Women's Studies teacher, she currently teaches English education and literacy courses at Adelphi University in New York. She was the recipient of the untenured Teaching Excellence Award in 2007. Her research interests include critical literacy, gender, and differentiated instruction and has presented her work at several international and national conferences. In addition, she has published in *English Journal, New England Reading Association Journal* and in several books.